On the Transcendent
The Yoga-Sūtra

महर्षि पतञ्जलि प्रणीतम्

योगसूत्रम्

व्यासभाष्यसमेतम्

With the Commentary of Vyāsa

Translated by David Shepheard

On the Transcendent: the Yoga-Sūtra

Translated by David Shepheard

Published by 1stWorld Publishing
P.O. Box 2211, Fairfield, Iowa 52556
tel: 641-209-5000 • fax: 866-440-5234
web: www.1stworldpublishing.com

First Edition

LCCN: 2012954826
SoftCover ISBN: 978-1-4218-8658-9
HardCover ISBN: 978-1-4218-8659-6
eBook ISBN: 978-1-4218-8660-2

This material has been written and published for educational purposes to enhance one's wellbeing. In regard to health issues, the information is not intended as a substitute for appropriate care and advice from health professionals, nor does it equate to the assumption of medical or any other form of liability on the part of the publisher or author. The publisher and author shall have neither liability nor responsibility to any person or entity with respect to loss, damages or injury claimed to be caused directly or indirectly by any information in this book.

CONTENTS

Note on the Translation 7

Chapter 1
Samādhipāda: The Transcendent 9

Chapter 2
Sādhanapāda: Technologies of Enlightenment......... 121

Chapter 3
Vibhūtipāda: All Possibilities.................................... 257

Chapter 4
Kaivalyapāda: Cosmic Consciousness 401

The Yoga-Sūtras... 475

Glossary.. 511

Further Reading 521

Note on the Translation

ऋचो अक्षरे परमे व्योमन् ।

The purpose of this translation is to provide an accurate version of the *Yogasūtra* of Patañjali, together with the commentary of Vyāsa, in cogent, modern English. The intention has been to present the original Sanskrit texts as they are, without notes, expansion or further commentary.

The inspiration for this work derives from my own understanding and practice, over many years, of the Transcendental Meditation technique and the TM-Sidhi programme, as taught by His Holiness Maharishi Mahesh Yogi.

David Shepheard

Cambridge

|| 1 ||

samādhipāda

Chapter 1

The Transcendent

atha yogānuśāsanam || 1.1 ||

athetyayamadhikārārthaḥ | yogānuśāsanaṃ śāstramadhikṛtaṃ veditavyam | yogaḥ samādhiḥ | sa ca sārvabhaumaścittasya dharmaḥ | kṣiptaṃ mūḍhaṃ vikṣiptamekāgraṃ niruddhamiti cittabhūmayaḥ | tatra vikṣipte cetasi vikṣepopasarjanībhūtaḥ samādhirna yogapakṣe vartate | yastvekāgre cetasi sadbhūtamarthaṃ pradyotayati kṣinoti ca kleśān karmabandhanāni ślathayati nirodhamabhimukhaṃ karoti sa saṃprajñāto yoga ityākhyāyate | sa ca vitarkānugato vicārānugata ānandānugato'smitānugata ityupariṣṭāt pravedayiṣyāmaḥ | sarvavṛttinirodhe tvasaṃprajñātaḥ samādhiḥ | 1.1 |

I.1. So: this is the exposition of yoga.

'So': the meaning is that the instruction which follows is authoritative. 'Exposition of yoga': this supreme teaching is worthy of knowing. 'Yoga': the Transcendent. Now, this is a characteristic of all levels of thought. The levels of thought are: directed outwards; undirected; surface wandering; one-pointed; silence. When the attention wanders on the surface, transcendental consciousness is overshadowed and is not considered within the purview of yoga. Yoga, however, refers to the procedure of transcending the thinking process which, as the mind becomes one-pointed, refines one's perception of reality, releases stress, dissolves the boundaries of mental activity, and settles into silence. As it progresses from gross, to subtle, to bliss, to Amness, we shall explain later. When all the impulses of the mind have settled, transcendental consciousness remains, without experience of thought.

lakṣaṇābhidhitsayedaṃ sūtraṃ pravavṛte |

yogaścittavṛttinirodhaḥ || *1.2* ||

sarvaśabdāgrahaṇāt saṃprajñāto'pi yoga ityākhyāyate | cittaṃ hi prakhyāpravṛttisthitiśīlatvāt triguṇam | prakhyārūpaṃ hi cittasattvaṃ rajastamobhyāṃ saṃsṛṣṭamaiśvaryaviṣayapriyaṃ bhavati | tadeva tamasā'nuviddhamadharmājñānāvairāgyānaiśvaryopagaṃ bhavati | tadeva prakṣīṇamohāvaraṇaṃ sarvataḥ pradyotamānamanuviddhaṃ rajomātrayā dharmajñānavairāgyaiśvaryopagaṃ bhavati | tadeva rajoleśamalāpetaṃ svarūpapratiṣṭhaṃ sattvapuruṣānyatākhyātimātraṃ dharmameghadhyānopagaṃ bhavati | tatparaṃ prasaṃkhyānamityācakṣate dhyāyinaḥ | citiśaktirapariṇāminyapratisaṃkramā darśitaviṣayā śuddhā cānantā ca sattvaguṇātmikā ceyamato viparītā vivekakhyātiriti | atastasyāṃ viraktaṃ cittaṃ tāmapi khyātiṃ niruṇaddhi | tadavasthaṃ saṃskāropagaṃ bhavati | sa nirbījaḥ samādhiḥ | na tatra kiṃcitsaṃprajñāyata ityasaṃprajñātaḥ | dvividhaḥ sa yogaścittavṛttinirodha iti | 1.2 |

This *sūtra* seeks to provide a definition:

I.2. Yoga is the settling of the impulses of the mind.

Since the word 'all' is not mentioned, transcending while experiencing impulses of thought is also referred to. The mind is made of the three *guṇas*, since it has the ability to be clear, active and stable. The aspect of clarity comes from the *sattva* in the mind; when mixed with *rajas* and *tamas*, it is drawn to power and to external objects. Dominated by *tamas*, it tends to incoherence, ignorance, non-detachment, incapacitation. Released from the veil of delusion, fully energised, animated by *rajas* only, it is drawn to evolution, to knowledge, to detachment, to power. And when the final trace of *rajas* is eliminated, established in its own nature, aware only of the difference between the mind and the Self, it enters a level of awareness supported by the Unified Field of Natural Law. Experts in consciousness regard this as supreme, total knowledge. However, this state of Pure Knowledge is suffused with *sattva* and is thus distinct from Pure Consciousness, which is unchanging, unmoving, ever-aware, pure and unbounded. Next, letting go of this state as well, the mind transcends it too. In this state, past impressions remain, but this level of transcendental consciousness is seedless. Here there is no thinking at all; it is beyond thought. So this yoga — the settling of the impulses of the mind into silence — has two aspects.

tadavasthe cetasi viṣayābhāvādbuddhibodhātmā puruṣaḥ kiṃsvabhāva iti ।

***tadā draṣṭuḥ svarūpe'vasthānam* || *1.3* ||**

svarūpapratiṣṭhā tadānīṃ citiśaktiryathā kaivalye | vyutthānacitte tu sati tathā'pi bhavantī na tathā | 1.3 |

— When the awareness is in that state, when there is no object of thought, what is the nature of the Self, the Knower of the intellect? —

I.3. Then consciousness is established in Self-referral.

At that time, Pure Consciousness is established in Self-referral, as in Cosmic Consciousness. Even when the mind is active, It remains so, though It does not appear so.

kathaṃ tarhi | darśitaviṣayatvāt |

vṛttisārūpyamitaratra || *1.4* ||

vyutthāne yāścittavṛttayastadaviśiṣṭavṛttiḥ puruṣaḥ | tathā ca sūtram | ekameva darśanaṃ khyātireva darśanamiti | cittamayaskāntamaṇikalpaṃ saṃnidhimātropakāri dṛśyatvena svaṃ bhavati puruṣasya svāminaḥ | tasmāccittavṛttibodhe puruṣasyānādiḥ saṃbandho hetuḥ | 1.4 |

— How is that? — Because It witnesses thoughts.

I.4. Otherwise, It takes on the form of mental activity.

When the mind is active, the Self is not distinguished from thoughts. There is a *sūtra* on this: 'Consciousness is one. It is conscious of the activity in the mind' (*Pañcaśikha*). As with a magnet, just being brought up close, once it is perceived, the mind becomes the property of the Self, its owner. It is because of this fixed relationship that the Self comes to experience the thoughts which arise in the mind.

tāḥ punarniroddhavyā bahutve sati cittasya |

***vṛttayaḥ pañcatayyaḥ kliṣṭākliṣṭāḥ* || *1.5* ||**

kleśahetukāḥ karmāśayapracayakṣetrībhūtāḥ kliṣṭāḥ | khyātiviṣayā guṇādhikāravirodhinyo'kliṣṭāḥ | kliṣṭapravāhapatitā apyakliṣṭāḥ | kliṣṭacchidreṣvapyakliṣṭā bhavanti akliṣṭācchidreṣu kliṣṭā iti | tathājātīyakāḥ saṃskārā vṛttibhireva kriyante | saṃskāraiśca vṛttaya iti | evaṃ vṛttisaṃskāracakramaniśamāvartate | tadevaṃbhūtaṃ cittamavasitādhikāramātmakalpena vyavatiṣṭhate pralayaṃ vā gacchatīti | 1.5 |

Although there are many thoughts to settle in the mind:

I.5. Thoughts are of five kinds, negative or positive.

Negative thoughts are caused by suffering and form the basis for the accumulation of stress. Positive thoughts derive from Pure Knowledge and counter the influences of the *guṇas*. Positive thoughts can occur within a chain of negative thoughts; such positive thoughts occur in the gaps between negative thoughts, and negative thoughts may occur in the gaps between positive thoughts. Either way, impressions are generated, created by corresponding thoughts; and thoughts are generated by impressions. Thus proceeds the endless cycle of thought and impression. But when the mind becomes silent as described, as its activity comes to rest, it remains still like the Self, or it dissolves.

tāḥ kliṣṭāścākliṣṭāśca pañcadhā vṛttayaḥ |

pramāṇaviparyayavikalpanidrāsmṛtayaḥ || *1.6* ||

tatra |

pratyakṣānumānāgamāḥ pramāṇāni || *1.7* ||

indriyapraṇālikayā cittasya bāhyavastūparāgāttadviṣayā sāmānyaviśeṣātmano'rthasya viśeṣāvadhāraṇapradhānā vṛttiḥ pratyakṣaṃ pramāṇam | phalamaviśiṣṭaḥ pauruṣeyaścittavṛttibodhaḥ | buddherpratisaṃvedī puruṣa ityupariṣṭādupapādayiṣyāmaḥ | anumeyasya tulyajātiyeṣvanuvṛtto bhinnajātiyebhyo vyāvṛttaḥ saṃbandho yastadviṣayā sāmānyāvadhāraṇapradhānā vṛttiranumānam | yathā deśāntaraprāptergatimaccandratārakaṃ caitravat vindhyāścāprāptiragatiḥ | āptena dṛṣṭo'numito vā'rthaḥ paratra svabodhasaṃkrāntaye śabdenopadiśyate | śabdāttadarthaviṣayā vṛttiḥ śroturāgamaḥ | yasyā'śraddheyārtho vaktā na dṛṣṭānumitārthaḥ sa āgamaḥ plavate | mūlavaktari tu dṛṣṭānumitārthe nirviplavaḥ syāt | 1.6-7 |

These are the five negative and positive types of thought:

I.6. True knowledge, false knowledge, mental constructs, sleep, memory.

Of these:

I.7. The types of true knowledge are: direct perception, inference, and authoritative testimony.

Through the channel of the senses an external object overshadows the mind. The object itself is composed of generic and specific features. When the thought mainly picks up on the specific, this type of true knowledge is direct perception. The result is an undifferentiated experience on the part of the Self of the thought in the mind. Later we shall explain how the Self knows the mind by reflection.

Inference is a form of thought which foregrounds the generic traits in the inferent that are common to items of the same series but absent from items of different series. Thus, the moon and stars are mobile because they move, say, into the asterism *Citrā*; but the *Vindhya* hills are immobile because they do not change position.

Something seen or inferred by a reliable person is reported verbally to another in order to transmit such experience; testimony is the form of thought engendered in the hearer by the verbal report. If the speaker is untrustworthy or has not himself seen or inferred the thing, the testimony is unreliable. But when the original speaker has himself seen or inferred the thing, it is reliable.

viparyayo mithyājñānamatadrūpapratiṣṭham || 1.8 ||

sa kasmānna pramāṇam | yataḥ pramāṇena bhādyate | bhūtārthaviṣayatvāt pramāṇasya | tatra pramāṇena bādhanamapramāṇasya dṛṣṭam | tadyathā dvicandradarśanaṃ sadviṣayeṇaikacandradarśanena bādhyata iti | seyaṃ pañcaparvā bhavatyavidyā | avidyā'smitārāgadveṣābhiniveśāḥ kleśā iti | eta eva svasaṃjñābhistamomoho mahāmohastāmisraḥ andhatāmisra iti | ete cittamalaprasaṅgenābhidhāsyante | 1.8 |

I.8. False knowledge is flawed knowledge, not based on the reality of its object.

— Why is it not true knowledge? — Because it is invalidated by true knowledge. Knowledge is true because its object is real. So untrue knowledge is seen to be invalidated by true knowledge — just as the sighting of two moons is confuted by the sighting of one moon, which is based on the reality. There are five kinds of such unknowing: ignorance, the sense of separate individuality, desire, aversion, and the will to live are the causes of suffering. These are also known by technical terms: negativity (*illusion*), delusion (*lust for power*), grand delusion (*glamour*), darkness (*depravity*), blind darkness (*desolation*). They will be described in the context of impurities in the mind.

śabdajñānānupātī vastuśūnyo vikalpaḥ || *1.9* ||

sa na pramāṇopārohī | na viparyayopārohī ca | vastuśūnyatve'pi śabdajñānamāhātmyanibandhano vyavahāro dṛśyate | tadyathā caitanyaṃ puruṣasya svarūpamiti | yadā citireva puruṣastadā kimatra kena vyapadiśyate | bhavati ca vyapadeśe vṛttiḥ | yathā caitrasya gauriti | tathā pratiṣiddhavastudharmo niṣkriyaḥ puruṣaḥ | tiṣṭhati bāṇaḥ sthāsyati sthita iti gatinivṛttau dhātvarthamātraṃ gamyate | tathā anutpattidharmā puruṣa iti | utpattidharmasyābhāvamātramavagamyate na puruṣānvayī dharmaḥ | tasmādvikalpitaḥ sa dharmastena cāsti vyavahāra iti | 1.9 |

I.9. Mental constructs are devoid of reality, being derived from an understanding created within language.

These are not a part of true knowledge; and they are not a form of false knowledge. Although devoid of reality, we can see that they have a function which is that of the value of knowledge produced within the order of language. For example, in saying, 'The essential nature of the Self is consciousness', since consciousness is the Self, what is predicated on what? Nonetheless, a tautology creates a thought in the mind, just as a phrase such as 'Caitra's cow' does. 'The Self is without activity, without qualities,' is another such example. Likewise: '*Bāṇa* is standing still, will stand still, did stand still', where the verbal root conveys no other meaning than an absence of movement. Also, when the Self is declared to be 'unborn', we understand only the absence of birth, but not a positive feature of the Self. Therefore, such a feature is a mental construct, and such is its *modus operandi*.

abhāvapratyayālambanā vṛttirnidrā || 1.10 ||

sā ca samprabodhe pratyavamarśāt pratyayaviśeṣaḥ | katham | sukhamahamasvāpsam | prasannaṃ me manaḥ prajñāṃ me viśāradī karoti | duḥkhamahamasvāpsaṃ styānaṃ me mano bhramatyanavasthitam | gāḍhaṃ mūḍho'hamasvāpsam | gurūṇi me gātrāṇi | klāntaṃ me cittam | alasaṃ muṣitamiva tiṣṭhatīti | sa khalvayaṃ prabuddhasya pratyavamarśo na syādasati pratyayānubhave tadāśritāḥ smṛtayaśca tadviṣayā na syuḥ | tasmātpratyayaviśeṣo nidrā | sā ca samādhāvitarapratyayavanniroddhavyeti | 1.10 |

I.10. The mental activity based on the experience of non-presence is sleep.

This is a special kind of experience because one only becomes aware of it upon waking. — How? — We say: 'I slept well. My mind feels rested. My brain is alert.' Or: 'I slept badly. My mind feels fuzzy, I can't focus, I'm unsettled. I slept heavily, I'm all over the place. My body feels heavy. My mind is exhausted, it feels faint, like I have mislaid it.' In fact, one could not recall sleep upon waking unless the experience of it left an impression, or there would be no memory of it. Therefore sleep is a specific kind of experience. And like other mental activity, it too needs to settle into transcendental consciousness.

anubhūtaviṣayāsaṃpramoṣaḥ smṛtiḥ || *1.11* ||

kiṃ pratyayasya cittaṃ smarati āhosvid viṣayasyeti | grāhyoparaktaḥ pratyayo grāhyagrahaṇobhayākāranirbhāsastathājātīyakaṃ saṃskāramārabhate | sa saṃskāraḥ svavyañjakāñjanastadākārameva grāhyagrahaṇobhayātmikāṃ smṛtiṃ janayati | tatra grahaṇākārapūrvā buddhiḥ | grāhyākārapūrvā smṛtiḥ | sā ca dvayī | bhāvitasmartavyā cā'bhāvitasmartavyā ca | svapne bhāvitasmartavyā | jāgratsamaye tvabhāvitasmartavyeti | sarvāḥ smṛtayaḥ pramāṇaviparyayavikalpanidrāsmṛtīnāmanubhavāt prabhavanti | sarvāścaitā vṛttayaḥ sukhaduḥkhamohātmikāḥ | sukhaduḥkhamohāśca kleśeṣu vyākhyeyāḥ | sukhānuśayī rāgaḥ duḥkhānuśayī dveṣaḥ mohaḥ punaravidyeti | etāḥ sarvā vṛttayo niroddhavyāḥ | āsāṃ nirodhe saṃprajñāto vā samādhirbhavati asaṃprajñāto veti | 1.11 |

I.11. Non-loss of the object experienced is memory.

Does the mind remember the experience or the object? Coloured by the object, the experience is shaped by the imprint of both the object perceived and the process of perception and forms a correspondingly inscribed impression. When the impression comes to remanifest, it generates a memory which has the same double inscription as the object perceived and the process of perception. When the imprint of the process of perception is foregrounded, there is a thought. When the imprint of the object perceived is foregrounded, there is a memory. Memory is of two kinds, depending on whether what is remembered is imaginary or not. In dreams, what is remembered is imagined; whereas in waking, what is remembered is not imagined. All such memories arise from the experience of true knowledge, false knowledge, mental construct, sleep or memory. And all such memories are by nature pleasurable, painful or delusional. Pleasure, pain and delusion will be described along with the causes of suffering. Desire follows pleasure. Aversion follows pain. Delusion is ignorance.

All these various impulses are to be transcended. When they settle, there is transcendental consciousness with or without accompanying thought.

athā'sāṃ nirodhe ka upāya iti |

***abhyāsavairāgbhyāṃ tannirodhaḥ* || *1.12* ||**

cittanādī nāma ubhatovāhinī | vahati kalyāṇāya vahati pāpāya ca | yā tu kaivalyaprāgbhārā vivekaviṣayanimnā sā kalyāṇāvahā | saṃsāraprāgbhārā avivekaviṣayanimnā pāpavahā | tatra vairāgyeṇa viṣayasrotaḥ khilī kriyate | vivekadarśanābhyāsena vivekasrota udghāṭyate | ityubhayādhīnaścittavṛttinirodhaḥ | 1.12 |

— So what is the technique for them to settle? —

I.12. To transcend, repeat and take it as it comes.

Now, the current of thought can flow in two directions. It can flow towards what is beneficial or towards what is harmful. When it is directed towards what is conducive to enlightenment and the deepening of Pure Knowledge, it is beneficial. When it flows towards the world of illusion and not towards deepening Pure Knowledge, it is harmful. Taking it easy dispels the whirlpool of the Relative. Repeated exposure to the experience of non-involvement opens the floodgate of Pure Knowledge. Transcending is effected with these two principles.

***tatra sthitau yatno'bhyāsaḥ* || *1.13* ||**

cittasya avṛttikasya praśāntavāhitā sthitiḥ | tadarthaḥ prayatnaḥ vīryamutsāhaḥ | tatsaṃpipādayiṣayā tatsādhanānuṣṭhānamabhyāsaḥ | 1.13 |

I.13. To achieve integration, a commitment to regular practice is required.

Integration is achieved when a sense of peacefulness permeates the settled mind. To achieve this, commitment, focus and resolve are required. Regular practice means adopting these means with a desire to succeed.

sa tu dīrghakālanairantaryasatkārāsevito dṛḍhabhūmiḥ || 1.14 ||

dīrghakālāsevito nirantarāsevitaḥ satkārāsevitaḥ | tapasā brahmacaryeṇa vidyayā śraddhayā ca saṃpāditaḥ satkāravāndṛḍhabhūmirbhavati | vyutthānasaṃskāreṇa drāgityeva anabhibhūtaviṣaya ityarthaḥ | 1.14 |

I.14. But it can be steadily acquired over time when practised carefully and consistently.

Kept up for a long time; kept up without break; kept up with application. When pursued diligently, together with self-purification, celibacy, intellectual understanding, and confidence, it becomes firmly established. The meaning is that it is not easily overshadowed by incoming impressions.

dṛṣṭānuśravikaviṣayavitṛṣṇasya vaśīkārasaṃjñā vairāgyam || *1.15* ||

striyaḥ annapānam aiśvaryam iti dṛṣṭaviṣayavitṛṣṇasya svargavaidehyaprakṛtilayatvaprāptāvānuśravikaviṣaye vitṛṣṇasya divyādivyaviṣayasaṃprayoge'pi cittasya viṣayadoṣadarśinaḥ prasaṃkhyānabalād anābhogātmikā heyopādeyaśūnyā vaśīkārasaṃjñā vairāgyam | 1.15 |

I.15. An inner freedom, termed 'self-sufficiency', is acquired when the thirst for personal experience and for the goals enjoined by the Vedas is quenched.

One who is not carried away by personal inclinations (such as women, food, power), who does not thirst for the goals enjoined by the Vedic texts (such as the attainment of heaven, disembodied existence, the state of absorption into Nature), recognising the limitations of the Relative, even though this might involve contact with divine and non-divine things, and exercising the power of discernment, enjoys an inner freedom, technically known as 'self-sufficiency', which is characterised by non-involvement, where nothing can be added or taken away.

tatparaṃ puruṣakhyāterguṇavaitṛṣṇyam || *1.16* ||

dṛṣṭānuśravikaviṣayadoṣadarśī viraktaḥ puruṣa-darśanābhyāsāt tacchuddhipravivekāpyāyitabuddhir-guṇebhyo vyaktāvyaktadharmakebhyo virakta iti | taddvayaṃ vairāgyam | tatra yaduttaraṃ tajjñānaprasāda-mātraṃ | yasyodaye sati yogī pratyuditakhyātirevaṃ manyate | prāptaṃ prapanīyam | kṣiṇāḥ kṣetavyāḥ kleśāḥ | cchinnaḥ śliṣṭaparvā bhavasaṃkramaḥ | yasyāvicchedājjanitvā mriyate mṛtvā ca jāyata iti | jñānasyaiva parā kāṣṭhā vairāgyam | etasyaiva hi nāntarīyakaṃ kaivalyamiti | 1.16 |

I.16. Beyond that, the realisation of the Self brings complete freedom from the Relative.

Recognising the limitations of personal experiences and the goals enjoined in the Vedic texts, one is not attracted to them. From repeated exposure to the Self, as the mind abounds in the purity of self-sufficiency, one remains uninvolved in the manifest or unmanifest activities of the *guṇas*. These are the two aspects of inner freedom. The latter is but the light of Pure Knowledge. When it shines within him, the yogi thinks, 'The achievable is achieved. Suffering is overcome. If left unbroken, the chain of successive existences ensures that being born one dies, and dying one is born again; but its soldered links have been smashed open.' This form of inner freedom is the highest summit of knowledge. Enlightenment requires nothing more.

atha upāyadvayena niruddhacittavṛtteḥ kathamucyate saṃprajñātaḥ samādhiriti |

vitarkavicārānandāsmitārūpānugamāt saṃprajñātaḥ || *1.17* ||

vitarkaścittasyā'lambane sthūla abhogaḥ | sūkṣmo vicāraḥ | ānando hlādaḥ | ekātmikā saṃvid asmitā | tatra prathamaścatuṣṭayānugataḥ samādhiḥ savitarkaḥ | dvitīyo vitarkavikalaḥ savicāraḥ | tṛtīyo vicāravikalaḥ sānandaḥ | caturthastadvikalaḥ asmitāmātra iti | sarve ete sālambanāḥ samādhayaḥ | 1.17 |

— So, when the impulses of the mind have started to settle by implementing the two principles mentioned, how can the process of transcending the experience of thinking be described? —

I.17. Transcending the levels of thought ranges from gross, to subtle, to bliss, to Amness.

Surface thinking is the experience of the gross object of thought. Thinking expands to the subtle level. Bliss is an experience of joy. Amness is the fullness of knowledge of the Self alone. Of these states, the first of the four levels of transcending is gross. Leaving behind the gross, the second is subtle. Leaving behind the subtle, the third is bliss. Leaving behind bliss, the fourth is pure Amness. All these levels of transcending involve the experience of levels of thought.

athāsaṃprajñātasamādhiḥ kimupāyaḥ kiṃsvabhāvo veti |

virāmapratyayābhyāsapūrvaḥ saṃskāraśeṣo'nyaḥ || 1.18 ||

sarvavṛttipratyastamaye saṃskāraśeṣo nirodhaścittasya samādhiḥ asaṃprajñātaḥ | tasya paraṃ vairāgyamupāyaḥ | sālambano hi abhyāsastatsādhanāya na kalpate iti | virāmapratyayo nirvastuka ālambanī kriyate | sa ca arthaśūnyaḥ | tadabhyāsapūrvakaṃ hi cittaṃ nirālambanamabhāvaprāptamiva bhavatīti | eṣa nirbījaḥ samādhirasaṃprajñātaḥ | 1.18 |

— As for transcending beyond thought, what is the technique, and what is it like? —

I.18. The repeated experience of the state of least excitation culminates in the other form of transcendental consciousness, where only impressions remain.

When all the impulses have subsided, the settled state of the mind is Pure Consciousness, which is beyond thought, and where only impressions remain. The technique for it is complete letting go. Repetition of a vehicle of thought does not enable one to arrive at this goal. The experience of silence occurs when the vehicle of thought has no object. It has no meaning. Having previously experienced the repetition, the mind is now without any object, as if non-existent. This seedless transcendental consciousness is beyond thought.

sa khalvayaṃ dvividhaḥ | upāyapratyayo bhavapratyayaśca | tatra upāyapratyayo yogināṃ bhavati |

***bhavapratyayo videhaprakṛtilayānām** || 1.19 ||*

videhānāṃ devānāṃ bhavapratyayaḥ | te hi svasaṃskāramātropayogena cittena kaivalyapadamivānubhavantaḥ svasaṃskāravipākaṃ tathājātīyakamativāhayanti | tathā prakṛtilayāḥ sādhikāre cetasi prakṛtilīne kaivalyapadamivānubhavanti yāvanna punarāvartate adhikāravaśāccittamiti | 1.19 |

This is of two types: one attained by the use of techniques, one acquired by status. Yogis attain it through techniques.

I.19. Disembodied beings and those immersed in the subtle levels of Nature experience this by virtue of their status.

Divine beings with no physical nervous system have it by virtue of their status. They spend a period of time experiencing a state similar to enlightenment, while the impressions which condition their awareness come to fruition. Likewise, those entities which abide within the subtler levels of Nature also experience a state similar to enlightenment in a collapsed state of awareness within Nature, but only for as long as their mind is not forced to reincarnate in order to fulfil its assigned role.

śraddhāvīryasmṛtisamādhiprajñāpūrvaka itareṣām || *1. 20* ||

upāyapratyayo yogināṃ bhavati | śraddhā cetasaḥ saṃprasādaḥ | sā hi jananīva kalyāṇī yoginaṃ pāti | tasya hi śraddadhānasya vivekārthino vīryamupajāyate | samupajātavīryasya smṛtirupatiṣṭhate | smṛtyupasthāne ca cittamanākulaṃ samādhīyate | samāhitacittasya prajñāviveka upāvartate | yena tathārthaṃ vastu jānāti | tadabhyāsāt tadviṣayācca vairāgyād asaṃprajñātaḥ samādhirbhavati | 1.20 |

I.20. For others, confidence, vigour, focus, practice of transcending, and clear experience lead to it.

Yogis use techniques. Confidence is assurance in the mind. It protects the yogi like a good mother. Vigour enlivens one who is confident and seeking knowledge. One who is vigorous acquires focus. And with focus, the mind transcends effortlessly. A mind that transcends enjoys clear experiences, through which one becomes a knower of Reality. With regular practice, and with no expectations about the practice and the outcome, transcendental consciousness, beyond thought, is realised.

te khalu nava yogino mṛdumadhyādhimātropāyā bhavanti | tadyathā mṛdūpāyaḥ madhyopāyaḥ adhimātropāya iti | tatra mṛdūpāyo'pi trividhaḥ mṛdusaṃvego madhyasaṃvegaḥ tīvrasaṃvega iti | tathā madhyopāyastathādhimātropāya iti | tatrādhimātropāyānām |

***tīvrasaṃvegānāmāsannaḥ** || **1.21** ||*

samādhilābhaḥ samādhiphalaṃ ca bhavatīti | 1.21 |

In fact, there are nine kinds of yogi: mild, moderate and intent in their practice. In turn, the mildly committed are of three degrees: mild, moderate and intent. And the same applies to the moderate and intent types. As for the highly intent:

I.21. For the serious-minded, it is easy to attain.

The Transcendent and its benefits are attained.

mṛdumadhyādhimātratvāttato'pi viśeṣaḥ || *1.22* ||

mṛdutīvro madhyatīvro'dhimātratīvra iti | tato'pi viśeṣaḥ | tad viśeṣānmṛdutīvrasaṃvegasyā'sannaḥ tato madhyatīvrasaṃvegasyā'sannataraḥ tasmādadhimātratīvrasaṃvegasyādhimātropāyasyā'sannatamaḥ samādhilābhaḥ samādhiphalaṃ ceti | 1.22 |

I.22. Although there is a difference between less, somewhat and highly committed.

The meaning is: 'there is a difference depending on a low level of commitment, a moderate level of commitment or an intense level of commitment'. Depending on the degree, attaining the Transcendent and its benefits is close at hand for those of less commitment, closer for those of moderate commitment, and closest for those of serious commitment.

kimetasmādevāsannataraḥ samādhirbhavati | athāsya lābhe bhavati anyo'pi kaścidupāyo na veti |

īśvarapraṇidhānādvā || *1.23* ||

praṇidhānād bhaktiviśeṣād āvarjita īśvarastamanugṛhṇāti abhidhyānamātreṇa | tadabhidhyānamātrādapi yogina āsannataraḥ samādhilābhaḥ samādhiphalaṃ ca bhavatīti | 1.23 |

— Is the Transcendent more accessible only because of this? Or is there some other means for attaining it, or not? —

I.23. Or by surrendering to the Absolute.

When the seeker surrenders to the Absolute, It is moved to support him in his desire. Simply by having this desire, the yogi gets closer to the Transcendent and its benefits.

atha pradhānapuruṣavyatiriktaḥ ko'yamīśvaro nāmeti |

***kleśakarmavipākāśayairaparāmṛṣṭaḥ puruṣaviśeṣa īśvaraḥ* || *1.24* ||**

avidyādayaḥ kleśāḥ | kuśalākuṣalāni karmāṇi | tatphalaṃ vipākaḥ | tadanuguṇā vāsanā āśayāḥ | te ca manasi vartamānāḥ puruṣe vyapadiśyante | sa hi tatphalasya bhokteti | yathā jayaḥ parājayo vā yoddhṛṣu vartamānaḥ svāmini vyapadiśyate | yo hyanena bhogenāparāmṛṣṭaḥ sa puruṣaviśeṣa īśvaraḥ | kaivalyaṃ prāptāstarhi santi ca bahavaḥ kevalinaḥ | te hi trīṇi bandhanāni cchittvā kaivalyaṃ prāptāḥ | īsvarasya ca tatsaṃbandho na bhūto na bhāvī | yathā muktasya pūrvā bandhakoṭiḥ prajñāyate naivamīśvarasya | yathā vā prakṛtilīnasyottarā bandhakoṭiḥ saṃbhāvyate naivamīśvarasya | sa tu sadaiva muktaḥ sadaiveśvara iti | yo'sau prakṛṣṭasattvopādānādīśvarasya śāśvatika utkarṣaḥ sa kiṃ sanimitta āhosvinnnirnimitta iti | tasya śāstraṃ nimittam | śāstraṃ punaḥ kiṃ nimittam | prakṛṣṭasattvanimittam | etayoḥ śāstrotkarṣayorīśvarasattve vartamānayoranādiḥ saṃbandhaḥ | etasmādetadbhavati sadaiveśvaraḥ sadaiva mukta iti | tacca tasyaiśvaryaṃ sāmyātiśāyavinirmuktam | na tāvadaiśvaryāntareṇa tadatiśayyate | yadevātiśāyi syāttadeva ca tatsyāt | tasmādyatra kāṣṭhāprāptiraiśvaryasya sa īśvara iti |

— So how is what is called the Absolute different from the Relative and the Self? —

I.24. The Absolute is a special Self that is untouched by suffering, action, its results and impressions.

The causes of suffering are ignorance and the other factors. Actions are evolutionary or non-evolutionary. Results are their fruit. Impressions, consonant with these, become deposits, which, entering the mind, are imputed to the Self, which experiences their consequences, in the same way as a victory or a defeat befalling an army is imputed to the commander. But there is a special Self which is untouched by this experience — the Absolute. For there are many who have Self-realised and attained enlightenment; they have attained enlightenment by sundering the three bonds. There has not been, and will not be, any such bond for the Absolute. One who has achieved liberation is presumed to have cut the knot, but not the Absolute. Likewise, an entity abiding within unmanifest Nature is expected to cut the knot in the future, but not the Absolute. For It is ever free, ever supreme. — Is the eternal self-sufficiency of the Absolute, upheld within Its supreme purity, proven or unproven? — The Teaching is Its proof. — How is the Teaching proof? — The proof is absolute purity. The connection between the two, between the Teaching and Its self-sufficiency, residing within the purity of the Absolute, is beginningless. Therefore it is that It is ever absolute, ever free. And Its supreme status is unequalled and unsurpassable. No other power could surpass It. What could surpass It *is* It. Therefore where the Absolute is found, there *is* the

na ca tatsamānamaiśvaryamiti | kasmād | dvayostulyayorekasminyugapatkāmite'rthe navamidamastu purāṇamidamastu ityekasya siddhāvitarasya prākāmyavighātādūnatvaṃ prasaktam | dvayośca tulyayoryugapatkāmitārthaprāptirnāsti | arthasya viruddhatvāt | tasmādyasya sāmyātiśayairvinirmuktam-aiśvaryaṃ sa evaiśvaraḥ | sa ca puruṣaviśeṣa iti | 1.24 |

Absolute. — How can there be no equal to the Absolute? — Because, if two equals rival in the same desire — the one saying 'This is new', the other saying 'It is old' — if one obtains his desire, the other's desire is thwarted, so he is inferior. Where there are two equals, different outcomes of desire cannot occur, since that would be a contradiction in terms. Therefore, the Absolute, unequalled and unsurpassable, is supreme. And It is a special kind of Self.

kiṃca |

***tatra niratiśayaṃ sarvajñabījam* || *1.25* ||**

yadidamatītānāgatapratyutpannapratyeka-samuccayātīndriyagrahaṇamalpaṃ bahviti sarvajñabījametadvivarddhamānaṃ yatra niratiśayaṃ sa sarvajñaḥ | asti kāṣṭhāprāptiḥ sarvajñabījasya sātiśayatvāt parimāṇavaditi | yatra kāṣṭhāprāptirjñānasya sa sarvajñaḥ sa ca puruṣaviśeṣa iti | sāmānyamātropasaṃhāre ca kṛtopakṣayamanumānaṃ na viśeṣapratipattau samarthamiti | tasya saṃjñādiviśeṣapratipattirāgamataḥ paryanveṣyā | tasyā'tmānugrahābhāve'pi bhūtānugrahaḥ prajoyanam | jñānadharmopadeśena kalpapralayamahāpralayeṣu saṃsāriṇaḥ puruṣānuddhariṣyāmīti | tathā coktam | ādividvānnirmāṇacittamadhiṣṭhāya kāruṇyādbhagavānparamarṣirāsuraye jijñāsamānāya tantraṃ provāca iti | 1.25 |

Moreover:

I.25. Within It is located the supreme home of all knowledge.

Whatever the extent of knowledge acquired beyond the senses of the past, future and present, both in terms of general outline and particular details, whether great or small — this is the seed of omniscience. Expanding this to the fullest extent, one becomes all-knowing. Since the seed of all knowledge can grow and expand, its extreme value can be measured. Where this extreme value is attained, the knower is omniscient, and such is the special Self. Only a general idea of It can be obtained using the methods of inference, which cannot furnish any of Its particular characteristics. An understanding of the technicalities and Its other features must be sought in the Teaching. Although the Absolute does not experience any lack of fulfilment, the fulfilment of created beings is a motive for It to say, 'I shall raise up those Selfs journeying through the cycles of dissolution of the ages and the universes with instruction in Pure Knowledge and the mechanics of evolution'. Thus it is said: 'Out of compassion, having assumed a manifested consciousness (Kapila), the Lord, the supreme seer, the first knower, expounded this science to Asuri who was desirous of receiving the knowledge' (*Pañcaśikha*).

sa eṣa pūrveṣāmapi guruḥ kālenānavacchedāt || 1.26 ||

pūrve hi guruvaḥ kālenāvacchidyante | yatrāvacchedārthena kālo nopāvartate sa eṣa pūrveṣāmapi guruḥ | yathā'sya sargasyā'dau prakarṣagatyā siddhastathā'tikrāntasargādiṣvapi pratyetavyaḥ | 1.26 |

I.26. It is the teacher of the sages of old, beyond time.

Teachers of the past are bound by time. Being unbounded, time has no effect on It. It is the teacher of former teachers. It is to be thought of as perfect in Its supreme status, from the beginning of this creation and all previous creations.

tasya vācakaḥ praṇavaḥ || 1.27 ||

vācya īśvaraḥ praṇavasya | kimasya saṃketakṛtaṃ vācyavācakatvamatha pradīpaprakāśavadavasthitamiti | sthito'sya vācyasya vācakena saha saṃbandhaḥ | saṃketastvīśvarasya sthitamevārthamabhinayati | yathā'vasthitaḥ pitāputrayoḥ saṃbandhaḥ saṃketenāvadyotyate ayamasya pitā ayamasya putra iti | sargāntareṣvapi vācyavācakaśaktyapekṣastathaiva saṃketaḥ kriyate | saṃpratipattinityatayā nityaḥ śabdārthasaṃbandha ityāgaminaḥ pratijānate | 1.27 |

I.27. The cosmic hum is Its expression.

The Absolute is expressed by the cosmic hum (*oṃ*). — Is the relation here between expression and expressed a convention, or is it inherent like the light and a lamp? — The link between this expression and what is expressed is fixed. However, it is a convention instituted by the Absolute that performs the role of a fixed meaning. Thus, the link between father and son is an inherent one, which the conventions of language only make explicit in phrases like, 'This is his father, this is his son'. The convention in question is the basis for the bond between expression and expressed, and it endures across creations. The custodians of the Tradition declare that, because they are forever inseparable, the link between the sound and Its meaning is eternal.

vijñātavācyavācakatvasya yoginaḥ |

tajjapastadarthabhāvanam || *1.28* ||

praṇavasya japaḥ praṇavābhidheyasya caiśvarasya bhāvanā | tadasya yoginaḥ praṇavaṃ japataḥ praṇavārthe ca bhāvayataścittamekāgraṃ saṃpadyate | tathā coktam | svādhyāyādyogamāsīta yogātsvādhyāyamāsate | svādhyāyayogasaṃpattyā paramātmā prakāśate iti | 1.28 |

For the yogi who knows the ground of expressed and expression:

I.28. Repeating it realises Its meaning.

Repeating *oṃ* realises the meaning of *oṃ*, the Absolute. The mind of the yogi who repeats *oṃ* and has his attention on *oṃ* becomes one-pointed. For it is said:

'Through recitation one perfects yoga.
Through yoga one perfects recitation.
By perfecting recitation and yoga,
The supreme Self is realised.'
(*Viṣṇupurāṇa VI. 2. 2*)

kiṃ cāsya bhavati |

tataḥ pratyak cetanādhigamo'pi antarāyābhāvaśca || 1.29 ||

ye tāvadantarāyā vyādhiprabhṛtayaste tāvadīśvarapraṇidhānānna bhavanti | svarūpadarśanamapyasya bhavati | yathaiveśvaraḥ puruṣaḥ śuddhaḥ prasannaḥ kevalo'nupasargastathā'yamapi buddheḥ pratisaṃvedī yaḥ puruṣa ityevamadhigacchati | 1.29 |

— Then what happens? —

I.29. The attention can dive within and obstacles dissolve.

Whatever the obstacles, such as illness and so on, they do not arise when attending to the Absolute. One realises one's own nature. Just as the Absolute is like the Self, pure, settled, uninvolved, unbounded, so the Knower of the intellect is one's Self: one attains That.

atha ke'ntarāyā ye cittasya vikṣepakāḥ | ke punaste kiyanto veti |

vyādhistyānasaṃśayapramādālasyāviratibhrānti-darśanālabhabhūmikatvānavasthitatvāni cittavikṣepāste'ntarāyāḥ || 1.30 ||

nava antarāyāścittasya vikṣepāḥ saha ete cittavṛttibhirbhavanti | eteṣāmabhāve na bhavanti | pūrvoktāścittavṛttayaḥ | tatra vyādhirdhāturasakaraṇavaiṣāmyam | styānamakarmaṇyatā cittasya | saṃśaya ubhayakoṭispṛgvijñānaṃ syādidamevaṃ naivaṃ syāditi | pramādaḥ samādhisādhanānāmabhāvanam | ālasyaṃ kāyasya cittasya ca gurutvādapravṛttiḥ | aviratiścittasya viṣayasaṃprayogātmā gardhaḥ | bhrāntidarśanaṃ viparyayajñānam | alabdhabhūmikatvaṃ samādhibhūmeralābhaḥ | anavasthitatvaṃ yallabdhāyāṃ bhūmau cittasyāpratiṣṭhā | samādhipratilambhe hi sati tadavasthitaṃ syāditi | ete cittavikṣepā nava yogamalā yogapratipakṣā yogāntarāyā ityabhidhīyante | 1.30 |

— So what are the obstacles that send the mind off course? What, and how many, are they? —

I.30. Sickness, apathy, doubt, neglect, listlessness, intemperance, confused misunderstandings, failure to make progress, failure to integrate, are the hindrances which distract the mind.

There are nine hindrances which distract the mind. They accompany excitations in the mind. When these are gone, they do not occur. The impulses of the mind have been described earlier. Sickness is some imbalance in the tissues, humours and organs. Apathy comes from not exercising the mind. Doubt is a kind of thinking which hovers between the two sides of an issue, shifting from 'It is so' to 'It is not so'. Neglect is the failure to make use of the technologies for transcending. Lethargy is disinclination that comes from heaviness in the body and mind. Intemperance is the craving of the mind for contact with the objects of the senses. Confused misunderstandings are the result of false knowledge. Failure to progress means not achieving transcendence. Having attained a certain level, failure to integrate is the inability to stabilise it; for once the Transcendent is attained, it needs to be stabilised. These hindrances in the mind are called the nine impurities in yoga, the opponents of yoga, the obstacles to yoga.

***duḥkhadaurmanasyāṅgamejayatvaśvāsapraśvāsā vikṣepasahabhuvaḥ* || *1.31* ||**

duḥkhamādhyātmikam ādhibhautikam ādhidaivakaṃ ca | yenābhihatāḥ prāṇinastadupaghātāya prayatante tadduḥkham | daurmanasyam icchābhighātāccetasaḥ kṣobaḥ | yadaṅgānyejayati kampayati tadaṅgamejayatvam | prāṇo yadbāhyaṃ vāyumācāmati sa śvāsaḥ | yatkautṣṭhyaṃ vāyuṃ niḥsārayati sa praśvāsaḥ | ete vikṣepasahabhuvo vikṣiptacittasyaite bhavanti | samāhitacittasyaite na bhavanti | 1.31 |

I.31. Pain, frustration, restlessness in the body, coarseness of the inward and the outward breath, accompany such distractions.

Pain can be self-inflicted, or caused by external agents, or result from natural causes. Living creatures are afflicted by it, and they seek to be free of it. Frustration is the disturbance in the mind that comes when desire is not fulfilled. Restlessness in the body causes the limbs to tremble and shake. Breath that draws air in is inhalation. Breath that expels air is exhalation. These phenomena occur when the mind is distracted. When the mind increases in coherence, they do not arise.

atha ete vikṣepāḥ samādhipratipakṣāstābhyām evābhyāsavairāgyābhyāṃ nirodhavyāḥ | tatrābhyāsasya viṣayamupasaṃharannidamāha |

***tatpratiṣedhārthamekatattvābhyāsaḥ* || *1.32* ||**

vikṣepapratiṣedhārthamekatattvālambanaṃ cittamabhyaset | yasya tu pratyarthaniyataṃ pratyayamātraṃ kṣaṇikaṃ ca cittaṃ tasya sarvameva cittamekāgraṃ nāstyeva viṣkiptam | yadi punaridam sarvataḥ pratyāhṛtya ekasminnarthe samādhiyate tadā bhavatyekāgramiti | ato na pratyarthaniyatam | yo'pi sadṛśapratyayapravāhena cittamekāgraṃ manyate tasya yadyekāgratā pravāhacittasya dharmastadaikaṃ nāsti pravāhacittam kṣaṇikatvāt | atha pravāhāṃśasyaiva pratyayasya dharmaḥ sa sarvaḥ sadṛśapratyayapravāhī vā visadṛśapratyayapravāhī vā pratyarthaniyatatvādekāgra eveti vikṣiptacittānupapattih | tasmādekamanekārthamavasthitaṃ cittamiti | yadi ca cittenaikenānvitāḥ svabhāvabhinnāḥ pratyayā jāyerannatha kathamanyapratyayadṛṣṭasyānyaḥ smartā

So these are the distractions which hold up the process of transcending. They can be obviated by regular practice and taking it easy. Summarising the issue of regular practice, he says this:

I.32. Repeated exposure to the wholeness of Reality removes them.

To counter distractions, the mind should entertain a specific thought that encapsulates the ultimate Reality. — There are those who maintain that the mind is only momentary, only a flow consisting in a constant succession of thoughts; so the mind is always one-pointed and cannot become distracted. — If you agree that the mind withdraws from without and then transcends on a thought, and thereby becomes one-pointed, then it cannot consist merely in a succession of thoughts. — But if you take the view that the mind is one-pointed because there is a flow of identical thoughts, then one-pointedness is a permanent feature of the mind as flow. — Then the mind, as flow, is not an autonomous entity at all; there is just a series of moments. Moreover, if one-pointedness is a feature of thought conceived as an item in a flow, then all thinking — whether the flow is made up of similar thoughts or of dissimilar thoughts — is one-pointed because it is limited to the particular object being entertained. And if that is the case, the phenomenon of the mind getting distracted cannot be explained. Therefore the mind is in fact unitary, and stable, and entertains different thoughts. Furthermore, if thoughts sprang up, each different in nature, but unconnected within one mind, then how could one thought recall what

bhavet | anyapratyayopacitasya ca karmāśayasyānyaḥ pratyaya upabhoktā bhavet | kathaṃcit samādhīyamānamapyetad gomayapāyasīyanyāyamākṣipati | kiṃca svātmānubhavāpahnavaścittasyānyatve prāpnoti | kathaṃ yadahamadrākṣaṃ tatspṛśāmi yaccāsprākṣaṃ tatpaśyāmyahamiti pratyayaḥ sarvasya pratyayasya bhede sati pratyayinyabhedenopasthitaḥ | ekapratyaya viṣayo'yamabhedātmā'hamiti pratyayaḥ | kathamatyantabhinneṣu citteṣu vartamānaṃ sāmānyamekaṃ pratyayinamāśrayet | svānubhavagrāhyaścā'yamabhedātmā'hamiti pratyayaḥ | na ca pratyakṣasya māhātmyaṃ pramāṇāntareṇabhibhūyate | pramāṇāntaraṃ ca pratyakṣabalenaiva vyavahāraṃ labhate | tasmādekamanekārthamavasthitaṃ ca cittam | 1.32 |

another thought has seen? One thought would experience the result of an action performed by another thought. Even with some finessing, such a line of argument is even more extravagant than the false syllogism of the milk and the dung (the fallacy that claims both are the same because both are produced by the cow). Moreover, to accept the premise of the changing momentaneity of the mind would put into question the experience of personal identity. How can the thought arise from the continuity of the thinker who thinks 'I touch what I have seen, I see what I have touched', if all thoughts are unconnected? The thought 'I am a self, undivided', would be one item within the flow; how could it occur to one and the same thinker persisting across different states of mind? The thought 'I am a self, undivided' is derived from personal experience. And there is no mode of true knowledge which has greater priority than that of direct perception; all other forms of true knowledge are based on the validity of direct perception. Therefore the mind is one, stable, and capable of experiencing a variety of objects.

yasya cittasya avasthitasya idaṃ śāstreṇa parikarma nirdiśyate tatkatham |

maitrīkaruṇāmuditopekṣāṇāṃ sukhaduḥkha-puṇyāpuṇyaviṣayāṇāṃ bhāvanātaścittaprasādanam || 1.33 ||

tatra sarvaprāṇiṣu sukhasaṃbhogāpanneṣu maitrīm bhāvayet | duḥkhiteṣu karuṇām | puṇyātmakeṣu muditām | apuṇyātmakeṣūpekṣām | evamasya bhāvayataḥ śuklo dharma upajāyate | tataśca cittaṃ prasīdati | prasannamekāgraṃ sthitipadaṃ labhate | 1.33 |

— Cleansing the mind, once stabilised, is recommended by the Teaching. What is this? —

I.33. Clarity of mind comes from cultivating friendliness, compassion, good will, and indifference towards the happy, the unhappy, the deserving and the undeserving.

Let him cultivate friendliness towards all creatures enjoying happiness, compassion towards the unhappy, good will towards the deserving, indifference towards the undeserving. Cultivating these, one's evolution is unencumbered. Also, the mind is calmed, and being calmed, attains a state of one-pointed stability.

praccchardanavidhāraṇābhyāṃ vā prāṇasya || *1.34* ||

koṣṭhyasya vāyornāsikāpuṭābhyāṃ prayatnaviśeṣādvamanaṃ pracchardanam | vidhāraṇaṃ prāṇāyāmaḥ | tābhyāṃ vā manasaḥ sthitiṃ sampādayet | 1.34 |

I.34. Or by exhaling and suspending the breath.

'Exhaling' involves a specific technique, expelling the breath from the stomach through the nostrils. 'Suspending' means retaining the breath. The mind may also be settled with these.

viṣayavatī vā pravṛttirutpannā manasaḥ sthitinibandhanī || 1.35 ||

nāsikāgre dhārayato'sya yā divyagandhasaṃvit sā gandhapravṛttiḥ | jihvāgre divyarasasaṃvit | tāluni rūpasaṃvit | jihvāmadhye sparśasaṃvit | jihvāmūle śabdasaṃvidityetāḥ pravṛttaya utpannāścittaṃ sthitau nibadhnanti saṃśayaṃ vidhamanti samādhiprajñāyāṃ ca dvārī bhavantīti | etena candrādityagrahamaṇipradīparaśmyādiṣu pravṛttirutpannā viṣayavatyeva veditavyā | yadyapi hi tattacchāstrānumānācāryopadeśairavagatamarthatattvaṃ sadbhūtameva bhavati eteṣāṃ yathābhūtārthapratipādanasāmarthyāttathā'pi yāvadekadeśo'pi kaścinna svakaraṇa saṃvedyo bhavati tāvatsarvaṃ parokṣamivāpavargādiṣu sūkṣmeṣvartheṣu na dṛḍhāṃ buddhimutpādayati | tasmācchāstrānumānācāryopadeśopodbalanārtham-evāśrayaṃ kaścidarthaviśeṣaḥ pratyakṣīkartavyaḥ | tatra tadupadiṣṭārthaikadeśapratyakṣatve sati sarvaṃ susūkṣmaviṣayamapi ā'pavargāt śraddhīyate | etadarthamevedaṃ cittaparikarma nirdiśyate | aniyatāsu vṛttiṣu tadviṣayāyāṃ vaśikārasaṃjñāyāmupajāyātāṃ

I.35. Or directing the attention to have the refined experience of certain objects also helps to settle the mind swiftly.

When the attention is on the tip of the nose, the faculty of smell produces an awareness of divine smell; on the tip of the tongue, awareness of divine taste; on the palate, awareness of colour; on the middle of the tongue, awareness of touch; on the root of the tongue, awareness of sound. These experiences quickly settle the mind, dissipate doubt, and become doorways to the experience of the Transcendent. In the same way, putting the attention on the moon, the sun, the planets, precious stones, the light of a lamp and so on, is known promptly to produce the direct experience of those objects. Although all that is learnt from the Teaching, from inference, and from the instructions of the masters is firmly grounded in reality — because they are competent in communicating the reality of things — nonetheless while one has not oneself had direct experience of the last particular aspect of a thing, then the whole thing is as if blocked from one's view, and so, as far as subtle matters, such as enlightenment and the like, are concerned, a reliable understanding cannot be obtained. Therefore, in order to confirm the Teaching, the inference, or the master's instruction, it is necessary to know things on the basis of one's own direct experience. Then, when just a small part of what has been taught is known by direct perception, the whole, even the most subtle matters, including enlightenment, can be accepted on trust. To this end alone, the cleansing of the mind is recommended. Thoughts arise spontaneously in the mind, but when control over them is acquired, the mind is capable of

cittaṃ samarthaṃ syāttasya tasyārthasya pratyakṣīkaraṇāyeti | tathā ca sati śraddhāvīryasmṛtisamādhayo'syāpratibandhena bhaviṣyantīti | 1.35 |

knowing anything by direct perception. And with this, confidence, vigour, focus and transcending develop without delay.

viśokā vā jyotiṣmatī || 1.36 ||

pravṛttirutpannā manasaḥ sthitinibandhanītyanuvartate | hṛdayapuṇḍarīke dhārayato yā buddhisaṃvid buddhisattvaṃ hi bhāsvaramākāśakalpaṃ tatra sthitivaiśāradyāt pravṛttiḥ sūryendugrahamaṇiprabhārūpākāreṇa vikalpate | tathā'smitāyāṃ samāpannaṃ cittaṃ nistaraṅgamahodadhikalpaṃ śāntamanantamasmitāmātraṃ bhavati | yatredamuktam | tamaṇumātramātmānamanuvidyā'smītyevaṃ tāvatsaṃpratijānīta iti | eṣā dvayī viśokā viṣayavatī asmitāmātrā ca pravṛttijyotiṣmatītyucyate yayā yoginaścittaṃ sthitipadaṃ labhata iti | 1.36 |

I.36. Or a pleasing, luminous object.

Add: 'Directing the attention to some pleasing, luminous object also helps to settle the mind'. Putting the attention on the lotus of the heart one obtains an experience of the mind, and the *sattva* in the mind shines brilliant as the ether. As proficiency in this is gained, the subtle experience of the radiance of the sun, the moon, the planets, or of precious stones becomes possible. As the mind settles to the level of Amness, like an ocean without waves, it becomes peaceful, unbounded, pure Amness. So it is said: 'Knowing the finest Self, verily he realises "I am"' (*Pañcaśikha*). This subtle experience of radiance can be of two kinds: the one associated with some pleasant object, the other with pure Amness. It produces a state of restful alertness in the mind.

vītarāgaviṣayaṃ vā cittam || 1.37 ||

vītarāgacittālambanoparaktaṃ vā yoginaścittaṃ sthitipadaṃ labhata iti | 1.37 |

I.37. Or by attuning oneself to the level of consciousness of one who is free from desire.

The yogi's mind becomes settled when the focus is an object free from desire.

svapnanidrājñānālambanaṃ vā || 1.38 ||

svapnajñānālambanaṃ nidrājñānālambanaṃ vā tadākāraṃ yoginaścittaṃ sthitipadaṃ labhata iti | 1.38 |

I.38. Or the experience of witnessing dreaming or sleep.

Or the yogi's mind can achieve the settled state when the awareness takes the form of the experience of dreaming or sleep.

yathābhimatadhyānādvā || 1.39 ||

yadevābhimataṃ tadeva dhyāyet | tatra labdhasthitikamanyatrāpi sthitipadaṃ labhata iti | 1.39 |

I.39. Or with a recognised technique of meditation.

One may meditate as one feels to. Using this means to settle, one can also attain the state of restful alertness.

paramāṇuparamamahattvānto'sya vaśīkāraḥ || *1.40* ||

sūkṣme niviśamānasya paramāṇvantaṃ sthitipadaṃ labhata iti | sthūle niviśamānasya paramamahattvāntaṃ sthitipadaṃ cittasya | evaṃ tāmubhayīṃ koṭimanudhāvato yo'syā'pratīghātaḥ sa paro vaśīkāraḥ | tadvaśīkārātparipūrṇaṃ yoginaścittaṃ na punarabhyāsakṛtaṃ parikarmāpekṣata iti | 1.40 |

I.40. One's mastery ranges from the smallest to the greatest.

Diving into the subtle, one gains a state of restful alertness at the finest transcendental level. Transferring the attention to the gross level, the mind enjoys a silent state of total unboundedness. Alternating between these two extremes, one acquires complete, unimpeded mastery. When the yogi is completely steeped in this mastery, he has no more need to cleanse the mind with his regular practice.

atha labdhasthitikasya cetasaḥ kiṃsvarūpā kiṃviṣayā vā samāpattiriti | taducyate |

kṣīṇavṛtterabhijātasyeva maṇergrahītṛgrahaṇagrāhyeṣu tatsthatadañjanatā samāpattiḥ || 1.41 ||

kṣīṇavṛtteriti pratyastamitapratyayasyetyarthaḥ | abhijātasyeva maṇeriti dṛṣṭāntopādānam | yathā sphaṭika upāśrayabhedāttattadrūpoparakta upāśrayarūpākāreṇa nirbhāsate tathā grāhyālambanoparaktaṃ cittaṃ grāhyasamāpannaṃ grāhyasvarūpākāreṇa nirbhāsate | tathā bhūtasūkṣmoparaktaṃ bhūtasūkṣmasamāpannaṃ bhūtasūkṣmasvarūpābhāsaṃ bhavati | tathā sthūlālambanoparaktaṃ sthūlarūpasamāpannaṃ sthūlarūpābhāsaṃ bhavati | tathā viśvabhedoparaktaṃ viśvabhedasamāpannaṃ viśvarūpābhāsaṃ bhavati | tathā grahaṇeṣvapi indriyeṣvapi draṣṭavyam | grahaṇālambanoparaktaṃ grahaṇasamāpannaṃ grahaṇasvarūpākāreṇa nirbhāsate | tathā grahītṛpuruṣālambanoparaktaṃ grahītṛpuruṣasamāpannaṃ grahītṛpuruṣasvarūpākāreṇa nirbhāsate | tathā muktapuruṣālambanoparaktaṃ muktapuruṣasamāpannaṃ muktapuruṣasvarūpākāreṇa nirbhāsata iti | tadevamabhijātamaṇikalpasya cetaso

— So what are the nature and the mechanics of the experience that occurs when the awareness is in that state of restful alertness? —

I.41. As mental activity is refined, the mind is like a precious stone, absorbing the image of whatever object is presented — be it observer, process of observation or object observed.

'As mental activity is refined': the meaning is when there is no excitation. The precious stone is an analogy. When a rock crystal is placed next to an object, it is coloured by whatever form the object has and it glows with the reflection of that object. Like that, the mind absorbs the image projected by the object observed, and attuning to it, it takes on the appearance of the object observed. In the same way, coloured by the image of a subtle object, it absorbs the subtle object and takes on the appearance of the subtle object. Similarly, coloured by a gross object, it absorbs the image of the gross object and takes on the appearance of the gross object. Likewise, coloured by the image of any kind of object, it absorbs that object and takes on the appearance of that object. The same occurs with the means of perception, the senses. Coloured by the image of the sense, it is attuned to that sense and takes on the appearance of that sense. Likewise, coloured by the image of the observer, the Self, it entrains with the observer Self and takes on the appearance of the observing Self. In the same way, coloured by the image of the liberated Self, it comes into phase with the liberated Self and takes on the appearance of the liberated Self. In this manner, the mind is like a precious stone, assuming the form of whatever is presented to it from either the

Yoga-Sūtra I.41

grahītṛgrahaṇagrāhyeṣu puruṣendriyabhūteṣu yā tatsthatadañjanatā teṣu sthitasya tadākārāpattiḥ sā samāpattirityucyate | 1.41 |

observer, the process of observation or the observed — the Self, the senses, the objects of sense. This is the mechanism whereby the mind gets absorbed and assumes different forms.

tatra śadbārthajñānavikalpaiḥ saṃkīrṇā savitarkā samāpattiḥ || 1.42 ||

tadyathā gauriti śabdogaurityartho gauriti jñānamityavibhāgena vibhaktānāmapi grahaṇaṃ dṛṣṭam | vibhajyamānāścānye śabdadharmā anye'rthadharmā anye jñānadharmā ityeṣāṃ vibhaktaḥ panthāḥ | tatra samāpannasya yogino yo gavādyarthaḥ samādhiprajñāyāṃ samārūḍhaḥ sa cecchabdārthajñānavikalpānuviddha upāvartate sā saṃkīrṇā samāpattiḥ savitarketyucyate | yadā punaḥ śabdasaṃketasmṛtipariśuddhau śrutānumānajñānavikalpaśūnyāyāṃ samādhiprajñāyāṃ svarūpamātreṇāvasthito'rthastatsvarūpākāra-mātratayaivāvacchidyate sā ca nirvitarkā samāpattiḥ | tatparaṃ pratyakṣam | tacca śrutānumānayor-bījam | tataḥ śrutānumāne prabhavataḥ | na ca śrutānumānajñānasahabhūtaṃ taddarśanam | tasmādasaṃkīrṇaṃ pramāṇāntareṇa yogino nirvitarkasamādhijaṃ darśanamiti | 1.42 |

I.42. The awareness may be absorbed in meanings, caught up in the associations of words, objects and ideas.

Take, for example, the word 'cow', the object 'cow' and the idea 'cow'. In ordinary perception, though they are distinct, they are not separated. But when they are distinguished, the respective properties of the word, the object and the idea are found to be different; their modes are different. When, at the start of the process of transcending, the yogi picks up on a thought — 'cow', for example — it is conflated with the construct of the word, the object and the idea. This experience involves the associations of meaning. But, when the awareness is freed from the boundaries of the conventions of language and the experience of the Transcendent is unencumbered by notions formed by the knowledge gained indirectly from authoritative teachings and from inference, the object of attention stands, disembedded, by itself, in its own status — and this kind of experience of being absorbed in meditation is beyond verbal thinking. This is the highest form of direct cognition. Indeed, it is the seed of all authoritative teaching and inference; it is the source of authoritative teaching and inference. This type of cognition is independent of authoritative teaching and inference. Therefore the yogi's awareness is one of transcendence beyond the level of meaning, unalloyed with any other mode of true knowledge.

nirvitarkāyāḥ samāpatterasyāḥ sūtreṇa lakṣanaṃ dyotyate |

smṛtipariśuddhau svarūpaśūnyevārthamātranirbhāsā nirvitarkā || *1.43* ||

yā śabdasaṃketaśrutānumānajñānavikalpasmṛti-pariśuddhau grāhyasvarūpoparaktā prajñā svamiva prajñārūpaṃ grahaṇātmakaṃ tyāktvā padārthamātrasvarūpa grāhyasvarūpāpanneva bhavati sā nirvitarkā samāpattiḥ | tathā ca vyākhyātam | tasyā ekabuddhyupakramo hyarthātmā'ṇupracayaviśeṣātmā gavādirghaṭādirvā lokaḥ | sa ca saṃsthānaviśeṣo bhūtasūkṣmāṇāṃ sādhāraṇo dharma ātmabhūtaḥ phalena vyaktenānumitaḥ svavyañjakāñjanaḥ prādurbhavati | dharmāntarodaye ca tirobhavati | sa eṣa dharmo'vayavītyucyate | yo'sāvekaśca mahāṃścāṇīyāṃśca sparśavāṃśca kriyādharmakaścānityaśca tenāvayavinā vyavahārāḥ kriyante | yasya punaravastukaḥ sa pracayaviśeṣaḥ sūkṣmaṃ ca kāraṇamanupalabhyamavikalpasya tasyāvayavyabhāvādatadrūpapratiṣṭhaṃ mithyājñānamiti

The characteristics of experiencing thought beyond the level of meaning are described in the following *sūtra*:

I.43. When the thinking refines into the vacuum state beyond the level of meaning, the awareness is lively just with the object of thought.

When the thinking is released from the knowledge that comes from the notions derived from linguistic convention, from authoritative teaching and from inference, the awareness is coloured by the reality of the object of perception. As if abandoning its status as knower, it takes on the form of the object designated by the word, and becomes as if entrained with the object of perception, absorbed at the level beyond meaning. This can be explained as follows: in this experience of being absorbed, an object in the world — a cow, for example, or a pot — provides the occasion for a particular experience. The object in question is composed of a specific collection of atoms. This specific arrangement is a manifestation of the subtle elements which are at the basis of the object's existence. This can be inferred from the mere fact of the object's presence, since the object only appears in accord with the causes of its manifestation, and then disappears when other properties are activated. It is this structure which is called the 'whole'. This 'whole' is unique: it may be large or small, tangible, fulfilling a specific function, ephemeral — a thing in the relative world we deal with in ordinary life. If someone maintains that this specific structure is unreal, then he can detect no subtle cause of it, and because, for him, there is no 'whole', he can only have equivocal knowledge of it, that is, knowledge with

prāyeṇa sarvameva prāptaṃ mithyājñānamiti | tadā ca samyagjñānamapi kiṃ syādviṣayābhāvāt | yadyadupalabhyate tattadavayavitvenāghrātam | tasmādastyavayavī yo mahattvādivyavahārāpannaḥ samāpatternirvitarkāyā viṣayo bhavati | 1.43 |

no basis in reality. From this point of view, all knowledge risks being baseless. Indeed, what true knowledge could there be of an object that does not exist? However, the fact is that whatever is perceived is sensed as a 'whole'. Therefore the 'whole' does exist, and it is this 'whole' with its everyday properties — 'large' or whatever — that is cognised at the level beyond verbal meaning during meditation.

etayaiva savicārā nirvicārā ca sūkṣmaviṣaya vyākhyātā || 1.44 ||

tatra bhūtasūkṣmeṣvabhivyaktadharmakeṣu deśakālanimittānubhavāvacchinneṣu yā samāpattiḥ sā savicāretyucyate | tatrāpyekabuddhinirgrāhyam-evoditadharmaviśiṣṭaṃ bhūtasūkṣmamālambanībhūtaṃ samādhiprajñāyāmupatiṣṭhate | yā punaḥ sarvathā sarvataḥ śāntoditāvyapadeśyadharmānavacchinneṣu sarvadharmānupātiṣu sarvadharmātmakeṣu samāpattiḥ sā nirvicāretyucyate | evaṃ svarūpaṃ hi tadbhūtasūkṣmametenaiva svarūpeṇā'lambanībhūtameva samādhiprajñāsvarūpamuparañjayati | prajñā ca svarūpaśūnyevārthamātrā yadā bhavati tadā nirvicāretyucyate | tatra mahadvastuviṣayā savitarkā nirvitarkā ca sūkṣmaviṣayā savicārā nirvicārā ca | evamubhayoretayaiva nirvitarkayā vikalpahānirvyākhyātā iti | 1.44 |

I.44. From this, the subtler experiences of expansion and unboundedness can be understood.

The experience of expansion concerns the subtle level of the elements where their properties begin to manifest and their differentiation into space, time, and causation can be experienced. In this case, the thought is experienced at the finest transcendental levels of awareness and apprehends the finest expressed values of the subtle elements of the object. On the other hand, with unbounded awareness, the experience encompasses all of time and space, with no differentiation of past, present or future values, in all their expressed and non-expressed potential. Thus, when the finest level of the subtle elements becomes the object of awareness, this finest aspect permeates the subtle level of transcendental consciousness; whereas, when the awareness is aware only of its own nature, as in a vacuum state, there is unboundedness. So, at the grosser levels the exploration of consciousness is either with associations or beyond the level of meaning; and at the subtle levels, the research is performed at the level of expanded awareness or unboundedness. The explanation given for transcending surface thinking by going beyond meaning also applies to the latter two stages.

sūkṣmaviṣayatvaṃ cāliṅgaparyavasānam || 1.45 ||

pārthivasyāṇorgandhatanmātraṃ sūkṣmo viṣayaḥ | āpyasya rasatanmātram | taijasasya rūpatanmātram | vāyavīyasya sparśatanmātram | ākāśasya śabdatanmātramiti | teṣāmahaṃkāraḥ | asyāpi liṅgamātraṃ sūkṣmo viṣayaḥ | liṅgamātrasyāpyaliṅgaṃ sūkṣmo viṣayaḥ | na āliṅgāt paraṃ sūkṣmamasti | nanvasti puruṣaḥ sūkṣma iti | satyam | yathā liṅgāt paramaliṅgasya saukṣmyaṃ na caivaṃ puruṣasya | kiṃtu liṅgasyānvayikāraṇaṃ puruṣo na bhavati | hetustu bhavatīti | ataḥ pradhāne saukṣmyaṃ niratiśayaṃ vyākhyātam | 1.45 |

I.45. And the finest subtle level in turn dissolves into undifferentiated pure Being.

The subtle aspect of a particle of earth is the element smell. Of water, the element taste. Of fire, the element colour. Of air, the element touch. Of ether, the element sound. Of all these, the subtle element is Amness. Subtler than that is the element of pure differentiation. And subtler than pure differentiation is undifferentiated pure Being. There is no further subtle element beyond non-differentiation. — But the Self is subtle. — True. However, the subtleness of pure Being which is beyond differentiation is not the subtleness of the Self. Although It provides the motive, the Self is not the underlying cause of differentiation. Thus, the subtleness within unmanifest Nature is considered unsurpassable.

tā eva sabījaḥ samādhiḥ || 1.46 ||

tāścatasraḥ samāpattayo bahirvastubījā iti samādhirapi sabījaḥ | tatra sthūle'rthe savitarko nivitarkaḥ sūkṣmo'rthe savicāro nirvicāra iti | sa caturdhopasaṃkhyātaḥ samādhiriti | 1.46 |

I.46. These occur at relative transcendental levels.

The four aspects of the experience of transcending occur at levels of the Relative, so the transcending is relative. When the object of thought is gross, the awareness is absorbed in surface associations or just below the level of meaning; and when the object of thought is subtle, the experience is one of expansion or unboundedness. This explains the four levels of the process of transcending.

nirvicāravaiśāradye'dhyātmaprasādaḥ || *1.47* ||

aśuddhyāvaraṇamalāpetasya prakāśātmano buddhisattvasya rajastamobhyāmanabhibhūtaḥ svacchaḥ sthitipravāho vaiśāradyam | yadā nirvicārasya samādhervaiśāradyamidaṃ jāyate tadā yogino bhavatyadhyātmaprasādaḥ | bhūtārthaviṣayaḥ kramānanurodhī sphuṭaḥ prajñālokaḥ | tathā coktam | prajñāprasādamāruhyā'śocyaśśocato janān | bhūmiṣṭhāniva śailasthassarvānprājño'nupaśyati | 1.47 |

I.47. Familiarity with the calm of unboundedness brings sublime peacefulness.

When the layers of impurity are removed, when the Self is radiant and the mind is pure, the flow of simplest awareness is transparent, uninfluenced by *rajas* and *tamas*, then this is the state of proficiency. As this proficiency in transcending and unboundedness grows, then the yogi enjoys sublime inner peace. Awareness is fully awake, fully unfolded, fully comprehensive, cognisant of Reality. Thus it is said:

'From the vantage of the awareness of inner peace,
free from suffering, though seeing that others suffer,
the enlightened stands upon the mountain top
and looks down on those in the valley below.'
(*Mahābhārata XII.17.20*)

ṛtaṃbharā tatra prajñā || *1.48* ||

tasminn samāhitacittasya yā prajñā jāyate tasyā ṛtaṃbharā saṃjñā bhavati | anvarthā ca sā satyameva bibharti | na ca tatra viparyāsajñānagandho'pyastīti | tathoktam | āgamenānumānena dhyānābhyāsarasena ca | tridhā prakalpayanprajñāṃ labhate yogamuttamam iti | 1.48 |

I.48. Then the awareness is in accord with cosmic law.

In this state of coherent consciousness, the experience arises which is technically known as 'conveying cosmic order'. The etymology is that it conveys only truth. In that state there is not even a hint of error. Thus it is said:

'Through the Tradition, through inference,
and through zeal in regular meditation
— cultivating the awareness in these three ways —
one attains supreme enlightenment.'

sā punaḥ |

***śrutānumānaprajñābhyāmanyaviṣayā viśeṣārthatvāt* || *1.49* ||**

śrutāgamavijñānaṃ tatsāmānyaviṣayam | na hyāgamena śakyo viśeṣo'bhidātum | kasmāt | na hi viśeṣeṇa kṛtasaṃketaḥ śabda iti | tathā'numānaṃ sāmānyaviṣayameva | yatra prāptistatra gatiryatrāprāptistatra na bhavati gatirityuktam | anumānena ca sāmānyenopasaṃhāraḥ | tasmācchrutānumānaviṣayo na viśeṣaḥ kaścidastīti | na cāsya sūkṣmavyavahitaviprakṛṣṭasya vastuno lokapratyakṣeṇa grahaṇamasti | na cāsya viśeṣasyāpramānakasyābhāvo'stīti | samādhiprajñānirgrāhya eva sa viśeṣo bhavati puruṣagato vā bhūtasūkṣmagato vā | tasmācchrutānumāna-prajñābhyāmanyaviṣayā sā prajñā viśeṣārthatvāditi | 1.49 |

Furthermore:

I.49. This is qualitatively different in scope to the knowledge gained from authoritative testimony and inference.

Knowledge from authoritative testimony is general. The specific cannot be expressed by verbal means. — Why? — Words are the creations of convention and cannot deal in specifics. The same is true of inference, whose object is general. Thus it is said: 'Arriving means moving; no arrival, no movement'. Inference is limited to general deductions. Therefore nothing specific can be had from authoritative testimony and inference. Also, in ordinary perception there is no experience of subtle, hidden or distant objects. — But there can be no such thing, without the instruments of some mode of true knowledge. — Yes, there is. Cognition of specific things can be experienced in the state of transcendental consciousness, either from within the Self or at the level of the subtle elements. Therefore this experience is different to the knowledge gained from authoritative testimony or from inference, because it deals with the particular.

samādhiprajñāpratilambhe yoginaḥ prajñākṛtaḥ saṃskāro navo navo jāyate |

***tajjaḥ saṃskāro'nyasaṃskārapratibandhī* || *1.50* ||**

samādhiprajñāprabhavaḥ saṃskāro vyutthānasaṃskārāśayaṃ bādhate | vyutthānasaṃskārābhibhavāttatprabhavāḥ pratyayā na bhavanti | pratyayanirodhe samādhirupatiṣṭhate | tataḥ samādhijā prajñā tataḥ prajñākṛtāḥ saṃskārā iti navo navaḥ saṃskārāśayo jāyate | tataśca prajñā tataśca saṃskārā iti | kathamasau saṃskārāśayaścittaṃ sādhikāraṃ na kariṣyatīti | na te prajñākṛtāḥ saṃskārāḥ kleśakṣayahetutvāccittamadhikāraviśiṣṭaṃ kurvanti | cittaṃ hi te svakāryādavasādayanti | khyātiparyavasānaṃ hi cittaceṣṭitamiti | 1.50 |

The yogi receives more and more new impressions from the experience of the state of transcendental consciousness.

I.50. The effect of this experience is to prevent other impressions caused by stress.

An impression that is created by the experience of the Transcendent prevents stress from other impressions coming from outer activity. When impressions that come from outer activity do not leave traces, thoughts related to them do not arise. When thoughts subside, transcendental consciousness is accessible. Experiences of transcendental consciousness create impressions of transcendental consciousness. So a new set of impressions is laid down. As is the experience, so is the impression. — How is it that the residue of these impressions does not dispose the mind to activity? — The impressions created by the experience of the Transcendent do not impel the mind into activity because they eliminate the causes of suffering. They bring fulfilment to the functioning of the mind. The work of the mind ends with enlightenment.

kiṃcāsya bhavati |

***tasyāpi nirodhe sarvanirodhānnirbījassamādhiḥ* || *1.51* ||**

sa na kevalaṃ samādhiprajñāvirodhī prajñākṛtānāmapi saṃskārāṇāṃ pratibandhī bhavati | kasmāt | nirodhajaḥ saṃskāraḥ samādhijānsaṃskārānbādhata iti | nirodhasthitikālakramānubhavena nirodhacittakṛtasaṃskārāstitvamanumeyam | vyutthānanirodhasamādhiprabhavaiḥ saha kaivalyabhāgīyaiḥ saṃskāraiścittaṃ svasyāṃ prakṛtāvavasthitāyāṃ pravilīyate | tasmātte saṃskārāścittasyādhikāravirodhino na sthitihetavo bhavantīti | yasmādavasitādhikāraṃ saha kaivalyabhāgīyaiḥ saṃskāraiścittaṃ nivarttate | tasminnivṛtte puruṣaḥ svarūpamātrapratiṣṭhaḥ ataḥ śuddhaḥ kevalo mukta ityucyata iti | 1.51 |

iti śrīpātañjale sāṃkhyapravacane sāṃkhyaśāstre prathamaḥ samādhipādaḥ || 1 ||

— And then what happens? —

I.51. When that too dissolves, everything has dissolved, and there is Pure Consciousness.

This not only puts an end to the experience of transcending but it also prevents the impressions that are created by that experience. — How? — The impression created by Pure Consciousness releases the impression of transcending. The existence of the impression left in the mind by Pure Consciousness has to be inferred from the experience of the lapse of time that has passed in the state of Pure Consciousness. The mind is absorbed within its own eternal nature along with the impressions created by the inward and outward strokes of transcending and which structure enlightenment. Then, as these impressions bring fulfilment to the role of the mind, they do not contribute to sustaining it. As a result, since its role is fulfilled with the impressions which structure enlightenment, the mind is collapsed back into the Absolute. With this collapse, the Self is said to be established in Its own nature, pure, uninvolved, free.

End of the First Chapter on 'The Transcendent' in Maharṣi Patañjali's Treatise on the Teaching on Yoga

|| 2 ||

sādhanapāda

Chapter 2

Technologies of Enlightenment

uddiṣṭaḥ samāhitacittasya yogaḥ | kathaṃ vyutthitacitto'pi yogayuktaḥ syādityetadārabhyate |

tapaḥsvādhyāyeśvarapraṇidhānāni kriyāyogaḥ || 2.1 ||

nātapasvino yogaḥ sidhyati | anādikarmakleśavāsanācitrā pratyupasthitaviṣayajālā cāśuddhirnāntareṇa tapaḥ saṃbhedamāpadyata iti | tapasa upādānam | tacca cittaprasādanamabādhamānamanenā'sevyamiti manyate | svādhyāyaḥ praṇavādipavitrāṇāṃ japaḥ mokṣaśāstrādhyāyanaṃ vā | īśvarapraṇidhānaṃ sarvakriyāṇāṃ paramagurāvarpaṇaṃ tatphalasaṃnyāso vā | 2.1 |

Yoga is recommended to create coherence in the mind. How an active mind can achieve yoga is now broached.

II.1. Self-purification, study and surrender to the Absolute are the technologies for yoga.

Yoga cannot succeed without purifying the system. Impurities of many kinds resulting from actions, suffering and deep-rooted stresses from time immemorial restrict the physical system; they cannot be removed without going through a process of purification. One can make use of the techniques of purification. It is recommended that they be employed in a way that does not upset the balance of the mind. 'Study' means recitation of purifying primordial sounds or study of the teachings on liberation. 'Surrender to the Absolute' means offering all actions, or giving over their fruits, to the Supreme Teacher.

sa hi kriyāyogaḥ |

***samādhibhāvanārthaḥ kleśatanūkaraṇārthaśca* || *2.2* ||**

sa hyāsevyamānaḥ samādhiṃ bhāvayati | kleśāṃśca pratanūkaroti | pratanūkṛtān kleśānprasaṃkhyānāgninā dadgdhabījakalpānaprasavadharmiṇaḥ kariṣyatīti | teṣāṃ tanūkaraṇātpunaḥ kleśairaparāmṛṣṭā sattvapuruṣānyatāmātrakhyātiḥ sūkṣmā prajñā samāptādhikārā pratiprasavāya kalpiṣyata iti | 2.2 |

For this yoga technology:

II.2. The purpose is to integrate the Transcendent and to relieve suffering.

Its practice integrates the Transcendent and alleviates suffering. It will alleviate suffering as seeds roasted in the fire of Pure Knowledge no longer sprout. With this relief, being unburdened by suffering, the awareness becomes more refined. The difference between the mind and the Self is realised, and having fulfilled this objective, the awareness is able to regain its original wholeness.

atha ke kleśāḥ kiyanto veti |

***avidyā'smitārāgadveṣābhiniveśāḥ kleśāḥ* || *2.3* ||**

kleśāḥ iti pañca viparyayā ityarthaḥ | te syandamānā guṇādhikāraṃ draḍhayanti pariṇāmamavasthāpayanti kāryakāraṇasrota unnamayanti | parasparānugrahatantrī bhūtvā karmavipākaṃ cābhinirharantīti | 2.3 |

— So what, and how many, are the causes of suffering? —

II.3. Suffering is caused by ignorance, the sense of separate individuality, desire, aversion, and the will to live.

The meaning is that the causes of suffering are five types of mistakes of the intellect. When they are in play, they reinforce the workings of the *guṇas*, whose functions thereby become deeply rooted, and they drive on the flood of cause and effect. As they mutually reinforce each other, they bring about the fruits of action.

avidyā kṣetramuttareṣāṃ prasuptatanu-vicchinnodārāṇām || 2.4 ||

atrāvidyā kṣetraṃ prasavabhūmiruttareṣāmasmitādīnāṃ caturvidhakalpitānāṃ prasuptatanuvicchinnodārāṇām | tatra kā prasuptiḥ | cetasi śaktimātrapratiṣṭhānāṃ bījabhāvopagamaḥ | tasya prabodhālambane saṃmukhībhāvaḥ | prasaṃkhyānavato dagdhakleśabījasya saṃmukhībhūte'pyālambane nāsau punarasti | dagdhabījasya kutaḥ praroha iti | ataḥ kṣīṇakleśaḥ kuśalaścaramadeha ityucyate | tatraiva sā dagdhabījabhāvā pañcamī kleśāvasthā nānyatreti | satāṃ kleśānāṃ tadā bījasāmarthyaṃ dagdhamiti | viṣayasya saṃmukhībhāve'pi sati na bhavatyeṣāṃ prabodha ityuktā prasuptirdagdhabījānāṃ cāprarohaśca | tanutvamucyate | pratipakṣabhāvanopahatāḥ kleśāstanavo bhavanti | tathā vicchidya vicchidya tena tenā'tmanā punaḥ punaḥ samudācarantīti vicchinnāḥ | katham | rāgakāle krodhasyādarśanāt | na hi rāgakāle krodhaḥ samudācarati | rāgaśca kvacid dṛśyamāno na viṣayāntare nāsti | naikasyāṃ striyāṃ caitro rakta ityanyāsu strīṣu viraktaḥ | kiṃtu tatra rāgo labdhavṛttiranyatra tu bhaviṣyadvṛttiriti | sa hi tadā prasuptatanuvicchinno bhavati | viṣaye yo labdhavṛttiḥ sa udāraḥ |

II.4. Ignorance is the breeding ground for the other causes, which may be dormant, attenuated, recurrent or active.

Ignorance is the breeding ground for the others — the sense of separateness and the rest — and these can be in any of four states: dormant, attenuated, recurrent, active. — What is 'dormant'? — When it is lodged in the mind in seed-state, a potential only. It awakens when triggered. When one has had experience of Pure Knowledge, even if brought into contact with a triggering mechanism, the predisposition is like a roasted seed and does not activate. How could a roasted seed sprout? Thus, when the roots of suffering are destroyed, the skilled yogi is said to be in his last incarnation. In him, but not in others, is found the fifth phase of the process of suffering, that of the roasted seed. In that condition, the potential of the seeds of extant suffering is burnt, so that even in the presence of a triggering mechanism, they do not activate. This is what is meant by 'dormant' — the non-germination of the roasted seeds. Next, 'attenuated': the causes of suffering are weakened when attacked by the administration of their opposite. When they keep remitting and re-present over and over in different guises, they are 'recurrent'. — How? — In love, anger is not displayed. For when a man is in love, his anger does not flare up. However, the love a man has for one thing does not exclude love for something else. Caitra's love for one woman does not prevent him from loving other women. Although for now his desire has a particular focus, that focus may shift elsewhere; and then his current desire will be either dormant, or attenuated, or in remission. When an impulse is focussed on an object, it is 'active'. All these conditions

sarvaite kleśāviṣayatvaṃ nātikrāmanti | kastarhi vicchinnaḥ prasuptastanurudāro vā kleśa ityucyate | satyamevaitat | kiṃtu viśiṣṭānāmevaiteṣāṃ vicchinnāditvam | yathaiva pratipakṣabhāvanāto nivṛttastathaiva svavyañjakāñjanenābhivyakta iti | sarva evāmī kleśā avidyābhedāḥ | kasmāt | sarveṣvavidyaivābhiplavate | yadavidyayā vastvākāryate tadevānuśerate kleśāḥ | viparyāsapratyayakāle upalabhyante kṣīyamāṇāṃ cāvidyāmanukṣīyanteti | 2.4 |

are constants in the realm of the Relative. — So what exactly causes suffering whose forms are said to be recurrent, dormant, attenuated, or active? — A good question. 'Recurrent' or whatever are its different modes of manifestation. Just as suffering can be eliminated by the administration of its opposite, so it can be stoked by an appropriate fuel. All the forms of suffering are varieties of ignorance. — Why? — Ignorance is inherent in them all. What is informed by ignorance is infused by suffering. Its forms take hold when misprision occurs, but they fade when ignorance is destroyed.

tatrāvidyāsvarūpamucyate |

***anityāśuciduḥkhānātmasu nityaśucisukhātma-khyātiravidyā* || *2.5* ||**

anitye kārye nityakhyātiḥ | tadyathā dhruvā pṛthivī dhruvā sacandratārakā dyauḥ amṛtā divaukasa iti | tathā'śucau paramabībhatse kāye śucikhyātiḥ | uktaṃca | sthānādbījādupaṣṭambhānniḥ syandānnidhānādapi | kāyamādheyaśaucatvātpaṇḍitā hyaśuciṃ viduḥ | ityaśucau śucikhyātirdṛśyate | naveva śaśāṅkalekhā kamanīyeyaṃ kanyā madhvamṛtāvayavanirmiteva candraṃ bhitvā niḥsṛteva jñāyate | nīlotpalapatrāyatākṣī hāvagarbhābhyāṃ locanābhyāṃ jīvalokamāśvāsayantīveti | kasya kenābhisaṃbandhaḥ | bhavati caivamaśucau śuciviparyaya pratyaya iti | etenāpuṇye puṇyapratyayastathaivānarthe cārthapratyayo vyākhyātaḥ | tathā duḥkhe sukhakhyātiṃ vakṣyati | pariṇāmatāpasaṃskāraduḥkhairguṇa-vṛttyavirodhācca duḥkhameva sarvaṃ vivekinaḥ iti | tatra sukhakhyātiravidyā | tathā'nātmanyātmakhyātir-bāhyopakaraṇeṣu cetanācetaneṣu bhogādhiṣṭhāne vā śarīre puruṣopakaraṇe vā manasyanātmanyātmakhyātiriti | tathaitadatroktam | vyaktamavyaktaṃ vā sattvamātmatvenābhipratītya tasya saṃpadamanunandati ātmasaṃpadaṃ manvānastasya

Now the nature of ignorance is explained:

II.5. Ignorance mistakes impermanence, impurity, suffering, and the non-Self for eternity, purity, happiness, and the Self.

Taking something impermanent to be everlasting is like thinking the earth stands still, or the heavens and the moon and the stars are stationary, or the inhabitants of heaven are immortal. Likewise, thinking the body is pure, when it is an extremely disgusting thing. For it is said: 'Its origin, its mode of conception, its needs, its secretions, its disposal — the fact that the body must be kept clean — the wise known it is impure' (*cf. Maitryupaniṣad II.4).* So purity is seen in impurity. Likewise: 'This beautiful young girl is like the crescent of the new moon. Her limbs are fashioned of honey and ambrosia. Her eyes, wide like blue lotus leaves, dart flirtatiously. She seems to have fallen from the broken moon, as if despatched to soothe the world of mortal men' — what is the connection between any of this? It is but the mistranslation of purity into impurity. Similarly, we can see that good is transposed onto non-good, the useful onto the useless. In similar vein, Patañjali will later characterise seeing happiness in suffering: 'One who has learnt Pure Knowledge knows that all is sorrow — the banes of transience, pain, stress, and the implacable operations of the *guṇas*' (*Yoga-Sūtra II.15*). Seeing happiness in such things is ignorance. So too seeing the Self in the non-Self. In external things, animate or inanimate, or in the body (which is the instrument of experience), or in the mind (which is the instrument of the Self) — the non-Self is mistaken for the Self. Thus it is said: 'A man mistakes his conscious or unconscious mind for the Self. He enjoys its

vyāpadamanuśocatyātmavyāpadaṃ manyamānaḥ sa sarvo'pratibuddha iti | eṣā catuṣpadā bhavatyavidyā mūlamasya kleśasantānasya karmāśayasya ca savipākasyeti | tasyāścāmitrāgoṣpadavad vastusatattvaṃ vijñeyam | yathā nāmitro mitrābhāvo na mitramātraṃ kiṃtu tadviruddhaḥ sapatnaḥ tathā'goṣpadam na goṣpadābhāvo na goṣpadamātraṃ kiṃtu deśa eva tābhyāmanyadvastvantaram | evamavidyā na pramāṇaṃ na pramāṇābhāvaḥ kiṃtu vidyāviparītaṃ jñānāntaram-avidyeti | 2.5 |

success, thinking it to be the success of the Self, and then bemoans its failure, thinking it the failure of the Self — such a man is far from enlightened' (*Pañcaśikha*). This fourfold ignorance is the basis of the unending succession of suffering and the chain of action and reaction. It should be understood that ignorance is an active reality, like an enemy or a cow's footprint. An enemy is not just someone who is not a friend — not just a non-friend — but its active opposite, an opponent. To say that something does 'not cover a cow's footprint' means not just that there is no footprint of a cow, nor that there is no area of ground the size of a cow's footprint, it means something very different from both — namely, a vast expanse of land. In the same way, ignorance is not just not a form of true knowledge, nor just the absence of knowledge, but a different mode of knowing that is contrary to real knowledge.

dṛgdarśanaśaktyorekātmatevā'smitā || *2.6* ||

puruṣo dṛkśaktirbuddhirdarśanaśaktirityetayor-ekasvarūpāpattirivā'smitā kleśa ucyate | bhoktṛbhogya-śaktyoratyantavibhaktayoratyantāsaṃkīrṇayor-avibhāgaprāptāviva satyāṃ bhogaḥ kalpate | svarūpapratilambhe tu tayoḥ kaivalyameva bhavati kuto bhoga iti | tathā coktam | buddhitaḥ paraṃ puruṣamākāraśīlavidyādibhirvibhaktamapaśyan-kuryāttatrā'tmabuddhiṃ mohena iti | 2.6 |

II.6. The sense of individual identity comes from thinking that the functions of Seer and seeing are the same.

The Self has the function of Seer; the mind has the function of seeing. The confusion of the natures of the two is the cause of suffering called individuality. When the functions of observer and observed, which are totally separate, with no overlap, appear not to be distinct, then experience takes place. But when the real nature of the two is realised, there is only separation. What could be experienced? Thus it is said: 'Through delusion, not seeing that the highest Self is beyond the intellect and is without form, or tendencies, or knowledge, and so on, a man mistakes the mind for the Self' (*Pañcaśikha*).

sukhānuśayī rāgaḥ || *2.7* ||

sukhābhijñasya sukhānusmṛtipūrvaḥ sukhe tatsādhane vā yo garddhastṛṣṇā lobhaḥ sa rāga iti | 2.7 |

II.7. Desire follows pleasure.

Having had an experience of pleasure, or recalling a previous experience of pleasure, there is a longing, a thirst, a hankering for pleasure and its modes: that is desire.

***duḥkhānuśayī dveṣaḥ* || *2.8* ||**

duḥkhābhijñasya duḥkhānusmṛtipūrvo duḥkhe tatsādhane vā yaḥ pratigho manyurjighāṃsā krodhaḥ sa dveṣa iti | 2.8 |

II.8. Aversion follows pain.

Having had an experience of pain, or recalling a previous experience of pain, there is resistance, indignation, vindictiveness, anger: that is aversion.

***svarasavāhī viduṣo'pi tathārūḍho'bhiniveśaḥ* || *2.9* ||**

sarvasya prāṇina iyamātmāśirnityā bhavati mā na bhūvaṃ bhūyāsamiti | na cānanubhūtamaraṇadharmakasyaiṣā bhavatyātmāśiḥ | etayā ca pūrvajanmānubhavaḥ pratīyate | sa cāyamabhiniveśaḥ kleśaḥ svarasavāhī kṛmerapi jātamātrasya pratyakṣānumānāgamairasaṃbhāvito maraṇatrāsa ucchedadṛṣṭyātmakaḥ pūrvajanmānubhūtaṃ maraṇaduḥkhamanumāpayati | yathā cāyamatyantamūḍheṣu dṛśyate kleśastathā viduṣo'pi vijñātapūrvāparāntasya rūḍhaḥ | kasmāt | samānā hi tayoḥ kuśalākuśalayormaraṇaduḥkhānubhavādiyaṃ vāsaneti | 2.9 |

II.9. The will to live is spontaneous and inborn, even among the wise.

All living beings have the constant desire: 'Let me not not live; please let me live'. This wish would not exist if one had not experienced dying. From this can be deduced the existence of previous lives and the cause of suffering which is the spontaneous will to live. Even a newly-born worm experiences the terror of dying when it feels that it might be annihilated, a fear which cannot be instilled by direct perception, or by inference or by the tradition of the Teaching. The painfulness of dying must therefore be inferred from the fact of having already experienced it in previous lives. And this form of suffering is seen both in the most benighted and among the aware, even those who know the beginning and end of all things. — Why? — Because the deep impression made by the experience of the pain of dying is the same for both the gifted and the challenged.

te pratiprasavaheyāḥ sūkṣmāḥ || *2.10* ||

te pañca kleśā dagdhabījakalpā yoginaścaritādhikāre cetasi pralīne saha tenaivāstaṃ gacchanti | 2.10 |

II.10. The subtle aspects of suffering can be released by returning to the source of thought.

When the yogi's awareness is at rest in the state of least excitation, absorbed in the Absolute, the five causes of suffering become like roasted seeds, and cease to exist.

sthitānāṃ tu bījabhāvopagatānām |

dhyānaheyāstadvṛttayaḥ || *2.11* ||

kleśānāṃ yā vṛttayaḥ sthūlāstāḥ kriyāyogena tanūkṛtāḥ satyaḥ prasaṃkhyānena dhyānena hātavyāḥ yāvat sūkṣmīkṛtā yāvaddagdhabījakalpā iti | yathā vastrāṇāṃ sthūlo malaḥ pūrvaṃ nirdhūyate paścātsūkṣmo yatnenopāyena vā'panīyate tathā svalpapratipakṣāḥ sthūlā vṛttayaḥ kleśānāṃ sūkṣmāstu mahāpratipakṣā iti | 2.11 |

As for those that persist in seed-sate:

II.11. Release these fluctuations through meditation.

When the gross levels of stress have been softened by the technologies of yoga, they can then be tackled with Pure Knowledge, with meditation, until they become subtle, until they are turned into roasted seeds. Just like the surface dirt on a piece of cloth, first shake it off, then carefully remove the deeper layers of ingrained dirt, if necessary with some detergent. So the surface levels can be addressed easily but the subtle layers of the causes of suffering require more thorough treatment.

***kleśamūlaḥ karmāśayo dṛṣṭādṛṣṭajanmavedanīyaḥ* || *2.12* ||**

tatra puṇyāpuṇyakarmāśayaḥ kāmalobha-mohakrodhaprabhavaḥ | sa dṛṣṭajanmavedanīyaś-cādṛṣṭajanmavedanīyaśca | tatra tīvrasaṃvegena mantratapaḥsamādhibhirnirvartita īśvaradevatāmaharṣi-mahānubhāvānāmārādhanādvā yaḥ pariniṣpannaḥ sa sadyaḥ paripacyate puṇyakarmāśaya iti | yathā tīvrakleśena bhītavyādhitakṛpaṇeṣu viśvāsopagateṣu vā mahānubhāveṣu vā tapasviṣu kṛtaḥ punaḥ punarapakāraḥ sa cāpi pāpakarmāśayaḥ sadya eva paripacyate | yathā nandīśvaraḥ kumāro manuṣyapariṇānaṃ hitvā devatvena pariṇataḥ | tathā nahuṣo'pi devānāmindraḥ svakaṃ pariṇāmaṃ hitvā tiryaktvena pariṇata iti | tatra nārakāṇāṃ nāsti dṛṣṭajanmavedanīyaḥ karmāśayaḥ | kṣīṇakleśānāmapi nāsti adṛṣṭajanmavedanīyaḥ karmāśaya iti | 2.12 |

II.12. At the basis of suffering is the storehouse of karma which has to be worked out either in the present or in future lives.

The storehouse of positive and negative karma has its origins in desire, greed, delusion and anger. It has to be worked off in the present or a future life. The reward for positive deeds — those performed with serious intent using mantras, self-purification, or the practice of transcending, or those accumulated by surrendering to the Absolute, to a deity, a great seer or an exalted adept — is guaranteed. Likewise, the payback on negative deeds — such as repeated misdemeanours, or unjustifiable crimes against the terror-stricken, the sick, or the destitute; or acts of trickery against the gullible, or against intent seekers — is also ineluctable. This is how the young Nandīśvara was instantly transformed from the human state into a divinity. Similarly, Nahuṣa was instantly removed from holding the office of Indra among the gods, and transformed into a beast. However, those who have been consigned to the netherworlds cannot work out their karma there, while those who have eliminated the roots of their suffering have no karma to work off in a future life.

sati mūle tadvipāko jātyāyurbhogāḥ || *2.13* ||

satsu kleśeṣu karmāśayo vipākārambhī bhavati | nocchinnakleśamūlaḥ | yathā tuṣāvanaddhāḥ śālitaṇḍulāḥ adagdhabījabhāvāḥ prarohasamarthā bhavanti nāpanītatuṣā dagdhabījabhāvā vā tathā kleśāvanaddhaḥ karmāśayo vipākaprarohī bhavati nāpanītakleśo na prasaṃkhyānadagdhakleśabījabhāvo veti | sa ca vipākastrividho jātirāyurbhoga iti | tatredaṃ vicāryate | kimekaṃ karmaikasya janmanaḥ kāraṇamathaikaṃ karmānekaṃ janmā'kṣipatīti | dvitīyā vicāraṇā kimanekaṃ karmānekaṃ janma nirvartayati athānekaṃ karmaikaṃ janma nirvartayatīti | na tāvadekaṃ karmaikasya janmanaḥ kāraṇam | kasmād | anādikālapracitasyāsaṃkhyeyasyāviśiṣṭakarmaṇaḥ sāṃpratikasya ca phalakramāniyamādanāśvāso lokasya prasaktaḥ | sa cāniṣṭa iti | na caikaṃ karmānekasya janmanaḥ kāraṇam | kasmād | anekeṣu karmasvekaikameva karmānekasya janmanaḥ kāraṇamityaviśiṣṭasya vipākakālābhāvaḥ prasaktaḥ | sa cāpyaniṣṭa iti | na cānekaṃ karmānekasya janmanaḥ kāraṇam | kasmāt | tadanekaṃ janma yugapanna saṃbhavatīti | krameṇa vācyam tathā ca

II.13. While the roots of suffering subsist, the resolution of karma is expressed in the birth-chart, the lifespan, and the types of experience undergone.

The resolution of karma continues for as long as the potential for suffering has not been uprooted. Like grains of rice encased in the chaff can germinate if the seed is not roasted — unlike grains which have been winnowed or where the seeds have been roasted — so the effects of karma retain the potential for suffering and need to be resolved. (Although this is no longer the case where the possibilities for suffering have been eliminated or when the seed of suffering has been roasted in Pure Knowledge). There are three aspects to the working out of karma: in the birth-chart, in the lifespan, and in the experiences to be undergone. It is a matter for debate whether one deed is the cause of one lifetime, or whether one deed precipitates several rebirths. A second debate turns on whether many acts result in a corresponding number of rebirths, or whether many acts culminate in one rebirth. First, one isolated deed is not the cause of one life. — Why? — Belief would be strained if there was no ordered correlation between the innumerable acts performed since time immemorial and their effects in the present; and that would be undesirable. Second, one deed is not the cause of several lives. — Why? — If each of the myriad acts one has performed was the cause of several lives, there is a risk that time would run out before all actions found their reward. So this is also untenable. Third, several deeds are not the cause of several lives. — Why? — Because one does not live parallel lives; they must follow sequentially, otherwise the incoherences already

pūrvadoṣānuṣaṅgaḥ | tasmājjanmaprāyaṇāntare kṛtaḥ puṇyāpuṇyakarmāśayapracayo vicitraḥ pradhānopasarjanabhāvenāvasthitaḥ prāyanābhivyakta ekapraghaṭṭakena militvā maraṇaṃ prasādhya saṃmūrcchita ekameva janma karoti | tacca janma tenaiva karmaṇā labdhāyuṣkaṃ bhavati | tasminnāyuṣi tenaiva karmaṇā bhogaḥ saṃpadyata iti | asau karmāśayo janmāyurbhogahetutvāt trivipāko'bhidhīyata iti | ata ekabhavikaḥ karmāśaya ukta iti | dṛṣṭajanmavedanīyastvekavipākārambhī bhogahetutvāt dvivipākārambhī vā bhogāyurhetutvāt trivipākārambhī vā janmabhogāyurhetutvānnandīśvaravannahuṣavadveti | kleśakarmavipākānubhavanirvartitābhistu vāsanābhiranādikālasaṃmūrcchitamidaṃ cittaṃ vicitrīkṛtamiva sarvato matsyajālaṃ granthibhirivā'tatamityetā anekabhavapūrvikā vāsanāḥ | yastvayaṃ karmāśaya eṣa evaikabhavika ukta iti | ye saṃskārāḥ smṛtihetavastā vāsanāstāścānādikālīnā iti | yastvasāvekabhavikaḥ karmāśayaḥ sa niyatavipākaścāniyatavipākaśca | tatra dṛṣṭajanmavedanīyasya niyatavipākasyaivāyaṃ niyamo na tvadṛṣṭajanmavedanīyasyāniyatavipākasyaiva | kasmāt | yo hyadṛṣṭajanmavedanīyo'niyatavipākastasya

mentioned would persist. Consequently — lastly — what happens is that the mixed bag of positive and negative deeds performed between birth and death are collected together and divided into actions of major and minor consequence. At death, that stock of karma is usually synthesised into one package which is carried forward into the next rebirth. The new lifetime, with that stock of karma, is allotted a certain span. And with that stock of karma, during that lifespan, certain experiences are garnered. The legacy of karma thus works out in the triple modes of birth-chart, lifespan and experience. The stock of karma as a whole is said to be carried forward into the next existence. The resolution of karma in the present life may focus on the one aspect — the experiences to be faced — if that is the purpose; or it may focus on the two aspects of lifespan and experience; or on all three aspects of birth, span and experience, as was the case for Nandīśvara and Nahuṣa. The mind is muddied as with the precipitate of the deep impressions, accumulated from time immemorial, which have been produced by the experience of suffering and previous deeds; like a fisherman's net, it is a tangle of knots. These deeply-lodged impressions may date from many lifetimes ago; nonetheless, it is said that the whole of one's karma is brought forward into each existence. Such deep after-images from long ago are impressions that take the form of memories. As karma is carried forward into the next lifetime, it will be either fully resolved or held over. The general rule is that the consequences of karma can be resolved in the present life. However, some things are not ripe for resolution and will only be worked through in a future life. — Why? — There are three possibilities for

trayī gatiḥ | kṛtasyāvipākasya vināśaḥ pradhānakarmaṇyāvāpagamanaṃ vā niyatavipākapradhānakarmaṇā'bhibhūtasya vā ciramavasthānamiti | tatra kṛtasyā'vipakvasya nāśo yathā śuklakarmodayādihaiva nāśaḥ kṛṣṇasya | yatredamuktam | dve dve ha vai karmaṇī veditavye pāpakasyaiko rāśiḥ puṇyakṛto'pahanti | tadicchasva karmāṇi sukṛtāni kartumihaiva te karma kavayo vedayante | pradhānakarmaṇyāvāpagamanam | yatredamuktam | syātsvalpassaṃkaraḥ saparihārassapratyavamarṣaḥ kuśalasya nāpakarṣāyālam | kasmāt | kuśalaṃ hi me bahvanyadasti yatrāyamāvāpaṃ gatassvarge'pyaprakarṣamalpaṃ kariṣyati iti | niyatavipākapradhānakarmaṇābhibhūtasya vā ciramavasthānam | kathamiti | adṛṣṭajanmavedanīyasyaiva niyatavipākasya karmaṇaḥ samānaṃ maraṇamabhivyaktikāraṇamuktam na tvadṛṣṭajanmavedanīyasyāniyatavipākasya | yattvadṛṣṭajanmavedanīyaṃ karmāniyatavipākaṃ tannaśyedāvāpaṃ vā gacchedabhibhūtaṃ vā ciramapyupāsīta yāvatsamānaṃ karmābhivyañjakaṃ nimittamasya na vipākābhimukhaṃ karotīti | tadvipākasyaiva deśakālanimittānavadhāraṇādiyaṃ karmagatirvicitrā durvijñānā ceti | na cotsargasyāpavādānnivṛttiriti ekabhavikaḥ karmāśayo'nujñāyata iti | 2.13 |

what can be delayed for resolution in a future life. The consequence of a deed may be obliterated before it is resolved; or it may be incorporated as a minor component into a more dominant wave of karma; or it may be held over for a period of time because it is displaced by another dominating wave of karma. The obliteration, instead of the resolution, of the consequence of an act can occur because a bundle of bad karma can be neutralised by the arrival of a bundle of good karma. Thus it is said: 'Action and reaction should be understood pairwise. A measure of good deeds cancels a measure of wrong deeds. So desire to do good deeds; the wise will teach you what they are.' As for the inmixing of a minor wave of karma within a major wave of karma, it is said: 'A tiny blemish may be concealed or absorbed, for it is not so much as to disgrace a good man' (*Pañcaśikha*). — Why? — We can say, 'I have so many good points to my credit that even in heaven some tiny imperfection will hardly be noticed'. — How is it possible that the resolution of some item of karma can be held over for a time while a more dominant wave of karma is taken care of? — It was stated that usually death is the trigger for karma to return in the next life but this is not so where the reaction is not ready to manifest in the next life. The consequences of an act may be annihilated; or incorporated into another dominant wave of returning karma; or it may be some time before favourable circumstances allow for its return. Because the place, time, and occasion of maturation is not straightforward, the course of action and reaction is complicated and hard to fathom. However, although there are always exceptions to general rules, the whole stock of karma is considered to be brought forward into one's next lifetime.

te hlādaparitāpaphalāḥ puṇyāpuṇyahetutvāt || *2.14* ||

te janmāyurbhogāḥ puṇyahetukāḥ sukhaphalāḥ | apuṇyahetukāḥ duḥkhaphalā iti | yathā cedaṃ duḥkhaṃ pratikūlātmakamevaṃ viṣayasukhakāle'pi duḥkhamastyeva pratikūlātmakaṃ yoginaḥ | 2.14 |

II.14. As one's deeds are positive or negative, so the rewards are joy or sorrow.

When birth, lifespan, and experience are the rewards of positive actions, they bring joy; when actions are negative, they result in sorrow. Just as pain is always unwelcome, so for the yogi there is always an element of sorrow in the midst of any joy afforded by the Relative.

kathaṃ tadupapadyate |

***pariṇāmatāpasaṃskāraduḥkhairguṇavṛttyavirodhācca duḥkhameva sarvaṃ vivekinaḥ** || 2.15 ||*

sarvasyāyaṃ rāgānuviddhaścetanācetanasādhanādhīnaḥ sukhānubhava iti tatrāsti rāgajaḥ karmāśayaḥ | tathā ca dveṣṭi duḥkhasādhanāni muhyati ceti dveṣamohakṛto'pyasti karmāśayaḥ | tathā coktam | nānupahatya bhūtāni upabhogaḥ saṃbhavatīti hiṃsākṛto'pyasti śārīraḥ karmāśaya iti | viṣayasukhaṃ cāvidyetyuktam | yā bhogeṣvindriyānāṃ tṛpter upaśāntistatsukham | yā laulyādanupaśāntistadduḥkham | na cendriyāṇāṃ bhogābhyāsena vaitṛṣṇyaṃ kartuṃ śakyam | kasmāt | yato bhogābhyāsamanuvivardhante rāgāḥ kauśalāni cendriyāṇāmiti | tasmādanupāyaḥ sukhasya bhogābhyāsa iti | sa khalvayaṃ vṛścikaviṣabhīta ivāśīviṣeṇa daṣṭo yaḥ sukhārthī viṣayānuvāsito mahati duḥkhapaṅke nimagna iti | eṣā pariṇāmaduhkhatā nāma pratikūlā sukhāvasthāyāmapi yoginameva kliśnāti | atha kā tāpaduḥkhatā | sarvasya dveṣānuviddhaścetanācetanasādhanādhīnastāpānubhava iti tatrāsti dveṣajaḥ

— How is that? —

II.15. One who has learnt Pure Knowledge knows that nothing in the Relative can be fulfilling, because of the banes of transience, pain, stress, and the implacable operations of the guṇas.

Everyone's experience of pleasure, consciously or unconsciously, is shaped by desire, and with desire is created a store of karma. In the same way, everyone dislikes suffering and everyone is deluded, and a store of karma is likewise created by these dislikes and delusions. This has been analysed earlier. There is no enjoyment which does not entail harm to others; and acts of violence also create stress in one's own physiology. It has also already been explained that ignorance is the search for pleasure in external things. The calm that ensues from the satisfaction of the senses in external objects is pleasurable; while the agitation that comes from lust is painful. It is not possible to quench this thirst by continuing to repeat the experiences of the senses. — Why? — Because in the wake of repeated enjoyments, desires multiply and the acuity of the senses is heightened. Therefore repeated indulgence is not the way to happiness. Indeed if one's goal is pleasure, one gets caught up in external things and sinks into the mud of suffering like a man who, fearing the poison from a scorpion's sting, gets bitten by the fangs of a viper. Such is the unhappy misfortune that is transience which even in the midst of pleasure affects the yogi. — So what about the problem of pain? — Everyone's experience of pain, whether conscious or unconscious, is characterised by aversions, which create deposits. Addicted

karmāśayaḥ | sukhasādhanāni ca prāthayamānaḥ kāyena vācā manasā ca parispandate tataḥ paramānugṛhṇātyupahanti ca iti parānugrahapīḍābhyāṃ dharmādharmāvupacinoti | sa karmāśayo lobhānmohācca bhavatītyeṣā tāpaduḥkhatocyate | kā punassaṃskāraduḥkhatā | sukhānubhavātsukhasaṃskārāśayo duḥkhānubhavādapi duḥkhasaṃskārāśaya iti | evaṃ karmabhyo vipāke'nubhūyamāne sukhe duḥkhe vā punaḥ karmāśayapracaya iti | evamidamanādi duḥkhasroto viprasṛtaṃ yoginameva pratikūlātmakatvādudvejayati | kasmāt | akṣipātrakalpo hi vidvāniti | yathorṇātanturakṣipātre nyastaḥ sparśena duḥkhayati nānyeṣu gātrāvayaveṣu
evametāni duḥkhāni akṣipātrakalpaṃ yoginameva kliśnanti netaraṃ pratipattāram | itaraṃtu svakarmopahṛtaṃ duhkhamupāttamupāttaṃ tyajantaṃ tyaktaṃ tyaktamupādadānamanādivāsanāvicitrayā cittavṛttyā samantato'nuviddhamivāvidyayā hātavya evāhaṃkāramamakārānupātinaṃ jātaṃ jātaṃ bāhyādhyātmikobhayanimittāstriparvāṇastāpā anuplavante | tadevamanādiduḥkhasrotasā vyūhyamānamātmānaṃ bhūtagrāmaṃ ca dṛṣṭvā yogī sarvaduḥkhakṣayakāraṇaṃ samyagdarśanaṃ śaraṇaṃ prapadyata iti | guṇavṛttyavirodhācca duḥkhameva sarvaṃ vivekinaḥ | prakhyāpravṛttisthitirūpā buddhiguṇāḥ parasparānugrahatantrā bhūtvā śāntaṃ ghoraṃ mūḍhaṃ vā pratyayaṃ triguṇamevārabhante |

to the pursuit of happiness, a man frenetically engages in thought, speech and action, and so does good or harm to others. Accordingly, his evolution is promoted, or hindered. So a storehouse of karma is created by desire or delusion — this is called the curse of suffering. — And what is the misery of stress? — The experience of pleasure creates a storehouse of impressions of pleasure, and the experience of pain creates a storehouse of impressions of pain. When the associated karma returns to be experienced as pleasure or pain, a new set of impressions is generated. The yogi shudders at the unending, surging tide of suffering, because it is inimical to his nature. — Why? — A Knower of Reality is as sensitive as the pupil in the eye. A falling eyelash hurts the eye, but no other part of the body. Like that, these miseries affect the yogi who is as sensitive as the pupil, but they do not affect others to whom they may occur. Others can brush off whatever pain comes their way as a result of their actions, though it may keep returning to them. As if permanently agitated by the mental excitations of endless myriad stress and strain, propelled by ignorance, constrained by the sense of 'I' and 'mine', they are born again and again, tossed around both within and without by the three types of misery described. The yogi who has beheld himself and the multitude of other creatures borne along in the tide of endless misery, avails himself of that true vision of reality which alone destroys suffering. For the Knower of Reality, the implacable operations of the *guṇas* mean that nothing can be truly fulfilling. In spinning their web, the *guṇas* are responsible for the purity, the activity and the stability of the mind, creating thereby the experiences of calm, agitation or lethargy. As the combinations of the

calaṃ ca guṇavṛttamiti kṣipraparināmi cittamuktam | rūpātiśayā vṛttyatiśayaśca parasparena virudhyante sāmāyāni tvatiśayaiḥ saha pravartante | evamete guṇā itaretarāśrayeṇopārjitasukhaduḥkhamohapratyayā iti sarve sarvarūpā bhavanti | guṇapradhānabhāvakṛtastveṣāṃ viśeṣa iti | tasmād duḥkhameva sarvaṃ vivekina iti | tadasya mahato duḥkhasamudāyasya prabhavabījamavidyā | tasyāśca samyagdarśanamabhāvahetuḥ | yathā cikitsāśāstraṃ caturvyūham | rogo rogaheturārogyaṃ bhaiśajyamiti | evamidamapi śāstraṃ caturvyūhameva | tadyathā saṃsāraḥ saṃsāraheturmokṣo mokṣopāya iti | tatra duḥkhabahulaḥ saṃsāro heyaḥ | pradhānapuruṣayoḥ saṃyogo heyahetuḥ | saṃyogasyātyantikī nivṛttirhānam | hānopāyaḥ samyagdarśanam | tatra hātuḥ svarūpamupādeyaṃ heyaḥ vā na bhavitumarhati | hāne tasyocchedavādaprasaṅgaḥ | upādāne ca hetuvādaḥ | ubhayapratyākhyāne śāśvatavāda ityetatsamyagdarśanam | tadetacchāstraṃ caturvyūhamityabhidhīyate | 2.15 |

guṇas are forever changing, so the mind is said to be fickle. While highly excited states of the mind and the intense moods they give rise to are mutually exclusive, nonetheless the integrated function of the *guṇas* is maintained in the midst of such extreme agitation. In this way, all mental states — pleasure, pain, delusion — created by their interplay, incorporate all three *guṇas*; but the particular quality of any given state is determined by the presence of the predominant *guṇa*. So none of this satisfies the Knower of Reality. Ignorance is the basis for all this enormous mass of suffering. True vision dispels it. Medical science has four divisions: diagnosis, etiology, remedy, and therapeutics. Like that, the Teaching also has four divisions: identifying the problem of Relative existence; analysing its genesis; establishing the reality of liberation; applying the technology of enlightenment. The problem: the Relative is thick with suffering. The cause: the confusion of the Self with the Relative. The solution: the definitive removal of this confusion. The means: enlightened vision. In this instance, one who would be free can neither win nor relinquish the freedom that is his essential nature. To reject It would imply that It can be destroyed. To appropriate It for oneself would indicate that It is dependent on one's actions. If one avoids both these pitfalls, one is led to conclude that It is everlasting: this is enlightened vision. This is why the Teaching is said to contain four divisions.

heyaṃ duḥkhamanāgatam || 2.16 ||

duḥkhamatītamupabhogenātivāhitaṃ na heyapakṣe vartate | vartamānaṃ ca svakṣaṇe bhogārūḍhamiti na tatkṣanāntare heyatāmāpadyate | tasmādyadevānāgataṃ duḥkhaṃ tadevākṣipātrakalpaṃ yoginaṃ kliśnāti netaraṃ pratipattāraṃ tadeva heyatāmāpadyate | 2.16 |

II.16. Avert the pain before it arises.

Past suffering has been processed by experience and can no longer be avoided. Present suffering is upon us and cannot be delayed to some other time. Therefore, only the unhappiness which has not yet arrived can be avoided, affecting as it does only the yogi who becomes as sensitive in his reactions as the pupil in the eye.

tasmādyadeva heyamityucyate tasyaiva kāraṇaṃ pratinirdiśyate |

draṣṭṛdṛśyayoḥ saṃyogo heyahetuḥ || 2.17 ||

draṣṭā buddheḥ pratisaṃvedī puruṣaḥ | dṛśya buddhisattvopārūḍhāḥ sarve dharmāḥ | tadetad dṛśyamayaskāntamaṇikalpaṃ saṃnidhimātropakari dṛśyatvena svaṃ bhavati puruṣasya dṛśirūpasya svāminaḥ | anubhavakarmaviṣayatāmāpannamanyasvarūpeṇa pratilabdhātmakaṃ svatantramapi parārthatvāt paratantram | tayordṛgdarśanaśaktyoranādirarthakṛtaḥ saṃyogo heyahetuḥ duḥkhasya kāraṇamityarthaḥ | tathā coktam | tatsaṃyogaheturvivarjanāt syādayamātyantiko duḥkhapratīkāraḥ | kasmāt | duḥkhahetoḥ parihāryasya pratīkāradarśanāt | tadyathā pādatalasya bhedyatā kaṇṭakasya bhettṛtvaṃ parihāraḥ kaṇṭakasya pādānadhiṣṭhānaṃ pādatrāṇavyavahitena vā'dhiṣṭhānam | etattrayaṃ yo veda loke sa tatra pratikāramārambhamāṇo bhedajaṃ duḥkhaṃ nāpnoti | kasmāt | tritvopalabdhisāmarthyāditi | atrāpi tāpakasya rajasaḥ sattvameva tapyam | kasmāt | tapikriyāyāḥ karmasthatvāt | sattve tu karmaṇi tapikriyā nāpariṇāmini niṣkriye kṣetrajñe | darśitaviṣayatvāt sattve tu tapyamāne tadākārānurodhī puruṣo'nutapyata iti dṛśyate | 2.17 |

Consequently, only the cause of what can be avoided is analysed:

II.17. Avoid confusing the Seer and the seen.

The Seer is the Self reflecting the intellect. What is 'seen' are all the phenomena impinging upon the mind. The object seen is like an iron filing placed next to a magnet; by being seen it becomes the property of its owner, the Self, whose true nature is that of Seer. The mind becomes an object of experience and, although it is an independent entity, it takes on a form which is not its own; it becomes dependent on something else, through object-referral. The meaning is that there is no inaugural moment to the confusion of the two functions of Seer and seen; and, although it has a purpose, it is to be avoided because it is the source of suffering. Thus it is said: 'By avoiding the cause of this confusion, suffering can be fully prevented' (*Pañcaśikha*). — Why? — Because by avoiding the cause of suffering, suffering is averted. It is like the vulnerable sole of the foot and the prickliness of the thorn; prevention means not stepping barefoot on the thorn, or putting on a shoe. If you know this triple mechanics of life, you can adopt a means of prevention and not get pricked. — Why? — By being able to understand the three elements involved. Moreover, *rajas* instigates the suffering and *sattva* undergoes the suffering. — Why? — The suffering befalls the recipient of the action. Although the act of suffering falls to *sattva*, it does not affect the immutable Knower of the Relative which is beyond all activity. It is just that when *sattva* is seen to be suffering, then it appears that the Self is suffering because It takes on the form of the *sattva*.

dṛśyasvarūpamucyate |

prakāśakriyāsthitiśīlaṃ bhūtendriyātmakaṃ bhogāpavargārthaṃ dṛśyam || 2.18 ||

prakāśaśīlaṃ sattvam | kriyāśīlaṃ rajaḥ | sthitiśīlaṃ tama iti | ete guṇāḥ parasparoparaktapravibhāgāḥ pariṇāminaḥ saṃyogaviyogadharmāṇa itaretaropāśrayeṇopārjita-mūrtayaḥ parasparāṅgāṅgitve'pyasaṃbhinnaśakti-pravibhāgāstulyajātīyātulyajātīyaśaktibhedānupātinaḥ pradhānavelāyāmupadarśitasannidhānā guṇatve'pi ca vyāpāramātreṇa pradhānāntarṇītānumitāstitāḥ puruṣārthakartavyatayā prayuktasāmarthyāḥ saṃnidhimātropakāriṇo'yaskāntamaṇikalpāḥ pratyayamantareṇaikatamasya vṛttimanuvartamānāḥ pradhānaśabdavācyā bhavanti | etaddṛśyamityucyate | tadetadbhūtendriyātmakaṃ bhūtabhāvena pṛthivyādinā sūkṣmasthūlena pariṇamate | tathendriyabhāvena śrotrādinā sūkṣmasthūlena pariṇamata iti | tattu nāprayojanamapi tu prayojanamurarīkṛtya pravartata iti bhogāpavargārthaṃ hi taddṛśyaṃ puruṣasyeti | tatreṣṭāniṣṭaguṇasvarūpāvadhāraṇamavibhāgāpannaṃ bhogaḥ bhoktuḥ svarūpāvadhāraṇamapavarga iti |

The nature of the 'observable universe' is described:

II.18. The observable universe is composed of the forms of the elements and the senses and is produced by the interplay of the creative, upholding and destructive tendencies of the guṇas. Its purpose is the enjoyment of life and to gain enlightenment.

Sattva is bright. *Rajas* is active. *Tamas* is stable. The *guṇas* are distinct. They interact. They are ever-changing. They combine and recombine. Together their operations create forms. Despite their mutual interplay, each has its specific function. Their respective functions inform all categories of objects. When one predominates, its operations are clearly visible; but when it is secondary, its presence alongside the dominant *guṇa* can be inferred. Like iron filings placed in front of a magnet, their creativity is harnessed to fulfil the objectives of the Self. Each merely responds to the impulses of the others without any external impetus. They are known as the basic constituents. All this goes to make up what is called the 'observable universe'. This latter is composed of the elements and the senses. On the objective side, it undergoes transformations at gross and subtle levels into earth and the other elements. On the subjective side, it undergoes transformations at gross and subtle levels into hearing and the other senses. But the universe does not exist without a purpose; on the contrary, it is launched into existence in order to provide experience and liberation for the Self. Experience occurs through identification and thus it involves the encounter with desirable, or not so desirable, realities produced by the *guṇas*. Enlightenment is the realisation of the essential nature of the Observer. There

dvayoratiraktamanyaddarśanaṃ nāsti | tathā coktam | ayaṃ tu khalu triṣu guṇeṣu kartṛṣvakartari ca puruṣe tulyātulyajātīye caturthe tatkriyāsākṣiny-upanīyamānānsarvabhāvānupapannānanupaśyanna darśanamanyacchaṅkate iti | tāvetau bhogāpavargau buddhikṛtau buddhāveva vartamānau kathaṃ puruṣe vyapadiśyete iti | tathā vijayaḥ parājayo vā yoddhṛṣu vartamānaḥ svāmini vyapadiśyete sa hi tatphalasya bhokteti | evaṃ bandhamokṣau buddhāveva vartamānau puruṣe vyapadiśyete sa hi tatphalasya bhokteti | buddhereva puruṣārthā'parisamāptirbandhastadarthāvasāyo mokṣa iti | etena grahaṇadhāraṇohāpohatattvajñānābhiniveśā buddhau vartamānāḥ puruṣe'dhyāropitasadbhāvāḥ sa hi tatphalasya bhokteti | 2.18 |

is no experience which does not partake of these two goals. Thus it is said: 'The ignorant man does not suspect the possibility of any other state of consciousness; whereas the reality is that three factors — the *guṇas* — are active, while a fourth element, which is similar yet dissimilar to them — the non-active Self — is the witness of their activities, merely observing all the phenomena presented to It' (*Pañcaśikha*). — How is it that these two, experience and liberation, which are invented by the mind and unfold only within the mind, get imputed to the Self? — In the same way as victory or defeat befalling an army is attributed to the commander, because he is the one who sees the outcome of the battle. Even though they take place only within the mind, bondage and liberation are attributed to the Self, which merely witnesses that process. Bondage is only the affair of the mind, when it is incapable of carrying out the design of the Self, whereas liberation is the realisation of Its design. Thus, perception, reasoning, the retaining and discarding of arguments, the knowledge of the real nature of things, the will to live — all these only take place in the mind and are projected onto the Self because It is the enjoyer of their rewards.

dṛśyānāṃ tu guṇānāṃ svarūpabhedāvadhāraṇārtham-idamārabhyate |

***viśeṣāviśeṣaliṅgamātrāliṅgāni guṇaparvāṇi** || 2.19 ||*

tatrā'kāśavāyvagnyudakabhūmayo bhūtāni śabdasparśarūparasagandhatanmātrāṇāmaviśeṣāṇāṃ viśeṣāḥ | tathā śrotratvakcakṣurjihvāghrāṇāni buddhīndriyāṇi | vākpāṇipādapāyūpasthāni karmendriyāṇi | ekādaśaṃ manaḥ sarvārthamityetāny-asmitālakṣaṇasyāviśeṣasya viśeṣāḥ | guṇānāmeṣa ṣodaśako viśeṣapariṇāmaḥ | ṣaḍ aviśeṣāḥ | tadyathā | śabdatanmātraṃ sparśatanmātraṃ rūpatanmātraṃ rasatanmātraṃ gandhatanmātraṃ ceti ekadvitricatuṣpañcalakṣaṇāḥ śabdādayaḥ pañcāviśeṣāḥ | ṣaṣṭhaścāviśeṣo'smitāmātra iti | ete sattāmātrasyā'tmano mahataḥ ṣaḍaviśeṣapariṇāmāḥ | yattatparamaviśeṣebhyo liṅgamātraṃ mahattattvaṃ tasminnete sattāmātre mahatyātmanyavasthāya vivṛddhikāṣṭhāmanubhavanti | pratisaṃsṛjyamānāśca tasminneva sattāmātre mahatyātmanyavasthāya yattanniḥsattāsattaṃ niḥsadasad nirasad avyaktamaliṅgaṃ pradhānaṃ tatpratiyanti | eṣa teṣāṃ liṅgamātraḥ pariṇāmaḥ niḥsattāsattaṃ cāliṅgapariṇāma iti |

Next, the purpose is to examine the different forms of the *guṇas* which make up the observable universe.

II.19. The combinations of the guṇas operate at gross, subtle, subtlest and unmanifest levels.

Ether, air, fire, water, and earth are the gross elements which develop out of the subtle essences which are hearing, touch, sight, taste, and smell. The organs of sense are the ears, the skin, the eyes, the tongue and the nose. The organs of action are the mouth, the hands, the feet, and the organs of elimination and reproduction. The eleventh is the mind, which experiences all these. Such are the gross elements of the subtle sense of ego. This group of sixteen constitutes the gross expressions of the *guṇas*. The six subtle essences are the finest aspects of hearing, touch, sight, taste and smell. To these five subtle essences, which are associated to one, two, three, four or five special qualities, is added the sixth subtle essence which is the sense of Amness. These are the six subtle aspects of that great Self which is Pure Being. Beyond these subtle aspects is the subtlest field of pure differentiation — the cosmic principle — where they come to the final limit of their range of operation within the great Self that is Pure Being. When they are engaged in the work of decreating the cosmos back into the great Self of Pure Being, they dissolve into the cosmic source, which is the non-differentiated vacuum state, neither existence nor non-existence, neither existing nor non-existing, the Unmanifest. Such is their status within the field of pure differentiation and within the field of non-differentiation, which is neither existence nor non-existence. In the vacuum state, the Self

aliṅgavasthāyāṃ na puruṣārtho heturnāliṅgāvasthāyāmādau puruṣārthatā kāraṇaṃ bhavatīti | na tasyāḥ puruṣārthatā kāraṇaṃ bhavatīti | nāsau puruṣārthakṛteti nityā'khyāyate | trayāṇāṃ tvavasthāviśeṣāṇāmādau puruṣārthatā kāraṇam bhavati | sa cārtho heturnimittaṃ kāraṇaṃ bhavatītyanityā'khyāyate | guṇāstu sarvadharmānupātino na pratyastamayante tenopajāyante | vyaktibhirevātītānāgata-vyayāgamavatībhirguṇānvayiṇībhirupajananāpāya dharmakā iva pratyavabhāsante | yathā devadatto daridrāti | kasmāt | yato'sya mriyante gāva iti | gavāmeva maraṇāttasya daridrānaṃ na svarūpahānāditi | samaḥ samādhiḥ | liṅgamātramaliṅgasya pratyāsannaṃ tatra tatsaṃsṛṣṭaṃ vivicyate kramānativṛtteḥ | tathā ṣaḍaviśeṣā liṅgamātre saṃsṛṣṭā vivicyante pariṇāmakramaniyamāt | tathā teṣvaviśeṣu bhūtendriyāṇi saṃsṛṣṭāni vivicyante | tathā coktam purastāt | na viśeṣebhyaḥ paraṃ tattvāntaramastīti viśeṣāṇāṃ nāsti tattvāntarapariṇāmaḥ | teṣāṃtu dharmalakṣaṇāvasthāpariṇamā vyākhyāyiṣyante | 2.19 |

has no design. In the beginning, in the vacuum state, any design the Self may have does not cause the Unmanifest to manifest. Within That, there is no causality which could be the Self's design. Since That is not the product of any intention on the part of the Self, It is called eternal. But as the three elements begin to differentiate into manifestation, the intention of the Self does then become a cause. Since this intention has a purpose and is an efficient cause, the new level of manifestation is considered to be non-eternal. The *guṇas* are located at all the levels of creation; they do not wax or wane. They only seem to appear and disappear because the manifested products in which they feature come into being from out of the future and then disappear out of existence into the past. The process is like Devadatta's fall into poverty. — Why? — Because his cows died. The reason for his predicament is the loss of his cows, not the loss of his own existence. The situation is analogous. The level of pure differentiation is close to the level of the non-differentiated vacuum state. Being at one with That, it is nonetheless distinct from That, because the process of manifestation is upheld by a specific sequence. Likewise, the six subtle essences, although immersed within the level of differentiation, are nonetheless distinct from it because of the orderliness of the sequence of manifestation. Likewise, the elements and the organs of sense are immersed within the subtle essences, but are distinct from them. As was said before, there is no level which is grosser than material objects, and so forms which are grosser than material objects do not evolve. How evolution takes place as properties, phases and states undergo change will be explained later.

vyākhyātaṃ dṛśyam | atha draṣṭuḥ svarūpāvadhāraṇārthamidamārabhyate |

draṣṭā dṛśimātraḥ śuddho'pi pratyayānupaśyaḥ || *2.20* ||

dṛśimātra iti dṛkśaktireva viśeṣeṇāparāmṛṣṭetyarthaḥ | sa puruṣo buddheḥ pratisaṃvedī | sa buddherna svarūpo nātyantaṃ virūpa iti | na tāvatsarūpaḥ | kasmāt | jñātājñātaviṣayatvāt pariṇāminī hi buddhiḥ | tasyāśca viṣayo gavādighaṭādirvā jñātaścājnātaśceti pariṇāmitvaṃ darśayati | sadājñātaviṣayatvaṃ tu puruṣasyāpariṇāmitvaṃ paridīpayati | kasmāt | na hi buddhiśca nāma puruṣaviṣayaśca syādgṛhitā'gṛhītā ceti siddhaṃ puruṣasya sadājñātaviṣayatvaṃ tataścāpariṇāmitvamiti | kiñca parārthā buddhiḥ saṃhatyakāritvāt svārthaḥ puruṣa iti | tathā sarvārthādhyavasayakatvāt triguṇā buddhistriguṇatvādacetaneti | guṇānāṃ tūpadraṣṭā puruṣa ityato na svarūpaḥ | astu tarhi virūpa iti | nātyantaṃ virūpaḥ | kasmāt | śuddho'pyasau pratyayānupaśyo yataḥ pratyayaṃ bauddhamanupaśyati | tamanupaśyanna tadātmā'pi tadātmaka iva pratyavabhāsate | tathā coktam | apariṇāminī hi bhoktṛśaktirapratisaṃkramā ca

The structure of the observable universe has been described. Now the intention is to determine the nature of the Seer.

II.20. Ever pure, the Seer is the observer who just witnesses thoughts.

The meaning is that the function of the Seer is just to observe, unchanging. The Self knows the mind by reflection. It is not the same as the mind, but It is not entirely different either. — Why is It not the same? — The mind changes as the object of awareness is known and then not known. Its changeableness is demonstrated by the fact that the object — a cow or a pot — may be known or unknown, whereas the unchanging nature of the Self can be seen from the fact that It always knows the object before It. — Why? — The mind is the object of awareness for the Self; it is not first seen and then not seen. The invariable knowingness of the Self is perfect, and so It is by nature unchanging. Moreover, the mind is object-referral, because the role it has is to relay, while the Self is self-referral. The mind is composed of the three *guṇas* because it processes everything it perceives and, because it is subject to the three *guṇas*, it is not consciousness. But the Self is the witness of the three *guṇas*. So It is not the same. — So It is different? — Not entirely. — Why? — Although 'ever pure', It 'witnesses thoughts'. It takes on the form of the impulses in the mind. It takes on the form in the mind, and though different, It appears to be the same. Thus it is said: 'The function of the Seer, while unchanging and unmoving, appears to move with the changing object of thought and

pariṇāminyarthe pratisaṃkrāntevatadvṛttimanupatati tasyāśca prāptacaitanyopagraharūpāyā buddhivṛtteranukāramātratayā buddhivṛttyaviśiṣṭā hi jñānavṛttirityākhyāyate | 2.20 |

to take on the form of that impulse in the mind. The resultant wave of awareness is taken to be not different to the impulse in the mind because It takes on the form of the impulse in the mind' (*Pañcaśikha*).

***tadartha eva dṛśyasyātmā* || *2.21* ||**

dṛśirūpasya puruṣasya karmarūpatāmāpannaṃ dṛśyamiti tadartha eva dṛśyasyā'tmā svarūpaṃ bhavatītyarthaḥ | tatsvarūpaṃ tu pararūpeṇa pratilabdhātmakaṃ | bhogāpavargārthatāyāṃ kṛtāyāṃ puruṣeṇa na dṛśyata iti | svarūpahānādasya nāśaḥ prāpto na tu vinaśyati | 2.21 |

II.21. The role of creation is to serve the Self.

The nature of the object observed is to be the object of perception for the observer. The meaning is that the real role of the created universe is to serve the Self. It is there for the Other. When its purpose of providing experience of enjoyment and liberation is fulfilled, it is no longer perceived by the Self. When its mission is accomplished, it disappears from view, although it is not destroyed.

kasmāt |

kṛtārthaṃ prati naṣṭamapyanaṣṭaṃ tadanyasādharaṇatvāt || 2.22 ||

kṛtārthamekaṃ puruṣaṃ prati dṛśyaṃ naṣṭamapi nāśaṃ prāptamapyanaṣṭaṃ tad anyapuruṣasādhāraṇatvāt | kuśalaṃ puruṣaṃ prati nāśaṃ prāptamapyakuśalānpuruṣānpratyakṛtārthamiti | teṣāṃ dṛśeḥ karmaviṣayatāmāpannaṃ labhate evaṃ pararūpeṇā'tmarūpamiti | ataśca dṛgdarśanaśaktyornityatvādanādiḥ saṃyogo vyākhyāta iti | tathā coktam | dharmiṇāmanādisaṃyogād-dharmamātrāṇāmapyanādiḥ samyoga iti | 2.22 |

— Why? —

II.22. It disappears from view when this role is fulfilled, but it is not destroyed since it continues for others.

The object disappears when its role is fulfilled for one Self — its destruction is effected — but it remains for other Selfs. Although it disappears when one Self is freed, for unfreed Selfs its role is not yet fulfilled. For these others, it remains the object of perception for the Seer; its status continues to be for others. So the link between the function of the Seer and seeing was described as having had no beginning because it is permanent. Thus it is said: 'The link to phenomena is beginningless because the link to their source in objects is beginningless' (*Pañcaśikha*).

saṃyogasvarūpā'bhiditsayedaṃ sūtraṃ pravavṛte |

svasvāmiśaktyoḥ svarūpopalabdhihetuḥ saṃyogaḥ || *2.23* ||

puruṣaḥ svāmi dṛśyena svena darśanārthaṃ saṃyuktaḥ | tasmātsaṃyogād dṛśyasyopalabdhiryā sa bhogaḥ | yā tu draṣṭuḥ svarūpopalabdhiḥ so'pavargaḥ | darśanakāryāvasānaḥ saṃyoga iti darśanaṃ viyogasya kāraṇamuktam | darśanamadarśanasya pratidhvandvītyadarśanaṃ saṃyoganimittamuktam | nātra darśanaṃ mokṣakāraṇamadarśanābhāvādeva bandhābhāvaḥ sa mokṣa iti | darśanasya bhāve bandhakaraṇasyādarśanasya nāśa ityato darśanajñānaṃ kaivalyakāranam uktam | kiñcedamadarśanaṃ nāma | kiṃ guṇānāmadhikāra āhosvid dṛśirūpasya svāmino darśitaviṣayasya pradhānacittasyānutpādaḥ | svasmindṛśye vidyamāne darśanābhāvaḥ | kimarthavattā guṇānām |

The following *sūtra* seeks to elucidate the nature of the link:

II.23. It is the link that makes possible the conscious experience of the real nature of the mechanics of the 'property' (the object of perception) and of the 'owner' (the Self).

The Self, as 'owner', is linked to its 'property', the object seen, in order to achieve enlightened vision. Thus, when the link is in place, the perception of an object constitutes experience, whereas the perception of the true nature of the Seer brings fulfilment. The link ultimately issues in the advent of enlightened vision; this correct perception is said to be the cause of the unlinking. Since true vision is the opposite of wrong vision, wrong vision is said to bring about the link. However, for the purpose of this Teaching, it is not the case that correct vision 'causes' liberation, for liberation consists in there being no link at all, and this occurs in the absence of false perception. With true vision, the defective vision that causes bondage is destroyed. It is in this sense that the experience which comes from true vision is said to realise the singularity of consciousness.

— So what then is this 'lack of true vision'? Is it (a) the result of the operation of the *guṇas*? — Or is it (b) the absence of any perception at all that is occasioned when the mind — which presents objects to be observed by the 'owner' in Its capacity as Seer — is immersed in the Absolute, although the 'property' — the object observed — remains available to be known? — Or is it (c) the intention of the *guṇas*? — Or is it (d) ignorance, which subsides when the mind dissolves, but remains the seed at

athāvidyā svacittena saha niruddhā svacittasyotpattibījam | kiṃ sthitisaṃskārakṣaye gatisaṃskarābhivyaktiḥ | yatredamuktam | pradhānaṃ sthityaiva vartamānaṃ vikārākāraṇādapradhānaṃ syāttathā gatyaiva vartamānaṃ vikāranityatvādapradhānaṃ syāt | ubhayathā cāsya pravṛttiḥ pradhānavyavahāraṃ labhate nānyathā | kāraṇāntareṣvapi kalpiteṣveva samānaścarcaḥ | darśanaśaktirevādarśanamityeke | pradhānasyā'tmakhyāpanārthā pravṛttiriti śruteḥ | sarvabodhyabodhasamarthaḥ prākpravṛtteḥ puruṣo na paśyati sarvakāryakaraṇasamarthaṃ dṛśyaṃ tadā na dṛśyata iti | ubhayasyāpyadarśanaṃ dharma ityeke | tatredaṃ dṛśyasya svātmabhūtamapi puruṣapratyayāpekṣaṃ darśanaṃ dṛśyadharmatvena bhavati | tathā puruṣasyānātmabhūtamapi dṛśyapratyayāpekṣaṃ puruṣadharmatveneva darśanamavabhāsate | darśanaṃ jñānamevādarśanamiti kecitabhidadhati | ityete śāstragatā vikalpāḥ | tatra vikalpabahutvametatsarvapuruṣāṇāṃ guṇānāṃ saṃyoge sādhāraṇaviṣayam | 2.23 |

the basis of the mind when it remanifests? — Or is it (e) the manifestation of the impression of activity which follows when the impression of non-activity ends? (On this point, it is said: 'If almighty Nature was pure silence only, it would not be almighty, because it could not then promote evolutionary change. At the same time, if it was pure dynamism only, it could not be almighty either, because then change itself would be what was eternal.' But it is precisely because its *modus operandi* integrates both possibilities that it is called 'almighty' Nature and not some other name. The same reasoning may be applied to any other primal cause which might be adduced). — Or, as some say, is false vision (f) a function of true vision? For it says in the Veda: 'The purpose of the activities of Nature is to be known by the Self'. The Self is capable of knowing all that can be known, but It can see nothing before Nature becomes manifest; and before it does manifest, though Nature is capable of performing anything, it remains an object that cannot be seen. — Or, as others say, is defective vision (g) a function of both; of the knower and the known? On this view, although in essence it really pertains to an object of perception, this mode of consciousness must partake of the awareness of the Self — whereby it becomes an object observed. At the same time, although it is not really the same as the Self, this mode of consciousness must be aware of its objects of perception — whereby it appears to have the same status as the Self. — Or, as some hold, (h) is any knowledge, even 'true vision', a distortion of Reality?

All these various alternatives are found in the Teaching. But the common denominator in all these different views is that there is a link between the *guṇas* and all Selfs.

yastu pratyakcetanasya svabuddhisaṃyogaḥ |

tasya heturavidyā || *2.24* ||

viparyayajñānavāsanetyarthaḥ | viparyayajñānavāsanāvāsitā ca na kāryaniṣṭhaṃ puruṣakhyātiṃ buddhiḥ prāpnoti sādhikārā punarāvartate | sā tu puruṣakhyātirparyavāsanā kāryaniṣṭhaṃ prāpnoti caritādhikārā nivṛttādarśanā bandhakāraṇābhāvānna punarāvartate | atra kaścitṣaṇḍakopākhyānenodghāṭayati mugdhayā bhāryyayā'bhidhīyate ṣaṇḍakaḥ | āryaputra apatyavatī me bhaginī kimarthaṃ nāham iti | sa tāmāha | mṛtaste'hamapatyamutpādayiṣyāmīti | tathedaṃ vidyamānaṃ jñānaṃ cittanivṛttiṃ na karoti vinaṣṭaṃ kariṣyatīti kā pratyāśā | tatrā'cāryadeśīyo vakti | nanu buddhinivṛttireva mokṣaḥ adarśanakāraṇābhāvād buddhinivṛttiḥ | taccādarśanaṃ bandhakāraṇaṃ darśanānnivartate | tatra cittanivṛttireva mokṣaḥ kimarthamasthāna evāsya mativibhramaḥ | 2.24 |

The link is between one's mind and one's own Self, and:

II.24. Ignorance is its cause.

The meaning is that it is the deep impression left by false knowledge. The mind is permeated by the deep impressions made by false knowledge, and it cannot achieve its objective of realising the Self. As long as this task remains to be completed, the mind will continue to remanifest. But once its objective is attained — culminating in the realisation of the Self — its role is fulfilled, defective vision is ended, and as there is nothing to bind it, it does not remanifest. Some ridicule this aspect of the Teaching, quoting the anecdote of the impotent husband, whose artless wife complains: 'Darling, my sister has a baby; why don't I?' To which he replies: 'I'll give you a child when I'm dead'. The idea is that merely understanding this does not cause the mind to dissolve; so what expectation can there be that it will do so in the future? And a pseudo-master might say: 'So liberation occurs when the mind stops? The mind stops when there is no cause of defective vision. And wrong vision, which is the cause of bondage, is removed by true vision. So stopping the mind equals liberation.' What is the point of such misguided ramblings?

heyaṃ duḥkhaṃ heyakāraṇaṃ ca saṃyogākhyaṃ sanimmitamuktamataḥ paraṃ hānaṃ vaktavyam |

tadabhāvāt saṃyogābhāvo hānaṃ taddṛśeḥ kaivalyam || 2.25 ||

tasyādarśanasyābhāvād buddhipuruṣasaṃyogābhāvaḥ ātyantiko bandhanoparama ityarthaḥ | etadhānam | taddṛśeḥ kaivalyaṃ puruṣasyāmiśrībhāvaḥ punarasaṃyogo guṇairityarthaḥ | duḥkhakāraṇanivṛttau duḥkhoparamo hānam | tadā svarūpapratiṣṭhaḥ puruṣa ityuktam | 2.25 |

The pain that can be avoided and what is called the bond that is at its basis, as well as their cause, have been analysed. Now supreme freedom is described.

II.25. When ignorance is removed, there is no link. This means freedom — the singularity of consciousness.

The meaning is that in the absence of distorted vision, there is no link between the mind and the Self, and that brings a definitive end to bondage. This is freedom. 'Singularity of consciousness' means that there is no inmixing of the Self, no more connection to the *guṇas*. When the cause of unhappiness is gone, unhappiness comes to an end. It just stops. Then the Self is said to be established in Its own nature.

atha hānasya kaḥ prāptyupāya iti |

vivekakhyātiraviplavā hānopāyaḥ || 2.26 ||

sattvapuruṣānyatāpratyayo vivekakhyātiḥ | sā tvanivṛttamithyājñānā plavate | yadā mithyājñānaṃ dagdhabījabhāvaṃ bandhyaprasavaṃ saṃpadyate tadā vidhūtakleśarajasaḥ sattvasya pare vaiśāradhye parasyāṃ vaśikārasaṃjñāyāṃ vartamānasya vivekapratyayapravāho nirmalo bhavati | sā vivekakhyātiraviplavā hānopāyaḥ | tato mithyājñānasya dagdhabījabhāvopagamaḥ punaścāprasava ityeṣa mokṣasya mārgo hānasyopāya iti | 2.26 |

— So what is the way to end it? —

II.26. The way to end it is with the unbroken awareness of separation.

Awareness of separation is the experience of the difference between the *sattva* in the mind and the Self. This comes and goes as long as the awareness is not stabilised. When the habit of misperception has become like a roasted seed and no longer germinates, then there is an unbroken flow of awareness of the separation, absolutely pure, which is technically known as 'self-possession' — a state of supreme peacefulness — when the *sattva* in the mind is free from the *rajas* which causes suffering. This continuous flow of the awareness of separation is the means to freedom. In this way, this means of putting an end to bondage is the highway to liberation — achieved when the seed is roasted and does not germinate.

tasya saptadhā prāntabhūmiḥ prajñā || *2.27* ||

tasyeti pratyuditakhyāteḥ pratyāmnāyaḥ | saptadheti | aśuddhyāvaraṇamalāpagamāccittasya pratyayāntarānutpāde sati saptaprakāraiva prajñā vivekino bhavati | tadyathā | parijñātaṃ heyaṃ nāsya punaḥ parijñeyamasti | kṣīṇā heyahetavo na punareteṣāṃ kṣetavyamasti | sākṣātkṛtaṃ nirodhasamādhinā hānam | bhāvito vivekakhyātirūpo hānopāya iti | eṣā catuṣṭayī kāryā vimuktiḥ prajñāyāḥ | cittavimuktistu trayī | caritādhikārā buddhiḥ | guṇā giriśikharakūṭacyutā iva grāvāṇo niravasthānāḥ svakāraṇe pralayābhimukhāḥ saha tenāstaṃ gacchanti | na caiṣāṃ pravilīnānāṃ punarastyutpādaḥ prayojanābhāvāditi | etasyāmavasthāyāṃ guṇasaṃbandhātītaḥ svarūpamātrajyotiramalaḥ kevalī puruṣa iti | etāṃ saptavidhāṃ prāntabhūmiprajñāmanupaśyanpuruṣaḥ kuśala ityākhyāyate | pratiprasave'pi cittasya muktaḥ kuśala ityeva bhavati guṇātītatvād | 2.27 |

II.27. One's experience progresses through seven stages.

'One's' recaps 'one in whom this realisation has dawned'. 'Seven': when the layers of impurity in the mind have been removed and other thoughts do not arise, realisation grows and one's experience passes through seven stages. They are as follows: — 1. He knows what is to be avoided. He has nothing further to learn in this regard. — 2. The causes of what is to be avoided have been weakened. They require no further attention. — 3. The end of bondage has become a matter of direct perception, because of the experience of Pure Consciousness. — 4. The means of ending bondage is established in the form of awareness of separation. (These are the four aspects of liberation that come from action; freedom in the mind has the following three aspects.) — 5. The mind has fulfilled its role. — 6. The *guṇas*, like loose boulders tumbling down from a jagged mountain top, disintegrate back into their own source and return to non-existence along with the mind. Once dissolved, they do not appear again, there being no reason for them to do so. — 7. In this state, bondage to the *guṇas* is transcended, and the pure Self shines forth in Self-referral, in Unity. The Self is said to be free when one has passed through these seven stages of experience. When the mind demanifests, beyond the *guṇas*, the Self is liberated.

siddhā bhavati vivekakhyātirhānopāya iti | na ca siddhiranantareṇa sādhanamityetadārabhyate |

yogāṅgānuṣṭhānādaśuddhikṣaye jñānadīptir-āvivekakhyāteḥ || *2.28* ||

yogāṅgānyaṣṭāvabhidhāyiṣyamāṇāni | teṣāmanuṣṭhānātpañcaparvaṇo viparyayasyāśuddhirūpasya kṣayo nāśaḥ | tatkṣaye samyagjñānasyābhivyaktiḥ | yathā yathā ca sādhanānyanuṣṭhīyante tathā tathā tanutvamaśuddhirāpadyate | yathā yathā ca kṣīyate tathā tathā ca kṣayakramānurodhinī jñānasyāpi dīptirvivardhate | sā khalveṣā vivṛddhiḥ prakarṣamanubhavati ā vivekakhyāteḥ | ā guṇapuruṣasvarūpavijñānādityarthaḥ | yogāṅgānuṣṭhānamaśuddherviyogakāraṇam | yathā paraśuśchedyasya | vivekakhyātestu prāptikāraṇaṃ yathā dharmaḥ sukhasya nānyathā kāraṇam | kati caitāni kāraṇāni śāstre bhavanti | navaivetyāha | tadyathā | utpattisthityabhivyaktivikārapratyayāptayaḥ | viyogānyatvadhṛtayaḥ kāraṇannavadhā smṛtamiti | tatrotpattikāraṇaṃ | mano bhavati vijñānasya | sthitikāraṇaṃ manasaḥ puruṣārthatā śarīrasyevāhāra iti | abhivyaktikāraṇaṃ yathā rūpasyālokastathā rūpajñānam | vikārakāraṇaṃ manaso viṣayāntaraṃ yathāgniḥ pākyasya |

Perfect realisation of separation is the way to end bondage. Such perfection can only be achieved by adopting the technologies as described.

II.28. Exercising the limbs of yoga removes impurities and brings the light of consciousness to full realisation.

The eight limbs of yoga will now be explained. By adopting them, the five types of impure, false understanding are weakened or dissolved. Once weakened, true knowledge dawns. As the technologies are put into practice, so impurities are reduced. As the degree of purification grows, so the light of Pure Knowledge grows *pari passu.* Indeed, as Pure Knowledge grows, it leads to full enlightenment. This is because the nature of the Self as separate from the *guṇas* is realised. The practice of the limbs of yoga provides a methodology to remove impurities, just as an axe is an instrument used to fell a tree. Just as action in accord with Natural Law is the means whereby one achieves happiness, so yoga is a means to gain the awareness of separation; it is not an instrument for any other purpose. — How many such methodological principles does the Teaching acknowledge? — Nine are listed. They are recorded as follows: origination, conservation, manifestation, modification, association, attainment, disunion, diversification, maintenance. Origination: as the mind is the source of knowledge. Conservation: as the mind exists to serve the Self, or as the purpose of food is to feed the body. Manifestation: like a light shining reveals an object to view and also its colour. Modification: as when the mind changes when it experiences a different object, or as fire changes the food it cooks. Association: as seeing smoke makes one

pratyayakāraṇaṃ dhūmajñānamagnijñānasya | prāptikāraṇaṃ yogāṅgānuṣṭhānaṃ vivekakhyāteḥ | viyogakāraṇaṃ tadevaśuddheḥ | anyatvakāraṇaṃ yathā suvarṇasya suvarṇakāraḥ | evamekasya strīpratyayasyāvidyā mūḍhatve dveṣo duḥkhatve rāgaḥ sukhatve tattvajñānaṃ mādhyasthye | dhṛtikāraṇaṃ śarīramindriyāṇāṃ tāni ca tasya | mahābhūtāni śarīrāṇām tāni ca parasparaṃ sarveṣām | tairyagyonamānuṣadaivatāni ca parasparārthatvāditi | evaṃ nava kāraṇāni | tāni ca yathāsaṃbhavaṃ padārthāntareṣvapi yojyāni | yogāṅgānuṣṭhānaṃ tu dvidhaiva kāraṇatvaṃ labhata iti | 2.28 |

think of fire. Achievement: as when adopting the limbs of yoga one gains the experience of separation. Disunion: as with the removal of impurities. Diversification: as when the goldsmith produces a variety of artefacts from his gold. Or: as in one's changing attitude towards a woman, where ignorance leads to infatuation, antipathy to loathing, desire to joy, whereas knowledge of Reality ensures equanimity. Maintenance: the physiology maintains the senses, and *vice versa*. Also, the gross elements sustain material bodies, and *vice versa*. Likewise, the animal, the human and the divine kingdoms support one another. These are the nine principles, which can be equally well applied in other circumstances as appropriate. In adopting the limbs of yoga two of the above are brought into play: disunion and achievement.

tatra yogāṅgānyavadhāryante |

yamaniyamāsanaprāṇāyāmapratyāhāradhāraṇādhyāna-samādhayo'ṣṭāvaṅgāni || *2.29* ||

yathākramameṣāmanuṣṭhānaṃ svarūpaṃ ca vakṣyāmaḥ | 2.29 |

The limbs of yoga are enumerated.

II.29. The eight limbs of yoga are: observances, rules of living, posture, breathing, withdrawal, turning within, meditation, transcendence.

The nature and practice of each will be explained in turn.

tatrāhiṃsāsatyāsteyabrahmacaryāparigrahā yamāḥ || 2.30 ||

tatrāhiṃsā sarvathā sarvadā sarvabhūtānāmanabhidrohaḥ | uttare ca yamaniyamāstanmūlāstatsiddhiparatayaiva tatpratipādanāya pratipādyante | tadavadātarūpakaraṇāyaivopādīyante | tathā coktam | sa khalvayaṃ brāhmaṇo yathā yathā vratāni bahūni samāditsate tathā tathā pramādakṛtebhyo hiṃsānidānebhyo nivartamānastām-evāvadātarūpāmahiṃsāṃ karoti | satyaṃ yathārthe vāṅmanase | yathā dṛṣṭaṃ yathā'numitaṃ yathā śrutaṃ tathā vāṅmanaśceti | paratra svabodhasaṃkrāntaye vāguktā sā yadi na vañcitā bhrāntā vā pratipattivandhyā vā bhavediti | eṣā sarvabhūtopakārārthaṃ pravṛttā na bhūtopaghātāya | yadi caivamapyabhidhīyamānā bhūtopaghātaparaiva syānna satyaṃ bhavet pāpameva bhavet | tena puṇyābhāsena puṇyapratirūpakeṇa kaṣṭaṃ tamaḥ prāpnuyāt | tasmātparīkṣya sarvabhūtahitaṃ satyaṃ brūyāt | steyamaśāstrapūrvakaṃ dravyāṇāṃ parataḥ svīkaraṇaṃ tatpratiṣedhaḥ punaraspṛhārūpamasteyamiti | brahmacaryaṃ guptendriyasyopasthasya saṃyamaḥ | viṣayāṇāmarjanarakṣaṇakṣayasaṅgahiṃsādoṣadarśanād-asvīkaraṇamaparigraha ityete yamāḥ | 2.30 |

II.30. The observances are: non-violence, truthfulness, non-covetousness, celibacy, non-acceptance of others' possessions.

Non-violence is not harming any living creature, at any time and in any circumstances. The other observances and rules of living are based on this, and are practised in order to instil it firmly and to raise it to its fullest perfection. They are enjoined solely so it can be realised in its purest form. Thus it is said: 'Whatever the many vows he makes, a Brahman is only established in the purity of non-violence when he refrains from any careless act of harm'. Truthfulness is thought and speech in accord with one's reality — thought and speech which correspond to what one has seen, inferred or heard. Words are spoken to communicate one's knowledge to others and should not be deceitful, offensive or idle. Speech should be uplifting to all and not used to speak ill of others. Even though it be judged truthful, if in the end one's speech maligns others, it is wrong. Lending a veneer of virtue or a pretence of goodness to one's speech, one commits a sin. Therefore, one should speak the truth for the welfare of all. Theft is the appropriation to oneself of the possessions of others such as is not sanctioned by the Teaching. Refraining from stealing, not envying — that is non-covetousness. Celibacy is continence of the private organs of generation. Non-acceptance is the non-appropriation of possessions, given the burdens which they incur — acquiring, keeping, losing them, becoming attached to them, the harm done to others by obtaining them. These are the observances.

te tu |

jātideśakālasamayānavacchinnāḥ sārvabhaumā mahāvratam || 2.31 ||

tatrā'hiṃsā jātyavacchinnā matsyavadhakasya matsyeṣveva nānyatra hiṃsā | saiva deśāvacchinnā na tīrthe haniṣyāmīti | saiva kālāvacchinnā na caturdaśyāṃ na puṇye'hani haniṣyāmīti | saiva tribhiruparatasya samayāvacchinnā devabrāhmaṇārthe nānyathā haniṣyāmīti | yathā ca kṣatriyāṇāṃ yuddha eva hiṃsā nānyatreti | ebhir jātideśakālasamayairanavacchinnā ahiṃsādayaḥ sarvathaiva paripālanīyāḥ | sarvabhūmiṣu sarvaviṣayeṣu sarvathaivāviditavyabhicārāḥ sārvabhaumā mahāvratamityucyate | 2.31 |

As for these:

II.31. They apply in all circumstances, irrespective of class, place, time, or duty: this great law of life is universal.

The observance of non-violence may be set aside for reasons of profession, as when a fisherman is permitted to limit the exercise of violence to fish. Or it may be restricted by place, as when someone vows, 'I shall not kill in a holy site'. Or it may be restricted by time, as when someone vows, 'I shall not kill on the full-moon or a holy day'. Or if these three conditions are respected, the observance may nonetheless be waived out of duty, as when someone vows, 'I shall kill only in sacrifices to the gods or at the behest of Brahmans', or when warriors proclaim, 'Violence only on the field of battle'. Non-violence, and the other observances, without exemption of class, place, time or duty, are otherwise to be upheld in all circumstances. When they are practised unwaveringly, at all levels and in all areas of activity, they form what is called the 'great law of life'.

śaucasaṃtoṣatapaḥsvādhyāyeṣvarapraṇidhānāni niyamāḥ || *2.32* ||

tatra śaucaṃ mṛjjalādijanitaṃ medhyābhyavaharaṇādi ca bāhyam | ābhyantaraṃ cittamalānāmākṣālanam | saṃtoṣaḥ sannihitasādhanādadhikasyānupāditsā | tapo dvandvasahanam | dvandhvaṃ ca jighatsāpipāse śitoṣṇe sthānāsane kāṣṭhamaunākāramaune ca | vratāni caiṣāṃ yathāyogaṃ kṛcchracāndrāyaṇasāntapanādīni | svādhyāyaḥ mokṣaśāstrāṇāmadhyayanaṃ praṇavajapo vā | īśvarapraṇidhānaṃ tasminparamagurau sarvakarmārpaṇam | śayyāsanastho'tha pathi vrajanvā svasthaḥ parikṣīṇavitarkajālaḥ | saṃsārabījakṣayam-īkṣamāṇaḥ syānnityayukto'mṛtabhogabhāgī | yatredamuktam | tataḥ pratyakcetanādhigamo'pyantarāyābhāvaśca iti | 2.32 |

II.32. The rules of living are: purity, contentment, purification, study, surrender to the Absolute.

Purity is external when it is produced using soap, water and the like, and by consuming fresh food and drink. It is internal when the mind is washed clean. Contentment is the desire for no more means than are at hand. Purification comes from enduring extremes. Examples of extremes include: hunger and thirst, heat and cold, remaining seated or remaining standing, the practice of non-communication or of silence. Also, observing vows as are prescribed: fasting, for example, the lunar or the six-day observances (*Manu-Smṛti, XI. 212-222*). Study means learning the teachings on liberation or the recitation of primordial sounds. Surrender to the Absolute means offering all actions to the Supreme Teacher. Whether lying on a bed, or sitting in a chair, or walking on the road, the Self-possessed experiences the fog of mental chatter lift. Seeing the seeds of the cycle of life and death destroyed, ever united, he partakes of the joy of immortality. Thus it is said: 'Then the attention can dive within and obstacles are removed' (*Yoga-Sūtra I.29*).

eteṣāṃ yamaniyamānām |

vitarkabādhane pratipakṣabhāvanam || *2.33* ||

yadā'sya brāhmaṇasya hiṃsādayo vitarkā jāyeranhaniṣyāmyahamapakāriṇamanṛtamapi vakṣyāmi dravyamapyasya svī kariṣyāmi dāreṣu cāsya vyavāyī bhaviṣyāmi parigraheṣu cāsya svāmī bhaviṣyāmīti | evamunmārgapravaṇavitarkajvareṇātidīptena bādhyamānastatpratipakṣānbhāvayet | ghoreṣu saṃsarāṅgāreṣu pacyamānena mayā śaraṇamupagataḥ sarvabhūtābhayapradānena yogadharmaḥ | sa khalvahaṃ tyaktvā vitarkānpunastānādadānastulyaḥ śvavṛttena iti bhāvayet | yathā śvā vāntāvalehī tathā tyaktasya punarādadāna iti | evamādi sūtrāntareṣvapi yojyam | 2.33 |

As for the observances and the rules of living:

II.33. Neutralise negative thoughts if they arise.

When a Brahman is obsessed by thoughts of violence and similar temptations — such as 'I'm going to kill that man for speaking ill of me', or 'I shall lie about it', or 'I'll take his things', or 'I want to make love to his wife', or 'I want to take over his business' — being overpowered by the burning delirium of urges which threaten to lead him astray, he should entertain opposite notions. He should say to himself, 'I burn in the terrifying coals of the cycle of life and death; I take refuge in the practice of yoga which removes all fear from living beings. Were I to resume the ways I have now renounced, I should become addicted again, and be like a dog. For like a dog licking up his own vomit, I should take back what I have rejected.' The same approach should be applied to other *sūtras*.

vitarkā hiṃsādayaḥ kṛtakāritānumoditā lobhakrodhamohapūrvakā mṛdumadhyādhimātrā duḥkhājñānānantaphalā iti pratipakṣabhāvanam || 2.34 ||

tatra hiṃsā tāvat | kṛtakāritā'numoditeti tridhā | ekaikā punastrividhā | lobhena māṃsacarmārthena krodhena apakṛtamaneneti mohena dharmo me bhaviṣyatīti | lobhakrodhamohāḥ punastrividhā mṛdumadhyādhimātrā iti | evaṃ saptaviṃśatirbhedā bhavanti hiṃsāyāḥ | mṛdumadhyādhimātrāḥ punastrividhā | mṛdumṛduḥ madhyamṛduḥ tīvramṛduriti | tathā mṛdumadhyaḥ madhyamadhyaḥ tīvramadhya iti | tathā mṛdutīvraḥ madhyatīvraḥ adhimātratīvra iti | evamekāśītibhedā hiṃsā bhavati | sā punarniyamavikalpasamuccayabhedād-asaṃkhyeyā | prāṇabhṛdbhedasyāparisaṃkhyeyatvāditi evamanṛtādiṣvapi yojyam | te khalvamī vitarkā duḥkhājñānānantaphalā iti pratipakṣabhāvanam duḥkhamajñānaṃ cānantaṃ phalaṃ yeṣāmiti pratipakṣabhāvanam | tathā ca hiṃsakastāvatprathamaṃ vadhyasya vīryamākṣipati | tataśca saśtrādinipātena duḥkhayati | tato jīvitādapi mocayatīti | tato vīryākṣepādasya cetanācetanamupakaraṇaṃ kṣīṇavīryaṃ bhavati | duḥkhotpādānnarakatiryakpretādiṣu duḥkhamanubhavati |

II.34. Negative thoughts — about acts of violence and similar, which one has performed, caused, or condoned — come from lust, anger, and delusion. They are mild, moderate or high in intensity, and lead to unending suffering and ignorance. Neutralise them.

Take violence. It can be of three kinds: acts one performs oneself, acts one causes indirectly, or acts one condones. Each kind can take three forms: from lust (killing for food or hides); from anger (harming others); from delusion (imagining that one's evolution is being furthered). Lust, anger and delusion are themselves of three types: mild, moderate and intense. So there are 27 varieties of violence. Mild, moderate and intense are themselves subdivided into three degrees: low-mild, medium-mild, high-mild; then, low-moderate, medium-moderate, high-moderate; finally, low-intense, medium-intense, high-intense. So there are 81 varieties of violence. In fact, the possible variations implied by restrictive injunctions, optionality and collective performance during sacrifices are innumerable. The classification of the innumerable permutations in the case of harm done to living beings also applies to the other observances regarding untruthfulness, stealing and the rest. Negative thoughts can be neutralised by understanding that they lead to unending suffering and ignorance. Committing violence first involves constraining the victim, then inflicting injury with some implement, then taking its life. The act of constraining incurs a conscious or unconscious drain on the energy system of the perpetrator. The act of inflicting injury is met with suffering in hell, being born as an animal or as a living-dead or something similar. The act

jīvitavyaparopaṇātpratikṣaṇaṃ ca jīvitātyaye vartamāno maraṇamicchannapi duḥkhavipākasya niyatavipākavedanīyatvāt kathaṃ cidevocchvasiti | yadi ca kathaṃ citpuṇyāvāpagatā hiṃsā bhavettatra sukhaprāptau bhavedalpāyuriti | evamanṛtādiṣvapi yojyaṃ yathāsaṃbhavam | evaṃ vitarkāṇāṃ cāmumevānugataṃ vipākamaniṣṭaṃ bhāvayanna vitarkeṣu manaḥ praṇidadhīta | pratipakṣabhāvanādhetorheyā vitarkāḥ | yadāsya syuraprasavadharmāṇastadā tatkṛtamaiśvaryaṃ yoginaḥ siddhisūcakaṃ bhavati | 2.34 |

of taking life brings the constant threat of death upon oneself. Although one may be expecting to die, there will be some delay as the effect of karma takes shape before delivering suffering, so one will live on for some time. Even if the act of violence involved some positive aspect, and even though one may experience some happiness, life will be shortened. The same principles apply to untruthfulness and the other observances, as befits. So, given the undesirable consequences of negative thoughts, the mind should not dwell on them. Negative thoughts can be averted by neutralising them. When they are proven to be unproductive, then this sign of success shows that the yogi has achieved self-control.

tadyathā |

ahiṃsāpratiṣṭhāyāṃ tatsaṃnidhau vairatyāgaḥ || *2.35* ||

sarvaprāṇīnāṃ bhavati | 2.35 |

And so:

II.35. When non-violence is established, hostility melts away in its presence.

This applies to all living beings.

satyapratiṣṭhāyāṃ kriyāphalāśrayatvam || *2.36* ||

dhārmiko bhūyā iti bhavati dhārmikaḥ | svargaṃ prāpnuhīti svargaṃ prāpnoti | amoghā'sya vāgbhavati | 2.36 |

II.36. When truthfulness is established, action is guaranteed success.

Saying to someone, 'Be good', they behave responsibly. Saying 'Enjoy heaven', they enjoy heaven. Speech achieves the desired result.

asteyapratiṣṭhāyāṃ sarvaratnopasthānam || 2.37 ||

sarvadiksthānyasyopaniṣṭhante ratnāni | 2.37 |

II.37. When non-covetousness is established, affluence accrues.

Riches pour in from all sides.

***brahmacaryapratiṣṭhāyāṃ vīryalābhaḥ* || *2.38* ||**

yasya lābhādapratighānguṇānutkarśayati | siddhaśca vineyeṣu jñānamādhātuṃ samartho bhavati | 2.38 |

II.38. Established in celibacy, potency develops.

Acquiring this, one develops invincible powers. When it is perfected, one is able to confer enlightenment on one's followers.

aparigrahasthairye janmakathaṃtā saṃbodhaḥ || *2.39* ||

asya bhavati | ko'hamāsaṃ kathamahamāsaṃ kiṃsvididaṃ ke vā bhaviṣyāmaḥ kathaṃ vā bhaviṣyāma ityevamasya pūrvāntaparāntamadhyeṣvātmabhāvajijñāsā svarūpeṇopāvartate | etā yamasthairye siddhayaḥ | 2.39 |

II.39. With constancy in non-acceptance — clear understanding of one's purpose in life.

Add 'one obtains'. — 'Who am I? What was I like? What is this life? What will become of us? What will happen to us?' The desire to know one's status, during earlier stages of evolution, and those to come, and the periods between incarnations, is spontaneously fulfilled.

These powers come with steady practice of the observances.

niyameṣu vakṣyāmaḥ |

śaucātsvāṅgajugupsā parairasaṃsargaḥ || *2.40* ||

svāṅge jugupsāyāṃ śaucamārabhamāṇaḥ kāyāvadyadarśī kāyānabhiṣvaṅgī yatirbhavati | kiṃca parairasaṃsargaḥ kāyasvabhāvāvalokī svamapi kāyaṃ jihāsurmṛjjalādibhir-ākṣālayannapi kāyāśuddhimapaśyankathaṃ parakāyair-atyantamevāprayataiḥ saṃsṛjyeta | 2.40 |

Now we shall hear about the rules of living:

II.40. Purity entails attentiveness to the physiology and self-reliance from others.

While unattached to the body, the seeker recognises its imperfections and attends to maintaining its purity from a desire to care for the physiology. Moreover, dependence on others falls away. The aspirant becomes aware of the true nature of the physical body and sees that it is not purified by washing with soap and water or similar treatments; so why would he seek to get caught up with the totally unrefined systems of others?

kiṃca |

***sattvaśuddhisaumanasyaikāgryendriyajayātmadarśana-yogyatvāni ca* || *2.41* ||**

bhavantīti vākyaśeṣaḥ | śuceḥ sattvaśuddhistataḥ saumanasyaṃ tata ekāgryaṃ tata indriyajayastataścā'tmadarśanayogyatvaṃ buddhisattvasya bhavatīti | etacchautasthairyādadhigamyata iti | 2.41 |

Moreover:

II.41. And clarity of mind, positivity in outlook, the ability to concentrate, control of the senses, and witnessing.

Complete the sentence with 'develop'. With purity in the physiology comes clarity in the mind; then positivity in outlook; then the ability to concentrate; then control of the senses; then witnessing. This all follows from consistent purification.

saṃtoṣādanuttamasukhalābhaḥ || *2.42* ||

tathā coktam | yacca kāmasukhaṃ loke yacca divyaṃ mahatsukham | tṛṣṇākṣayasukhasyaite nārhataḥ ṣoḍaśīṃ kalām iti | 2.42 |

II.42. From contentment — unsurpassable joy.

Thus it is said: 'The joy from pleasures in this world and the supreme felicities of heaven do not compare to a tiny fraction of the joy that comes from inner fulfilment' (*Mahābhārata, XII.174.46*).

kāyendriyasiddhiraśuddhikṣayāttapasaḥ || *2.43* ||

nirvartyamānameva tapo hinastyaśuddhyāvaraṇamalaṃ tadāvaraṇamalāpagamātkāyasiddhiraṇimādyā | tathendriyasiddhirdūrācchravaṇadarśanādyeti | 2.43 |

II.43. With the elimination of impurities through the practice of purification — perfection of the body and the senses.

Practising the techniques of purification removes the layers of stress. When these layers are removed, physical powers develop — such as the ability to become as small as an atom, among others. Also cognitive powers, such as clairaudience and telepathy.

svādhyāyādiṣṭadevatāsaṃprayogaḥ || 2.44 ||

devā ṛṣayaḥ siddhāśca svādhyāyaśīlasya darśanaṃ gacchanti kārye cāsya vartanta iti | 2.44 |

II.44. In Vedic recitation — communion with the desired deity.

The gods, the *ṛṣis* and *siddhas* appear when one practises Vedic recitation and support one's undertakings.

samādhisiddhirīśvarapraṇidhānāt || *2.45* ||

īśvarārpitasarvabhāvasya samādhirsiddhiryayā sarvamīpsitamavitatathaṃ jānāti deśāntare dehāntare kālāntare ca | tato'sya prajñā yathābhūtaṃ prajñānātīti | 2.45 |

II.45. From surrender to the Absolute — perfect transcending.

Offering all thoughts to the Absolute, transcending is perfected, and from this one sees that all one desires comes to pass, whether in another place, another body, or another time. One's experience is that awareness is attuned to Reality.

uktāḥ saha siddhibhiryamaniyamāḥ | āsanādīni vakṣyāmaḥ | tatra |

***sthirasukhamāsanam* || *2.46* ||**

tadyathā padmāsanam vīrāsanam bhadrāsanam svastikam daṇḍāsanam sopāśrayam paryaṅkam krauñcaniṣadanam hastiniṣadanam uṣṭraniṣadanam samasaṃsthānam sthirasukhaṃ yathāsukhaṃ cetyevamādīni | 2.46 |

The observances and the rules of living, and the powers that develop from them, have been described. Now we turn to posture and the other limbs.

II.46. Posture involves comfortably holding certain positions.

Examples include: the lotus position, the hero, the throne, the auspicious, the staff, the support, the corpse, the heron, the elephant, the camel, the equal pose. These and other positions can be practised and held easily, as feels comfortable.

***prayatnaśaitilyānantasamāpattibhyām* || *2.47* ||**

bhavatīty vākyaśeṣaḥ | prayatnoparamātsidhyatyāsanaṃ yena nāṅgamejayo bhavati | anante vā samāpannaṃ cittamāsanaṃ nirvartayatīti | 2.47 |

II.47. Without straining and with the awareness on unboundedness.

Complete the sentence with: 'It is practised'. The posture is perfected without effort so there is no strain on the body. Or by allowing the mind to sink into the unbounded, the practice of posture is facilitated.

***tato dvandvānabhighātaḥ* || *2.48* ||**

śītoṣṇādibhirdvandvairāsanajayānnābhibhūyate | 2.48 |

II.48. Then one is not perturbed by the opposites.

When the posture is perfected, one is not overwhelmed by the opposites, hot and cold and so on.

tasminsati śvāsapraśvāsayorgativicchedaḥ prāṇāyāmaḥ || 2.49 ||

satyāsanajaye bāhyasya vāyorācamanaṃ śvāsaḥ |
kauṣṭhyasya vāyorniḥsāraṇaṃ praśvāsaḥ |
tayorgativicchedā ubhayābhāvaḥ prāṇāyāmaḥ | 2.49 |

II.49. Next, exercises to refine the breathing, inward and outward.

For after posture has been practised. Inhalation means breathing in air from outside. Exhalation is expelling air from inside. The purpose of breathing exercises is to settle their flow, refining both.

bāhyābhyantarastambhavṛttirdeśakālasaṃkhyābhiḥ paridṛṣṭo dīrghasūkṣmaḥ || 2.50 ||

yatra praśvāsapūrvako gatyabhāvaḥ sa bāhyaḥ | yatra śvāsapūrvako gatyabhāvaḥ sa ābhyantaraḥ | tṛtīyaḥ stambhavṛttiryatrobhayābhāvaḥ sakṛtprayatnād bhavati | yathā tapte nyastamupale jalaṃ sarvataḥ saṃkocamāpadyeta tathā dvayoryugapad gatyabhāva iti | trayo'pyete deśena paridṛṣṭāḥ iyānasya viṣayo deśa iti | kālena paridṛṣṭāḥ kṣaṇānāmiyattāvadhāraṇenāvacchinnā ityarthaḥ | saṃkhyābhiḥ paridṛṣṭāḥ etāvadbhiḥ śvāsapraśvāsaiḥ prathama udghātastadvan-nigṛhītasyaitāvadbhirdvitīya udghāta evaṃ tṛtīyaḥ evaṃ mṛdurevaṃ madhya evaṃ tīvra iti saṃkhyāparidṛṣṭaḥ | sa khalvayamevamabhyasto dīrghasūkṣmaḥ | 2.50 |

II.50. When the breathing — in, out and the pause between — is regulated by depth, rhythm, and count, it becomes relaxed and subtle.

When exhalation is complete, the breath is out. When inhalation is complete, the breath is in. The third aspect occurs spontaneously, as the gap in between these two. As water poured on to a hot stone instantly shrivels back from all sides, so both strokes of the breath become shallower together. In this way, the three aspects are regulated in terms of volume, measured as so much intake of air. When they are regulated in terms of duration, the meaning is that each phase is set to last so many seconds. When they are regulated in terms of count, a first round consists of so many inward and outward strokes with the corresponding number of pauses, followed by a second round, then a third, with so many soft, so many normal, so many brisk. Practised in this way, the breathing becomes relaxed and subtle.

***bāhyābhyantaraviṣayākṣepī caturthaḥ* || *2.51* ||**

deśakālasaṃkhyābhirbāhyaviṣayaḥ paridṛṣṭa ākṣiptaḥ | tathā'bhyantaraviṣayaḥ paridṛṣṭa ākṣiptaḥ | ubhayathā dīrghasūkṣmaḥ | tatpūrvako bhūmijayāt-krameṇobhayorgatyabhāvaścaturthaḥ prāṇāyāmaḥ | tṛtīyastu viṣayānālocito gatyabhāvaḥ sakṛdārabdha eva deśakālasaṃkhyābhiḥ paridṛṣṭo dīrghasūkṣmaḥ | caturthastu śvāsapraśvāsayorviṣayāvadhāranātkrameṇa bhūmijayādubhayākṣepapūrvako gatyabhāvaścaturthaḥ prāṇāyāma ityayaṃ viśeṣa iti | 2.51 |

II.51. The fourth aspect transcends the outward and the inward breaths.

The regulation of the outward stroke, by depth, speed and number, is transcended. Similarly, the regulation of the inward stroke is transcended. Both are long and subtle. When this preliminary stage has been progressively mastered, both cease, and a fourth form of breathing occurs. For the third aspect — the pause — is now unbounded: there is suddenly no flow of breath, which had been rendered refined and subtle through the regulation of volume, rhythm and count. This fourth aspect transcends both the earlier outward and inward breaths which had been progressively mastered, and it is breathless. This is what distinguishes the fourth aspect of breath.

tataḥ kṣīyate prakāśāvaraṇam || *2.52* ||

prāṇāyāmānabhyasyato'sya yoginaḥ kṣīyate vivekajñānāvaraṇīyaṃ karma | yattadācakṣate | mahāmohamayenendrajālena prakāśaśīlaṃ sattvamāvṛtya tadevākārye niyuṅkta iti | tadasya prakāśāvaraṇaṃ karma saṃsāranibandhanaṃ prāṇāyāmābhyāsāddurbalaṃ bhavati pratikṣaṇaṃ ca kṣīyate | tathā coktam | tapo na paraṃ prāṇāyamāttato viśuddhirmalānāṃ dīptaśca jñānasyeti | 2.52 |

II.52. Then the veil over the light is destroyed.

When the yogi has practised refining the breathing, excitations that tend to mask awareness of enlightenment are diminished. This can be explained by the fact that when the enlivening nature of the mind is shrouded by the spell of the grand delusion of glamour, it engages in action inappropriately. With the practice of refining the breath, the activity that hides the light and binds to the cycle of living and dying, becomes powerless and is gradually weakened. Thus it is said: 'There is no better form of purification than refining the breathing; it removes impurities and makes the light of knowledge to shine'.

kiñca |

dhāraṇāsu ca yogyatā manasaḥ || *2.53* ||

prāṇāyāmābhyāsādeva | pracchardanavidhāraṇābhyāṃ vā prāṇasya iti vacanāt | 2.53 |

Furthermore:

II.53. And the mind is ready to dive within.

From the refinement of the breath. As was said: 'by exhaling and suspending the breath' (*Yoga-Sūtra I.34)*.

atha kaḥ pratyāhāraḥ |

svaviṣayāsaṃprayoge cittasya svarūpānukāra ivendriyāṇāṃ pratyāhāraḥ || *2.54* ||

svaviṣayāsaṃprayogābhāve cittasvarūpānukāra iveti cittanirodhe cittavanniruddhānīndriyāṇi netarendriyajayavadupāyāntaramapekṣante | yathā madhukararājaṃ makṣikā utpatantamanūtpatanti niviśamānamanuniviśante tathendriyāṇi cittanirodhe niruddhānītyeṣa pratyāhāraḥ | 2.54 |

— And what is 'withdrawal'? —

II.54. The senses copy the mind and withdraw contact with their objects.

No longer in contact with their objects and as if copying the nature of the mind, the senses settle when the mind settles. No other means is required to achieve control of the senses. Like bees who fly off to follow the queen-bee and alight when she alights, so the senses settle when the mind settles. This is 'withdrawal'.

tataḥ paramā vaśyatendriyāṇām || *2.55* ||

śabdādiṣvavyasanamindriyajaya iti kecit | saktirvyasanaṃ vyasyatyenaṃ śreyasa iti | aviruddhā pratipattirnyayyā | śabdādisaṃprayogaḥ svecchayetyanye | rāgadveṣābhāve sukhaduḥkhaśūnyaṃ śabdādijñānamindriyajaya iti kecit | cittaikagryādapratipattireveti jaigīśavyaḥ | tataśca paramā tviyaṃ vaśyatā yaccittanirodhe niruddānīndriyāṇi netarendriyajayavatprayatnakṛtamupāyāntaramapekṣante yogina iti | 2.55 |

iti śrīpātañjale sāṃkhyapravacane sāṃkhyaśāstre dvitīyaḥ sādhanapādaḥ || 2 ||

II.55. Then comes complete control of the senses.

Some hold that control of the senses consists in non-attachment to sounds or other sensory stimuli; the force of the word 'attachment' here indicating what tends to separate one from the Good — so any experience is allowed except what is forbidden. Others say it implies contact with sounds and so on, without restriction, as one desires. Some say that mastery of the senses means being able to experience sound and so on while remaining free from pleasure and free from pain, without desire or aversion. Jaigīṣavya, however, says it means non-activity on the part of the senses when the mind is one-pointed. Complete control means that when the mind is settled, the senses settle, and yogis have no need of any other means to achieve mastery of the senses.

End of the Second Chapter on
'Technologies of Enlightenment' in
Maharṣi Patañjali's Treatise on the Teaching on Yoga

|| 3 ||

vibhūtipāda

Chapter 3

All Possibilities

uktāni pañca bahiraṅgāṇi sādhanāni | dhāraṇā vaktavyā |

deśabandhaścittasya dhāraṇā || *3.1* ||

nābhicakre hṛdayapuṇḍarīke mūrdhni jyotiṣi nāsikāgre jihvāgre ityevamādiṣu deśeṣu bāhye vā viṣaye cittasya vṛttimātreṇa bandha iti dhāraṇā | 3.1 |

The technologies for the five outer limbs have been described. Now diving within is defined.

III.1. The mind dives within by entertaining a specific impulse of thought.

The mind dives within when the attention is directed easily on to a focus of thought, such as the navel, the lotus of the heart, the light in the head, the tip of the nose, the tip of the tongue, and other sites, or some other external object.

tatra pratyayaikatānatā dhyānam || 3.2 ||

tasmindeśe dhyeyālambanasya pratyayasyaikatānatā sadṛśaḥ pravāhaḥ pratyayāntareṇāparāmṣṭo dhyānam | 3.2 |

III.2. Meditation involves the uniform flow of awareness on that thought.

Meditation is the process of fully expanding the conscious mind. A vehicle of thought provides a focus, which is experienced in a continuous flow, uninterrupted by other thoughts.

tadevārthamātranirbhāsaṃ svarūpaśūnyamiva samādhiḥ || *3.3* ||

dhyānameva dhyeyākāranirbhāsaṃ pratyayātmakena svarūpeṇa śūnyamiva yadā bhavati dhyeyasvabhāvāveśāttadā samādhirityucyate | 3.3 |

III.3. Transcending occurs when the vehicle of meditation is experienced as in a vacuum state of self-referral.

The process of meditation involves the conscious appreciation of the vehicle of meditation as if in a vacuum state of self-awareness. When the vehicle of meditation settles to that intimate level, it is called transcendental consciousness.

trayamekatra saṃyamaḥ || *3.4* ||

tadetaddhāraṇādhyānasamādhitrayamekatra saṃyamaḥ | ekaviṣayāṇi trīṇi sādhanāni saṃyama ityucyate | tadasya trayasya tāntrikī paribhāṣā saṃyama iti | 3.4 |

III.4. These three together is saṃyama — non-extravagance.

Saṃyama is the three together: inner focus, expansion, transcendence. The three aspects drawn together in synthesis is called 'non-extravagance'. *Saṃyama* is a specific technique involving all three.

tajjayātprajñālokaḥ || *3.5* ||

tasya saṃyamasya jayātsamādhiprajñāyā bhavatyālokaḥ | yathā yathā saṃyamaḥ sthirapado bhavati tathā tathā samādhiprajñā viśāradī bhavati | 3.5 |

III.5. Mastering this enlivens the finest transcendental level of the awareness.

The practice of *saṃyama* enlivens one's awareness at the finest transcendental level. As one is progressively habituated to *saṃyama*, so one's experience of the finest Transcendent matures.

***tasya bhūmiṣu viniyogaḥ* || *3.6* ||**

tasya saṃyamasya jitabhūmeryā'nantarā bhūmistatra viniyogaḥ | na hyajitā'dharabhūmirā'nantarabhūmiṃ vilaṅghya prāntabhūmiṣu saṃyamaṃ labhate | tadabhāvācca kutastasya prajñālokaḥ | īśvaraprasādāt jitottarabhūmikasya ca nādharabhūmiṣu paracittajñānādiṣu saṃyamo yuktaḥ | kasmāt | tadarthasyānyata evāvagatatvāt | bhūmerasyā iyamanantarā bhūmirityatra yoga evopādhyāyaḥ | katham | evaṃ hyuktam | yogena yogo jñātavyo yogo yogātpravartate | yo'pramattastu yogena sa yoge ramate ciramiti | 3.6 |

III.6. It can be applied across a range of all possibilities.

When *saṃyama* has been practised on one area, then one moves on to the next. One does not just jump around from one unexplored area to the next: one practises *saṃyama* in order to develop each area fully. Without this, how could the finest level of one's awareness be enlivened? If the support of the laws of Nature has spontaneously unlocked a particular channel, like reading another's mind, for example, there is no need to perform *saṃyama* to develop it further. — Why? — Because the desired objective has been attained through another means. The Transcendent itself will reveal if this is the case, as that channel will function flawlessly compared to another. — How? — It is said: 'Yoga is known from yoga. Yoga develops yoga. The wise enjoy more yoga through yoga' (*Saubhāgyalakṣmyupaniṣad II.1*).

trayamantaraṅgaṃ pūrvebhyaḥ || *3.7* ||

tadetad dhāraṇādhyānasamādhitrayam antaraṅgaṃ saṃprajñātasya samādheḥ pūrvebhyo yamādibhyaḥ pañcabhyaḥ sādhanebhya iti | 3.7 |

III.7. These three are more intimate that the earlier limbs.

The trio of focus, expansion and transcendence is more intimate to Pure Consciousness than the earlier five technologies, the observances and the rest.

tadapi bahiraṅgaṃ nirbījasya || 3.8 ||

tadapyantaraṅgaṃ sādhanatrayaṃ nirbījasya yogasya bahiraṅgaṃ bhavati | kasmāt | tadabhāve bhāvāditi | 3.8 |

III.8. Although this is grosser than Pure Consciousness.

Although the technique of the trio is subtle, it is gross in respect of Pure Consciousness. — Why? — Because Pure Consciousness remains when *saṃyama* is transcended.

atha nirodhacittakṣaṇeṣu calaṃ guṇavṛttamiti kīdṛśas tadā cittapariṇāmaḥ |

vyutthānanirodhasaṃskārayorabhibhavaprādurbhāvau nirodhakṣaṇacittānvayo nirodhapariṇāmaḥ || 3.9 ||

vyutthānasaṃskārāścittadharmā na te pratyayātmakā iti pratyayanirodhe na viruddhāḥ | nirodhasaṃskārā api cittadharmāḥ | tayorabhibhavaprādurbhāvau vyutthānasaṃskārā hīyante nirodhasaṃskārā ādhīyante | nirodhakṣaṇaṃ cittamanveti | tadekasya cittasya pratikṣaṇamidaṃ saṃskārānyathātvaṃ nirodhapariṇāmaḥ | tadā saṃskāraśeṣaṃ cittamiti nirodhasamādhau vyākhyātam | 3.9 |

— So, in the moments when the mind is silent, and the *guṇas* are still operative, what change takes place in the mind? —

III.9. At the junction point between the inward stroke of the mind settling and the outward stroke of mental activity, the experience of silence deepens the silence which infuses the mind.

Impressions from mental activity and from silence are lodged in the mind. Since they are not impulses of thought, they do not disappear when the impulses of thought subside. Silence also leaves an impression in the mind. The former are 'erased' and the latter 'grow': the impressions left in the mind by activity fade and impressions left by silence are laid down. Periods of silence have an effect on the mind. The silence in the mind deepens as gradually the one kind of impression is replaced by the other. That the mind retains impressions in the state of silent awareness has already been explained (*Yoga-Sūtras I.18*).

tasya praśāntavāhitā saṃskārāt || *3.10* ||

nirodhasaṃskārābhyāsapāṭavāpekṣā praśāntavāhitā cittasya bhavati | tatsaṃskāramāndye vyutthānadharmiṇā saṃskāreṇa nirodhadharma saṃskāro'bhibhūyata iti | 3.10 |

III.10. The effect of transcending is to produce restful alertness.

Restful alertness is established when the mind is habituated by repeated exposure to impressions of silence. When the impression left by silence is faint, it is overshadowed by the impression left by activity.

sarvārthataikāgratayoḥ kṣayodayau cittasya samādhi-pariṇāmaḥ || 3.11 ||

sarvāthatā cittadharmaḥ | ekāgratā cittadharmaḥ | sarvārthatāyāḥ kṣayastirobhāva ityarthaḥ | ekāgratāyā udaya āvirbhāva ityarthaḥ | tayordharmitvenānugataṃ cittam | tadidaṃ cittamapāyopajanayoḥ svātmabhūtayordharmayoranugataṃ samādhīyate sa cittasya samādhipariṇāmaḥ | 3.11 |

III.11. Transcendental consciousness is stabilised as the mind moves between the diversified state of awareness and the state of one-pointedness.

Wide-angled vision is a natural characteristic of the mind, and so is one-pointedness. The meaning is that its wide-angled vision decreases as its one-pointedness increases. Both tendencies are natural to the mind. Transcendental consciousness is transformed as the mind integrates these two otherwise alternating inherent tendencies.

tataḥ punaḥ śāntoditau tulyapratyayau cittasyaikāgratāpariṇāmaḥ || 3.12 ||

samāhitacittasya pūrvapratyayaḥ śāntaḥ uttarastatsadṛśa uditaḥ | samādhicittamubhayoranugatam punastathaiva ā samādhibhreṣāditi | sa khalvayam dharmiṇaścittasyaikāgratāpariṇāmaḥ | 3.12 |

III.12. And then the one-pointedness is transformed as the mind becomes able to maintain rest and activity both together.

When the mind is in the state of coherence, as one impulse of thought fades into silence, an identical impulse of thought can replace it. In the transcendental state, the mind is permeated by both that silence and that activity, until the transcendence is interrupted. In this way, the power of the attention is transformed within the fabric of the awareness.

etena bhūtendriyeṣu dharmalakṣanāvasthāpariṇāmā vyākhyātāḥ || 3.13 ||

etena pūrvoktena cittapariṇāmena dharmalakṣaṇāvasthārūpeṇa bhūtendriyeṣu dharmapariṇāmo lakṣaṇapariṇāmo'vasthāpariṇāmaścokto veditavyaḥ | tatra vyutthānanirodhayordharmayorabhibhavaprādurbhāvau dharmaṇi dharmapariṇāmaḥ | lakṣanapariṇāmaśca nirodhastrilakṣaṇastribhiradhvabhiryuktaḥ | sa khalvanāgatalakṣaṇamadhvānaṃ prathamaṃ hitvā dharmatvamanatikrānto vartamānalakṣaṇaṃ pratipanno yatrāsya svarūpeṇābhivyaktiḥ | eṣo'sya dvitīyo'dhvā | na cātītānāgatābhyāṃ lakṣaṇābhyāṃ viyuktaḥ | tathā vyutthānaṃ trilakṣaṇaṃ tribhiradhvabhiryuktaṃ vartamānaṃ lakṣaṇaṃ hitvā dharmatvamanatikrāntamatītalakṣaṇaṃ pratipannam | eṣo'sya tṛtīyo'dhvā | na cānāgatavartamānābhyāṃ lakṣaṇābhyāṃ viyuktam | evaṃ punarvyutthānamupasaṃpadyamānamanāgataṃ lakṣaṇaṃ hitvā dharmatvamanatikrāntaṃ vartamānaṃ lakṣaṇaṃ pratipannam | yatrāsya svarūpābhivyaktau tasyāṃ vyāpāraḥ | eṣo'sya dvitīyo'dhvā | na cātītānāgatābhyāṃ lakṣaṇābhyāṃ viyuktamiti | evaṃ punarnirodha evaṃ punarvyutthānamiti |

III.13. From this, changes in the qualities, temporal phases and states among the elements and the faculties of cognition can be understood.

'From this': from what has been said about changes to the qualities, the phasings and the status of the awareness, so changes in qualities, phases and states with regard to the elements and the faculties of cognition can also be understood. In this context, a change in qualities in the fabric of the awareness is effected by the alternation of silence and activity. Change in temporal phases is illustrated by the three moments of the silence. The first moment — that of its future state, what it has not yet become — though it is not discarded, is left behind as it emerges into the present, so that its potential becomes manifest. Now it is in its second phase, which is not completely disconnected from the aspects of its past and its future. In the same way, the mental activity of the outward stroke has three phases. Discarding its present, though this latter is not extinguished, it enters into its past phase. This is its third phase, which again is not completely disconnected from its future and present phases. Similarly, when a new wave of mental activity arises, although this facet is not destroyed, it discards its future and manifests in the present. As it comes to manifest in this way, it is actualised. Then it is in its second phase, which is not completely disconnected from its past and its future. And so on: another inward stroke of silence gives way to another outward stroke of mental activity.

tathā'vasthāpariṇāmaḥ | tatra nirodhakṣaṇeṣu nirodhasaṃskārā balavanto bhavanti durbalā vyuttānasaṃskārā iti | eṣa dharmāṇāmavasthāpariṇāmaḥ | tatra dharmiṇo dharmaiḥ pariṇāmaḥ dharmāṇāṃ lakṣaṇaiḥ pariṇāmaḥ lakṣaṇānāmapyavasthābhiḥ pariṇāma iti | evaṃ dharmalakṣaṇāvasthāpariṇāmaiḥ śūnyaṃ na kṣaṇamapi guṇavṛttamavatiṣṭhate | calaṃ ca guṇavṛttam | guṇasvābhāvyaṃ tu pravṛttikāraṇamuktaṃ guṇānāmiti |

etena bhūtendriyeṣu dharmadharmibhedāttrividhaḥ pariṇāmo veditavyaḥ | paramārthatastveka eva pariṇāmaḥ | dharmisvarūpamātro hi dharmaḥ dharmivikriyaivaiṣā dharmadvārā prapañcyata iti | tatra dharmasya dharmiṇi vartamānasyaivādhvasvatītānāgatavartamāneṣu bhāvānyathātvaṃ bhavati na tu dravyānyathātvam | yathā suvarṇabhājanasya bhittvā'nyathākriyamāṇasya bhāvānyathātvaṃ bhavati na suvarṇānyathātvamiti |

apara āha | dharmānabhyadhiko dharmī pūrvatattvānatikramāt | pūrvāparāvasthābhedam-anupatitaḥ kauṭasthyena viparivarteta yadyanvayī

Changes in state are similar. During the periods of silence, the impressions left by the silence become stronger and the impressions made by activity become weaker. This is how the state of awareness is transformed via its qualities. In this way, the underlying awareness is changed by the qualities; these qualities are changed through the temporal phases; and the temporal phases are changed by the state of the awareness. All this is because the operations of the *guṇas* never, not even for a moment, stop producing changes at the level of qualities, temporal phases and states. For the business of the *guṇas* is change. This function of the *guṇas* is said to be inherent in their very nature.

From this, the three aspects of change within the elements and the faculties of cognition can also be understood, based on the distinction between an object and its properties. Really, in the final analysis, there is only one mode of change. For a property is nothing other than an integral component of the object in which it inheres, and any modification in the object is effected only through the agency of its properties. The property inherent in the object is displayed differently as it progresses through its three phases of future, present and past, but this does not affect the underlying substance. It is like a gold goblet which is melted down and fashioned into something else: there is a change in appearance but not a change in the gold.

Someone may object: 'The substance is nothing other than its properties because it has no *a priori* existence. Though it may be a continuous entity, since it undergoes

syāditi | ayamadoṣaḥ | kasmāt | ekāntānabhyupagamāt | tadetat trailokyaṃ vyakterapaiti | kasmāt | nityatvapratiṣedhāt | apetamapyasti vināśapratiṣedhāt | saṃsargāccāsya saukṣmyaṃ saukṣmyāccānupalabdhiriti |

lakṣaṇapariṇāmo dharmo'dhvasu vartamāno'tīto'tītalakṣaṇayukto'nāgatavartamānābhyāṃ lakṣaṇābhyāmaviyuktaḥ | tathā'nāgato'nāgatalakṣaṇayukto vartamānātītābhyāṃ lakṣaṇābhyāmaviyukta iti | tathā vartamāno vartamānalakṣaṇayukto'tītānāgatābhyāṃ lakṣaṇābhyāmaviyukta iti | yathā puruṣa ekasyāṃ striyāṃ rakto na śeṣāsu virakto bhavatīti | atra lakṣaṇapariṇāme sarvasya sarvalakṣaṇayogādadhvasaṃkaraḥ prāpnotīti parairdoṣaścodyata iti | tasya parihāraḥ dharmāṇāṃ dharmatvamaprasādhyam | sati ca dharmatve lakṣaṇabhedo'pi vācyaḥ na vartamānasamaya evāsya dharmatvam | evaṃ hi na cittaṃ rāgadharmakaṃ syātkrodhakāle rāgasyāsamudācārāditi |

kiñca trayāṇāṃ lakṣaṇānāmyugapadekasyāṃ vyaktau nāsti saṃbhavaḥ | krameṇa tu svavyañjakāñjanasya bhāvo bhavediti | uktaṃ ca rūpātiśayā vṛttyatiśayāśca paraspareṇa virudhyante sāmānyāni tvatiśayaiḥ saha pravartante |

changes in appearance, before and after, in fact it is subject to change.' — There is no hole in our argument. — Why? — No object has an absolute unity. Everything in the three worlds is subject to change. — Why? — Nothing is eternal. Even so, although an object may disappear, it is not destroyed. As it demanifests, it remains in subtle form, where it is imperceptible.

With regard to temporal phases, the quality continues to exist at each stage. The past is what is connected to the past stage, but it is not divorced from the present and future phases. Likewise, the future is what is connected to the future phase and is not divorced from the present and past phases. It is like a man in love with a particular woman; he does not become indifferent to the attractions of others. In regard to changes in these temporal phases, some may object that there will be confusion among phases because everything is inextricably bound with every phase. The reply is that there is no need to prove the reality of a quality. Given that these exist, their modulation due to temporal change must also be admitted; their existence is not restricted to the present moment. The mind does not cease 'being in love' just because its love is not manifested in a moment of anger.

Moreover, it is not possible for the three temporal phases to manifest simultaneously within one phenomenon. They only emerge gradually as a result of the operations which produce their manifestation. Thus it is said: 'While highly excited states of mind and the intense moods they give rise to are mutually exclusive, nonetheless their integrated function is maintained in the midst of such

tasmādasaṃkaraḥ | yathā rāgasyaiva kvacit samudacārā iti na tadānīmanyatrābhāvaḥ kiṃtu kevalaṃ sāmānyeta samanvāgata ityasti tadā tatra tasya bhāvaḥ | tathā lakṣaṇasyeti |

na dharmī tryadhvā dharmāstu tryadhvānaḥ | te lakṣitā alakṣitāśca tāṃ tāmavasthāṃ prāpnuvanto'nyatvena pratinirdiśyante'vasthāntarato na dravyāntarataḥ | yathaikā rekhā śatasthāne ṣataṃ daśasthāne daśaikā caikasthāne | yathā caikatve'pi strī mātā cocyate duhitā ca svasā ceti |

avasthāpariṇāme kauṭasthyaprasaṅgadosaḥ kaiściduktaḥ | katham | adhvano vyāpāreṇa vyavahitatvād yadā dharmaḥ svavyāpāraṃ na karoti tadā'nagataḥ yadā karoti tadā vartamānaḥ yadā kṛtvā nivṛttastadā'tīta ityevaṃ dharmadharmiṇorlakṣaṇānāmavasthānāṃ ca kauṭasthyaṃ prāpnotīti parairdoṣa ucyate | nāsau doṣaḥ | kasmāt | guṇinityatve'pi guṇānāṃ vimardavaicitryāt | yathā saṃsthānamādimaddharmamātraṃ śabdādīnāṃ vināśyavināśināmevaṃ liṅgamādimaddharmamātraṃ

extreme agitation' (*Yoga-Sūtra II.15*). So the phases do not get confused. Like when a person gets very passionate about some topic, it does not mean that they have lost interest in everything else. At that moment, their other interests continue to exist but at an underlying level. The same applies to phases in time.

A substance is not subject to the three temporal phases, but its properties are. Properties are manifest or non-manifest and when they appear in different states they are known by different names. The condition changes but not the substance. Like the number '1' has a value of 100 in the 'hundreds' column, but in the 'tens' column its value is 10, and in the 'digits' column its value is 1. Or it is like one woman who is simultaneously a mother, a daughter and a sister.

Some say that the idea of change in state implies that the substance is forever immutable. — How? — Because the temporal phases are determined by activity on the part of the substance, and because when a property is not activated, it is said to be 'future', when it exercises its activity it is 'present', and when it is no longer activated it is 'past'. So some object that there is an inconsistency in our argument because substance and properties, phases and states, are immutable. But in fact there is no lacuna in our argument. — Why? — Although a product of the *guṇas* is stable, the interplay of the *guṇas* is always changing. Any assemblage of parts has a beginning and an end, for it is just the manifestation of the properties of the elements of sound and so on, which themselves are indeed indestructible. In the same way, the field of pure differentiation

sattvādīnāṃ guṇānāṃ vināśyavināśināṃ tasminvikārasaṃjñeti |

tatredamudāharaṇaṃ mṛddharmī piṇḍākārāddharmād dharmāntaramupasaṃpadyamāno dharmataḥ pariṇamate ghaṭākāra iti | ghaṭākāro'nāgataṃ lakṣaṇaṃ hitvā vartamāṇalakṣaṇaṃ pratipadyata iti lakṣaṇataḥ pariṇamate | ghaṭo navapūrāṇatāṃ pratikṣaṇamanubavannavasthāpariṇāmaṃ pratipadyata iti | dharmiṇo'pi dharmāntaramavasthā dharmasyāpi lakṣaṇāntaramavasthā ityeka eva dravyapariṇāmo bhedenopadarśita iti | evaṃ padārthāntareṣvapi yojyamiti | ta ete dharmalakṣaṇāvasthāpariṇāmā dharmisvarūpamanatikrāntā ityeka eva pariṇāmaḥ sarvānamūnviśeṣānabhiplavate | atha ko'yaṃ pariṇāmaḥ | avasthitasya dravyasya pūrvadharmanivṛttau dharmāntarotpattiḥ pariṇāmaḥ | 3.13 |

is technically a product of unmanifest Nature, for it has a beginning and an end, and it is only an expressed value of the *guṇas*, which are indestructible.

Here is an example. Clay is a substance which can be fashioned into a ball. When a different property is expressed, the material undergoes a change, and it becomes a pot. The pot has abandoned its future stage, it takes on a present form, and the temporal phase is changed. The pot, at each moment in time, experiences a dual condition of being old and being new, and undergoes a change of state. The state *is* a different property of the substance; and likewise the state *is* a different phase of the property. The substance undergoes one change, but it can be described in different ways. The same can be applied to other phenomena. However, changes in property, phase and state do not extend beyond the bounds of the potentiality of the substance. There is one change which encompasses all the different aspects of change described above. — So what then is change? — Change is the process which affects a permanent substance when a different property emerges to replace a previous property which fades.

tatra |

śāntoditāvyapadeśyadharmānupātī dharmī || *3.14* ||

yogyatāvacchinnā dharmiṇaḥ śaktireva dharmaḥ | sa ca phalaprasavabhedānumitasadbhāva ekasyā'nyo'nyaśca paridṛṣṭaḥ | tatra vartamānaḥ svavyāpāram-anubhavandharmo dharmāntarebhyaḥ śāntebhyaścāvyapadeśyebhyaśca bhidyate | yadā tu sāmānyena samanvāgato bhavati tadā dharmisvarūpamātratvātko'sau kena bhidyeta | tatra trayaḥ khalu dharmiṇo dharmāḥ śāntā uditā avyapadeśyāśceti | tatra śāntā ye kṛtvā vyāpārānuparatāḥ | savyāpārā uditāḥ | te cānāgatasya lakṣaṇasya samanantarāḥ | vartamānasyānantarāḥ atītāḥ | kimarthamatītasyānantarā na bhavanti vartamānāḥ | pūrvapaścimatāyā abhāvāt | yathā'nāgatavartamānayoḥ pūrvapaścimatā naivamatītasya | tasmānnātītasyāsti samanantaraḥ | tadanāgata eva samantantaro bhavati vartamānasyeti | athāvyapadeśyāḥ ke | sarvaṃ sarvātmakamiti | yatroktam | jalabhūmyoḥ pāriṇāmikaṃ rasādivaiśvarūpyaṃ dṛṣṭaṃ sthāvareṣu tathā sthāvarāṇāṃ jaṅgameṣu jaṅgamānāṃ sthāvareṣu iti | evaṃ jātyanucchedena sarvaṃ sarvātmakamiti | deśakālākāranimittāpabandhānna khalu samānakālamātmanāmabhivyaktiriti |

So:

III.14. An object contains within itself its own potential: past, present and future.

A property is an integral function of the potential of an object. The reality of its existence can be inferred from the changes in the manifested forms of a given substance, since it is observed to come and then go. A property is 'present' when its functionality is activated and then it is differentiated from other 'past' and 'future' properties. However, when it melts back into the underlying substance and is merged within the object, then what happens to it? How might it be identified? Properties have three aspects: past, present and future. They are 'past' when they have ceased to be active. A property is 'present' when its activity is lively; its 'present' follows upon its 'future'. 'Past' properties follow upon 'present' properties. — Why do present properties not follow past properties? — Because 'before' does not follow 'after'. In the case of the future and the present, there is a relationship of before and after, but not in the case of the past; the present does not follow the past. Only the future precedes the present. — So what are future properties? — Everything is everywhere. Thus it is said: 'In inanimate things, we observe an infinite variety of tastes and so on, that result from combinations of water and earth. So traces of inanimate things are present in animate beings, and vice-versa.' In this way, because creation is indestructible, everything is everywhere. However, the boundaries of time, space and causality mean that the totality of everything cannot manifest all at the same time.

ya eteṣvabhivyaktadharmamātramevedaṃ niranvayaṃ tasya bhogābhāvaḥ | kasmāt | anvyena vijñānena kṛtasya karmaṇo'nyat kathaṃ bhoktṛtvenādhikriyeta | tatsmṛtyabhāvaśca nānyadṛṣṭasya smaraṇamanyasyāstīti | vastupratyabhijñānācca sthitonvayī dharmī yo dharmānyathātvamabhyupagataḥ pratyabhijñāyate | tasmānnedaṃ dharmamātraṃ niranvayamiti | 3.14 |

The underlying substance contains both generic and specific values and displays manifest or unmanifest properties. In reality, experience is an impossibility for someone who holds that the universe is devoid of underlying continuity, composed only of properties. — Why? — How could a knowing subject claim to have experience of an action performed by another knowing subject? There would be no memory of it, for the one could not remember what the other had seen. Since objects are recognised, there must be an underlying substance which is being recognised when another of its properties has become visible. Therefore the universe is not just an array of phenomena without an underlying reality.

ekasya dharmiṇa eka pariṇāma iti prasakte |

***kramānyatvaṃ pariṇāmānyatve hetuḥ* || *3.15* ||**

tad yathā cūrṇamṛt piṇḍamṛd ghaṭamṛt kapālamṛt kaṇamṛditi ca kramaḥ | yo yasya dharmasya samanantaro dharmaḥ sa tasya kramaḥ | piṇḍaḥ pracyavate ghaṭa upajāyata iti dharmapariṇāmakramaḥ | lakṣaṇapariṇāmakramaḥ ghaṭasyānāgatabhāvād vartamānabhāvaḥ kramaḥ | tathā piṇḍasya vartamānabhāvādatītabhāvaḥ kramaḥ | natītasyāsti kramaḥ | kasmāt | pūrvaparatāyāṃ satyāṃ samanantaratvam sā tu nāstyatītasya | tasmāddvayoreva lakṣaṇayoḥ kramaḥ | tathā'vasthāpariṇāmakramo'pi ghaṭasyābhinavasya prānte purāṇatā dṛśyate | sā ca kṣaṇaparamparānupātinā krameṇabhivyajyamānā parāṃ vyaktimāpadyate iti | dharmalakṣaṇābhyāṃ ca viśiṣṭo'yaṃ tṛtīyaḥ pariṇāma iti |

ta ete kramāḥ dharmadharmibhede sati pratilabdhasvarūpāḥ | dharmo'pi dharmī bhavatyanyadharmasvarūpāpekṣayeti | yadā tu paramārthato dharmiṇyabhedopacārastaddvāreṇa sa evābhidhīyate dharmaḥ | tadāyamekatvenaiva kramaḥ pratyavabhāsate | cittasya dvaye dharmāḥ

On the proposition that there is only one type of change affecting one underlying matter:

III.15. Change is due to modulation in their sequence.

For instance, the sequence is: clay powder, a lump of clay, a jar, a shard, a broken chip. When one property aligns next to another property, there is a sequence. The lump of clay gives way to the appearance of the jar: there is a sequence to the changes of property. For the jar, the sequence of change in the temporal phases consists in the change from futurity to present manifestation. Similarly, for the lump of clay, the sequence lies in its passing from the present into the past. There is no sequence for the past. – Why? – There is contiguity only when there is a before and an after. This is not the case for the past. Therefore there is only sequence in the case of two of the three phases. The same holds for the sequence in the case of changes in state. The pot starts to get old as soon as it is new. Its ageing occurs in a sequence, moment after moment, until finally it becomes apparent. This is the third facet of change, distinct from that of properties and phases.

These sequences hold only as long as the distinction between an object and its properties is maintained. In point of fact, however, a given property is a substance when viewed from another, higher level of material manifestation. In the final analysis one is dealing with the indissociability of properties from matter. From this perspective, all matter can be thought of as a property; and on the basis of this identity, only its sequential modulation becomes visible to us. As for the mind, there

paridṛṣṭāścāparidṛṣṭāśca | tatra pratyayātmakāḥ paridṛṣṭāḥ | vastumātrātmakā aparidṛṣṭāḥ | te ca saptaiva bhavanti anumānena prāpitavastumātrasadbhāvāḥ | nirodhadharmasaṃskārāḥ pariṇāmo'tha jīvanam | ceṣṭā śaktiṣca cittasya dharmā darśanavarjitā iti | 3.15 |

are two kinds of property, those that are available to consciousness and those that are not. Those that are available to consciousness appear as thoughts. Those that are not so available are by nature abstract, although their existence can be proved by inference. They embody seven basic values: integration, stability, purification, adaptability, growth: plus intelligence and creativity. These are the values which are not directly perceptible.

ato yogina upāttasarvasādhanasya bubhutsitārtha-pratipattaye saṃyamasya viṣaya upakṣipyate |

***pariṇāmatrayasaṃyamādatītānāgatajñānam** || 3.16 ||*

dharmalakṣaṇāvasthāpariṇāmeṣu saṃyamād yogināṃ bhavatyatītānāgatajñānam | dhāraṇādhyānasamādhi-trayamekatra saṃyama uktaḥ | tena pariṇāmatrayaṃ sākṣātkriyamāṇamatītānāgatajñānaṃ teṣu saṃpādayati | 3.16 |

Now follows a discussion of the import of *saṃyama* when it is practised by a yogi who has adopted all the technologies mentioned so far, so as to experience whatever he desires.

III.16. Saṃyama on the three aspects of change develops knowledge of the past and future.

Saṃyama on changes of property, phase and state develops the yogi's knowledge of the past and the future. *Saṃyama* has been explained as the synthesis of directed focus, expansion, and transcendence. Through this technique, the three aspects of change can be perceived directly, and this provides knowledge of the past and the future.

śabdārthapratyayānāmitaretarādhyāsātsaṃkaras-tatpravibhāgasaṃyamātsarvabhūtarutajñānam || 3.17 ||

tatra vāg varṇeṣvevārthavatī | śrotraṃ ca dhvani-pariṇāmamātraviṣayam | padaṃ punarnādānusaṃhāra-buddhinirgrāhyamiti | varṇā ekasamayāsaṃbhavitvāt parasparaniranugrahātmanaḥ | te padam-asaṃspṛśyānupasthāpyā'virbhūtāstirobhūtāśceti pratyekamapadasvarūpā ucyante | varṇaḥ punarekaikaḥ padātma sarvābhidhānaśaktipracitaḥ sahakārivarṇāntara-pratiyogitvād vaiśvarūpyamivā'pannaḥ | pūrvaścottareṇottaraśca pūrveṇa viśeṣe'vasthāpita ityevaṃ bahavo varṇāḥ kramānurodhino'rthasaṃketenāvacchinnā iyanta ete sarvābhidhānaśaktiparivṛttā gakārokāravisarjanīyāḥ sāsnādimantamarthaṃ dyotayantīti | tadeteṣāmarthasaṃketenāvacchinnānām-upasaṃhṛtadhvanikramāṇāṃ ya eko buddhinirbhāsastatpadaṃ vācakaṃ vācasya saṃketyate | tadekaṃ padamekabuddhiviṣayamekaprayatnākṣiptam-abhāgamakramamavarṇaṃ bauddhamantyavarṇa-pratyayavyāpāropasthāpitaṃ paratra pratipipādayiṣayā varṇairevābhidhīyamānaiḥ śrūyamāṇaiśca śrotṛbhiranādivāgvyavahāravāsanānuviddhayā

III.17. The word, the meaning and the idea are confused because they are superimposed one upon the other. Saṃyama on the distinction between them develops understanding of the sounds of all creatures.

Speech conveys meaning when phonemes are articulated. The hearing decodes the sounds. Sounds are structured into words by the mind. Phonemes do not co-occur and are by nature mutually exclusive. They do not constitute or structure the word; they simply occur and then vanish. Taken in isolation they are non-lexical. However, each individual phoneme contains the essence of the word and possesses the potential to express everything. A phoneme can, so to speak, formulate everything by aligning with other phonemes. One phoneme links up with a following phoneme, and the next phoneme links up with the previous phoneme, and they are structured into a word. Thus, a series of many phonemes forms a sequence, which convention associates with an object. Although each phoneme is endowed with the ability to express everything, the specific Sanskrit series '*g*', '*au*', '*ḥ*', refers to that particular animal which has a dewlap (*i.e. [kou] 'cow'*). Thus a word — by convention a signifier expressing a signified — is the flashing in the mind of a sequence of sounds, which are structured into a whole, to which convention assigns a meaning. The word is a whole, linked to a meaning, evoked by one intention. It is indivisible, non-linear, non-phonemic, mental by nature, and realised as the final phoneme is articulated. Phonemes are enunciated with the purpose of communicating to another. When the listener hears them, they enter the mind, and are encoded by the deeply embedded psychic

lokabuddhyā siddhavatsaṃpratipattyā pratīyate | tasya saṃketabuddhitaḥ pravibhāgaḥ | etāvatāmevaṃ jātiyako'nusaṃhāra ekasyārthasya vācaka iti | saṃketastu padapadārthayoritaretarādhyāsarūpaḥ smṛtyātmakaḥ yo'yaṃ śabda so'yamarthaḥ | yo'yamarthaḥ so'yaṃ śabda iti | evamitaretarādhyāsarūpaḥ saṃketo bhavatīti | evamete śabdārthapratyayā itaretarādhyāsāt saṇkīrṇāḥ gauriti śabdo gaurityartho gauriti jñānam | ya eṣāṃ pravibhāgajñaḥ sa sarvavit |

sarvapadeṣu cāsti vākyaśaktiḥ vṛkṣa ityukte astīti gamyate | na sattāṃ padārtho vyabhicaratīti | yathā na hyasādhanā kriyā'stīti | tathā ca pacatītyukte sarvakārakāṇāmākṣepaḥ | niyamārtho'nuvādaḥ kartṛkaraṇakarmaṇāṃ caitrāgnitaṇḍulānāmiti | dṛṣṭaṃ ca vākyārthe padaracanaṃ śrotriyaś cchando'dhīte jīvati prāṇān dhārayati | tatra vākye padapadārthābhivyaktistataḥ padaṃ pravibhajya vyākaraṇīyaṃ krīyāvācakaṃ vā karakavācakaṃ vā | anyathā bhavati aśvaḥ ajāpaya ityevamādiṣu

structure which is the un-inaugurated institution of language. The word is ordered according to established convention. However, convention relies on memory, and memory superimposes the word upon the word's meaning, so that this word means this object, and that word means that object. Convention works by superimposition. Superimposition fuses word, object and idea together. For example, the word 'cow', the object 'cow' and the idea 'cow'. Separating these out, one can know everything.

All words contain the potential of a whole sentence. To say 'tree' assumes that trees exist; for signification does not depass existence. Likewise, a verb implies the means for performing it. Thus, when one says 'cooking', all the aspects of the action of cooking are implied. The meaning is explicated by specifying the agent (Caitra), the means (fire), and the object (rice). Also, the morphology of an individual word is seen to encapsulate the meaning of a whole sentence. The word '*śrotriya*' (from *śruti* 'scripture') means 'a Brahman who recites the Veda' (*cf. Pāṇini V.2.84*), just as the word 'alive' means 'being endowed with the vital forces of life'. With this one word, the meaning of a whole sentence has been expressed. The word has to be analysed grammatically in order to identify which morphemes express the action and which morphemes express features of the action. If this were not possible, homonyms such as '*bhavati*' ('madam', and 'he is'), or '*aśvas*' (aorist of √*śū/śvi*: 'thou inflatest', and 'horse'), or '*ajāpayaḥ*' ('goat's milk', and 'thou conquerest') — where nouns and verb forms are the same — would

nāmākhyātasārūpyādanirjñātaṃ kathaṃ kriyāyāṃ kārake vā vyākriyeteti |

teṣāṃ śabdārthapratyayānāṃ pravibhāgaḥ | tadyathā | śvetate prāsāda iti kriyārthaḥ śvetaḥ prāsāda iti kārakārthaḥ śabdaḥ | kriyākārakātmā tadarthaḥ pratyayaśca | kasmāt | so'yam ityabhisaṃbandhādekākāra eva pratyayaḥ saṃketa iti | yastu śyeto'rthaḥ sa śabdapratyayorālaṃbanībhūtaḥ sa hi svābhiravasthābhirvikrayamāṇo na śabdasahagato na buddhisahagataḥ | evaṃ śabda evaṃ pratyayo netaretarasahagata iti | anyathā śabdo'nyathārtho'nyathā pratyaya iti vibhāgaḥ | evaṃ tatpravibhāgasaṃyamād-yoginassarvabhūtarutajñānaṃ saṃpadyata iti | 3.17 |

remain ambiguous. How else would a word be analysed if not in terms of action and the features of action?

There is a distinction between word, object and idea. Take the sequences: '*śvetateprāsāda*' ('the house that is white' — where 'whiteness' is conveyed in the verb-phrase) and '*śvetaḥprāsāda*' ('the white house' — where 'whiteness' is conveyed by an adjective). The object and the mental image accommodate both verbal and adjectival inflections. — Why? — Because there is semantic equivalence, one and only one thought flashes up in the mind. Moreover, although 'whiteness' has served as the ground for both the word and the mental image, from its side the object may alter its appearance — so the object is not locked to the word or to the idea. Nor are the word and the idea bound to each other. The signifier is one thing; the referent is something else; the signified is something else again. There is a distinction.

Saṃyama on the distinction enables the yogi to understand the sounds of all creatures.

dvaye khalvamī saṃskārāḥ smṛtikleśahetavo vāsanārūpāḥ | vipākahetavo dharmādharmarūpāḥ | te pūrvabhavābhisaṃskṛtāḥ pariṇāmaceṣṭānirodhaśaktijīvanadharmavad-aparidṛṣṭāścittadharmāḥ | teṣu saṃyamaḥ saṃskārasākṣātkriyāyai samarthaḥ | na ca deśakālanimittānubhavairvinā teṣāmasti sākṣātkaraṇam | taditthaṃ |

saṃskārasākṣātkaraṇātpūrvajātijñānam || *3.18* ||

utpadyate yoginaḥ | paratrāpyevameva saṃskārasākṣātkaraṇātparajātijñānasaṃvedanam | atredamākhyānaṃ śrūyate | bhagavato jaigīṣavyasya saṃskārasākṣātkaraṇāddaśasu mahāsargeṣu janmapariṇāmakramamanupaśyato vivekajaṃ jñānaṃ prādurabhūt | atha bhagavānāvaṭyastanudharastamuvāca | daśasu mahāsargeṣu bhavyatvādanabhibhūta-buddhisattvena tvayā narakatiryaggarbhasaṃbhavaṃ duḥkhaṃ saṃpaśyatā devamanuṣyeṣu punaḥ punar-utpadyamānena sukhaduḥkhayoḥ kimadhikamupalabdhamiti | bhagavantamāvaṭyaṃ jaigīṣavya uvāca | daśasu mahāsargeṣu bhavyatvādanabhibhūtabuddhisattvena mayā narakatiryagbhavaṃ duḥkhaṃ saṃpaśyatā devamanuṣyeṣu punaḥ punarutpadyamānena yatkiṃcidanubhūtaṃ

There are two kinds of impression: those in the form of imprints which are caused by an overload of experience and by memory; and those in the form of positivity or negativity which are the result of the return of karma. The latter are formed in earlier stages of evolution and are unconscious latencies lodged deep within the mind, such as the qualities of adaptability, intelligence, integration, creativity, growth and stability (*cf. Yoga-Sūtras III.15*). *Saṃyama* on these is able to make these latencies directly perceivable. Since they cannot be directly cognised outside of the framework of space, time and causality, so:

III.18. The direct cognition of impressions provides knowledge of previous lives.

— to the yogi. In addition, from the direct cognition of the impressions which others have stored up within, knowledge of others' previous lives can be obtained. The following story is told: Direct cognition of his impressions brought enlightenment to the Great Jaigīṣavya, who had the vision of the sequence of the transmigration of his births through ten mega-eons of creation. The Great Āvaṭya, assuming bodily form, addressed him with these words: 'Throughout ten mega-eons of creation you have lived with pure heart, unmoved by the misery of being born in hell, as an animal, in the womb. You have incarnated again and again among gods and men. What have you seen most: joy or suffering?' — The Great Jaigīṣavya replied to Āvaṭya: 'I have lived through ten mega-eons of creation, with pure mind, unmoved by the misery of being born in hell, as an animal. I have been incarnated again and again among gods and men, and I

tatsarvaṃ duḥkhameva pratyavaimi | bhagavānāvaṭya uvāca | yadidamāyuṣmataḥ pradhānavaśitvamanuttamaṃ ca saṃtoṣasukhaṃ kimidamapi duḥkhapakṣe nikṣiptamiti | bhagavānjaigīṣavya uvāca | viṣayasukhāpekṣayaivedamanuttamaṃ saṃtoṣasukhamuktam | kaivalyasukhāpekṣayā duḥkhameva | buddhisattvasyāyaṃ dharmastriguṇaḥ triguṇaśca pratyayo heyapakṣe nyasta iti | duḥkhasvarūpastṛṣṇātantuḥ tṛṣṇāduḥkhasantāpāpagamāttu prasannamabādhaṃ sarvānukūlaṃ sukhamidamuktamiti | 3.18 |

hold that all is suffering.' — The Great Āvaṭya asked: 'O Great One! The mastery of Nature and the joy of unsurpassable contentment which are yours: do you count them too among the woes of suffering?' — The Great Jaigīṣavya said: 'It is only in terms of the pleasures of the senses that men speak of the joy of unsurpassable contentment. From the viewpoint of the joy of Unity consciousness, it is mere suffering. Such joy is but a property of the mind and is the doing of the three *guṇas*. Experience of it is produced by the three *guṇas* and belongs to the field of what is better avoided and is undesirable. The warp of desire is suffering. When the burning agony of desire has been cast off, the joy one experiences can be described as perfect peace, an effortless cosmic flow.'

pratyayasya paracittajñānam || *3.19* ||

pratyaye saṃyamāt pratyayasya sākṣātkaraṇāttataḥ paracittajñānam | 3.19 |

III.19. On an impulse of thought — knowledge of another's mind.

Saṃyama on thought, directly cognising the thought, brings knowledge of another's mind.

na ca tatsālambanaṃ tasyāviṣayībhūtatvāt || 3.20 ||

raktaṃ pratyayaṃ jānāti amuṣminnālambane raktamiti na jānāti | paracittasya pratyayasya yadālambanaṃ tad yogicittena nālambanīkṛtam | parapratyayamātraṃtu yogicittasya ālambanībhūtamiti | 3.20 |

III.20. But not its content, because that is not the object.

One cognises the impulse of love that the other experiences, but one does not know the object of the love. This is because the referent of the thought which occupies the other's mind does not become an object in the yogi's mind. It is only the mental impulse which the other has which becomes the object in the yogi's mind.

kāyarūpasaṃyamāttadgrāhyaśaktistambhe cakṣuḥprakāśā'saṃprayoge'ntardhānam || 3.21 ||

kāyasya rūpe saṃyamādrūpasya yā grāhyā śaktistāṃ pratiṣṭabhnāti | grāhyaśaktisstambhe sati cakṣuḥprakāśāsaṃprayoge'ntardhānamutpadyate yoginaḥ | etena śabdādyantardhānamuktaṃ veditavyam | 3.21 |

III.21. Saṃyama on the form of the body, blocking its ability to be seen, with no contact between its light and the eye, develops invisibility.

By practising *saṃyama* on the form of the body, the ability of the body to be seen is occluded. Once the ability to see the body has been removed, and there is no contact between the light it emits and the eye, the yogi becomes invisible. In the same way, it can be understood that the body cannot be heard, touched, and so on.

sopakramaṃ nirupakramaṃ ca karma tatsaṃyamādaparāntajñānamariṣṭebhyo vā || 3.22 ||

āyurvipākaṃ karma dvividhaṃ sopakramaṃ nirupakramaṃ ca | tatra yathā ādravastraṃ vitānitaṃ laghīyasā kālena śuṣyettathā sopakramam | yathā ca tadeva saṃpiṇḍitaṃ cireṇa saṃśuṣyedevaṃ nirupakramam | yathā vā'gniḥ śuṣke kakṣe mukto vātena samantato yuktaḥ kṣepīyasā kālena dahettathā sopakramam | yathā vā sa evāgnistṛṇarāśau kramaśo'vayaveṣu nyastaścireṇa dahettathā nirupakramam | tadaikabhavikamāyuṣkaraṃ karma dvividhaṃ sopakramaṃ nirupakramaṃ ca | tatsaṃyamādaparāntasya prāyaṇasya jñānam | ariṣṭebhyo veti | trividhamariṣṭamādhyātmikamādhibhautikam-ādhidaivikaṃ ca | tatrā'dhyātmikaṃ ghoṣaṃ svadehe pihitakarṇo na śṛṇoti jyotir vā netre'vaṣṭabdhe na paśyati | tathā'dhibhautikaṃ yamapuruṣānpaśyati pitṝnatītānāgatānakasmāt paśyati | tathā'dhidaivikaṃ svargamakasmāt siddhān vā paśyati | viparītaṃ vā sarvamiti | anena vā jānātyaparāntamupasthitamiti | 3.22 |

III.22. The effects of actions are slow or quick to return. From saṃyama on both — or from omens — comes knowledge of one's death.

The karma which determines the length of life is of two sorts: quick to return, or slow to return. Karma that returns quickly is like a wet garment that has been laid out; in a short time it is dry. But karma that is slow to return is like a garment which has been scrunched up into a ball; it takes a long time to dry. Or karma that returns quickly is like a fire ignited in dried grass fanned on all sides by the wind; it is quickly ablaze. Whereas karma that is slow to return is like a fire that is set going at several places in a pile of grass; it smoulders slowly. Such are the two kinds of karma which determine the span of a particular lifetime. *Saṃyama* on that develops knowledge of the timing of the end of one's life. 'Or from omens': there are three kinds of omen, depending on whether they concern oneself, or someone else, or divine beings. For oneself, two examples are: not being able to hear the sounds made by the body when covering the ears, or not being able to see light with the eyes closed. As for others, an example is seeing the servants of Yama or departed ancestors arriving unexpectedly. As for divine presages, having visions of heaven or of *siddhas* out of the blue. Or seeing that everything is topsy-turvy. From these signs one can know that one's end is nigh.

maitryādiṣu balāni || 3.23 ||

maitrīkaruṇāmuditeti tisro bhāvanāḥ | tatra bhūteṣu sukhiteṣu maitrīṃ bhāvayitvā maitrībalaṃ labhate | duḥkhiteṣu karuṇāṃ bhāvayitvā karuṇābalaṃ labhate | puṇyaśīleṣu muditāṃ bhāvayitvā muditābalaṃ labhate | bhāvanātaḥ samādhiryaḥ sa saṃyamaḥ tato balānyavandhyavīryāṇi jāyante | pāpaśīleṣu upekṣā na tu bhāvanā | tataśca tasyāṃ nāsti samādhiriti | ato na balamupekṣātastatra saṃyamābhāvāditi | 3.23 |

III.23. On friendliness and other feelings — the corresponding qualities.

The three feelings in question are friendliness, compassion and happiness. By enlivening friendliness towards those who are happy, one's capacity for friendliness grows. By enlivening compassion towards those who are unhappy, one's capacity for compassion grows. By enlivening happiness towards the deserving, one's capacity for joy grows. Since the Transcendent lies at the basis of these feelings, *saṃyama* on them is possible, and so these capacities can be developed into sources of inexhaustible energy. However, indifference towards wrong-doers is not a feeling as such (*cf. Yoga-Sūtra I.33*). Thus, the Transcendent cannot be located within it; and because therefore *saṃyama* cannot be performed on it, no capacity based on indifference can be developed.

***baleṣu hastibalādīni* || *3.24* ||**

hastibale saṃyamād hastibalo bhavati | vainateyabale saṃyamād vainateyabalo bhavati | vāyubale saṃyamād vāyubalo bhavatītyevamādi | 3.24 |

III.24. On the strength of an elephant, and other forms — the corresponding qualities.

Saṃyama on the strength of an elephant develops the strength of an elephant. *Saṃyama* on the strength of Vainateya develops strength like Vainateya's. *Saṃyama* on the power of the wind develops power like that of the wind — and so on.

*pravṛttyālokanyāsātsūkṣmavyavahitaviprakṛṣṭa-
jñānam* || *3.25* ||

jyotiṣmatī pravṛttiruktā manasaḥ | tasyāṃ ya ālokastaṃ yogī sūkṣme vā vyavahite vā viprakṛṣṭe vā arthe vinyasya tamarthamadhigacchati | 3.25 |

III.25. Directing the faculty of attention develops knowledge of what is subtle, hidden, or distant.

The enlivening power of attention has been mentioned before. The yogi who directs his attention on to a subtle, hidden or distant object can find it out.

***bhuvanajñānaṃ sūrye saṃyamāt* || *3.26* ||**

tatprastāraḥ sapta lokāḥ | tatrāvīceḥ prabhṛti meru-pṛṣṭhaṃ yāvadityevaṃ bhūrlokaḥ merupṛṣṭhādārabhya | ādhruvād grahanakṣatratārāvicitro'ntarikṣalokaḥ | tatparaḥ svarlokaḥ pañcavidho māhendras tṛtīyo lokaḥ | caturthaḥ prājāpatyo maharlokaḥ | trividho brāhmaḥ | tadyathā | janalokastapolokaḥ satyaloka iti | brāhmastribhūmiko lokaḥ prājāpatyastato mahān | māhendraśca svarityukto divi tārā bhuvi prajā iti saṃgrahaślokaḥ | tatrāvīceruparyupari niviṣṭāḥ ṣaṇmahānarakabhūmayo ghanasalilānalānilākāśatamaḥ pratiṣṭhā mahākālāmbarīṣarauravamahāraurava-kālasūtrāndhatāmisrāḥ | yatra svakarmopārjitaduḥkha-vedanāḥ prāṇinaḥ kaṣṭhamāyudīrghakālamākṣipya jāyante | tato mahātalarasātalātalasutalavitalatalātalapātālākhyāni sapta pātalāni | bhūmirayamaṣṭamī saptadvīpā vasumatī yasyāḥ sumerurmadhye parvatarājaḥ kāñcanaḥ | tasya rājatavaidūryasphaṭikahemamāṇimayāni śṛṅgāṇi | tatra vaidūryaprabhānurāgānnīlotpalapatraśyāmo

III.26. Saṃyama on the sun develops knowledge of the universe.

The universe contains seven worlds. From the nadir to the top of Mount Meru is our world. From the top of Mount Meru to the polestar extends the intermediate world, which includes the planets, the asterisms and the stars. Beyond lies heaven, which has five levels. Thus, the third world is the world of the great Indra. The fourth is the *mahar* world of Prajāpati. Finally, there are the three worlds of Brahmā: *jana*, *tapas*, *satya*. There is a verse:

'The world of Brahmā with its three levels.
The *mahar* world of Prajāpati.
And the heaven of the great Indra.
In the firmament are the stars.
On earth, people.
Together all this is called the universe.'
(*Cf. Viṣṇu-Purāṇa II.4.97*)

Below the nadir, one beneath the other, there are six major divisions of the netherworlds, built upon solid matter, water, fire, air, ether, and darkness, and called, respectively, *mahākālā*, *ambarīṣa*, *raurava*, *mahāraurava*, *kālasūtra*, and *andhatāmisra*. Creatures are born into these spheres to endure long periods of misery in recompense for their past actions. Next come seven hells: *mahātala*, *rasātala*, *atala*, *sutala*, *vitala*, *talātala*, *pātāla*. This earth is the eighth, with its seven continents abounding in riches, with at its centre the golden Sumeru, king of mountains. Its peaks are made of silver, lapis lazuli, crystal and gold. The southern sky is dark blue like a lotus, from the brilliant

nabhaso dakṣiṇo bhāgaḥ | śvetaḥ pūrvaḥ svacchaḥ paścimaḥ kuraṇḍakābha uttaraḥ | dakṣiṇapārśve cāsya jambūḥ yato'yaṃ jambūdvīpaḥ | tasya sūryapracārādrātriṃdivaṃ lagnamiva vartate | tasya nīlaśvetaśṛṅgvanta udīcīnāstrayaḥ parvatā dvisāhasrāyāmāḥ | tadantareṣu trīṇi varṣāṇi nava nava yojanasāhasrāṇi ramaṇakaṃ hiraṇmayamuttarāḥ kurava iti | niṣadhahemakūṭahimaśailā dakṣiṇato dvisāhasrāyāmāḥ | tadantareṣu trīṇi varṣāṇi nava nava yojanasāhasrāṇi harivarṣaṃ kiṃpuruṣaṃ bhāratamiti | sumeroḥ prācīnā bhadrāśvā mālyavatsīmānaḥ | pratīcīnāḥ ketumālā gandhamādanasīmānaḥ | madhye varṣamilāvṛtam | tadetad yojanaśatasāhasraṃ sumerordiśi diśi tadardhena vyūḍham | sa khalvayaṃ śatasāhasrāyāmo jambūdvīpastato dviguṇena lavaṇodadhinā valayākṛtinā veṣṭitaḥ | tataśca dviguṇā dviguṇāḥ śākakuśakrauñcaśālmalagomedhapuṣkaradvīpāḥ sapta samudrāśca sarṣaparāśikalpāḥ savicitraśailāvataṃsā ikṣurasasurāsarpirdadhimaṇḍakṣīrasvādūdakāḥ | sapta samudrapariveṣṭitā valayākṛtayo lokālokaparvataparivārāḥ pañcāśadyojanakoṭiparisaṃkhyātāḥ | tadetatsarvaṃ supratiṣṭhitasaṃsthānamaṇḍamadhye vyūḍham | aṇḍaṃ

reflection of the lapis lazuli; while the eastern sky is white, the western clear, and the northern amarantine. On its southern flank towers a rose-apple *jambu* tree, whence the name 'Jambu Island'. The course of the sun rotates day and night as if affixed to the summit. To the north stretch three ranges of the White, the Blue and the Horned Mountains. Around these chains, extending for some 9,000 leagues are three subcontinents, the Fair, the Gold, and the Northern *Kurus*. To the south rise the *Niṣadha* Mountains, the Mountains of Ice, and the Mountains of the Snows, each 2,000 leagues long; and between the three subcontinents open out for 9,000 leagues, the Isle of Gold, the Small Man, and *Bhārata*.

To the east of Mount Meru, the *Bhadrāśva* Mountains are bordered by the *Mālyavat* Mountains. To the west, the *Ketumālā* mountains are enclosed by the *Gandhamādhanas*. In the middle lies the island of *Ilāvṛta*. *Jambudvīpa* extends for 100,000 leagues in every direction and for half this distance from Mount Meru. This 100,000 league-long *Jambudvīpa* is surrounded by the garland-shaped Sea of Salt, which is twice as large. The seven continents are each double the size of the preceding one: *śāka*, *kuśa*, *krauñca*, *śālmala*, *gomedha*, *puṣkara*. The seven oceans surround them, overflowing like a mountain of mustard seeds enclosed by stunning hills, their waters made of cane juice, liquor, clarified butter, yoghurt, butter, milk and sugar. In turn, the seven oceans are encircled by the World-Non-World Mountains which measure fifty crores of leagues. The foundation of the whole universe is fixed in the centre of the cosmic egg,

ca pradhānasyāṇuravayavo yathā'kāśe khadyota iti |

tatra pātāle jaladhau parveteṣveteṣu devanikāyā asuragandharvakinnarakiṃpuruṣayakṣarākṣasabhūtapreta-piśācāpasmārakāpsarobrahmarākṣasakūṣmāṇḍavināyakāḥ prativasanti | sarveṣu dvipeṣu puṇyātmano devamanuṣyāḥ | sumerustridaśānāmudyānabhūmiḥ | tatra miśravanaṃ nandanaṃ caitrarathaṃ sumānasamityudyānāni | sudharmā devasabhā | sudarśanaṃ puram | vaijayantaḥ prāsādaḥ | grahanakṣatratārakāstu dhruve nibaddhā vāyuvikṣepaniyamenopalakṣitapracārāḥ | sumeroruparyupari sanniviṣṭā divi viparivartante |

māhendranivāsinaḥ ṣaḍ eva devanikāyāḥ | tridaśā agniṣvāttā yāmyāḥ tuṣitā aparinirmitavaśavartinaḥ parinirmitavaśavartinaśceti | te sarve saṃkalpasiddhā aṇimādyaiśvaryopapannāḥ kalpāyuṣo vṛndārakāḥ kāmabhogina aupapādikadehā uttamānūkūlābhirapsarobhiḥ kṛtaparivārāḥ | mahati loke prājāpatye pañcavidho devanikāyaḥ | kumudā ṛbhavaḥ pratardanā añjanābhāḥ pracitābhā iti | ete mahābhūtavaśino dhyānāhārāḥ kalpasahasrāyuṣaḥ |

and the cosmic egg is a minuscule particle of almighty Nature, like a tiny firefly in the vastness of space.

In the infernal regions, in the oceans, and in the mountains live various groups of divine beings: the *asuras*, the *gandharvas*, the *kinnaras*, the *kiṃpuruṣas*, the *yakṣas*, the *rākṣasas*, the elements, the living dead, the *piśācas*, the *apasmārakas*, the *apsarasas*, the *brahmarākṣasas*, the *kūṣmāṇḍas*, the *vināyakas*. On the continental mainlands live virtuous gods and men. Mount Meru is paradise, the abode of the thrice eleven gods. The zones of paradise are: *miśravana*, *nandana*, *caitraratha*, *sumānasa*. The assembly of the gods is *sudharma*. Their city is Belle-Vue. Their palace is Victoria. The planets, the asterisms and the stars are connected to the polestar. Located one above another over Mount Meru, they revolve around the sky, driven by the power of the blowing wind.

The inhabitants of the world of the great Indra are six sets of divine beings: the thrice eleven gods, the *agniṣvattas*, the *yāmyas*, the *tuṣitas*, the *aparinirmitavaśavartins*, and the *parinimitavaśavartins*. All of them are proficient in realising their desires by mere intention. They have all acquired the major powers, such as becoming as small as an atom and so on. They live for a *kalpa* (4,294,080,000 years). They are highly evolved and enjoy all delights. Their bodies are unborn. They are attended by a retinue of gorgeous and compliant nymphs. In the *mahar* world of Prajāpati there are five classes of divine being: the *kumudas*, the *ṛbhus*, the *pratardanas*, the *añjanābhas*, the *pracitābhas*. These beings have mastery over the elements,

prathame brahmaṇo janaloke caturvidho devanikāyaḥ | brahmapurohitā brahmakāyikā brahmamahākāyikā ajarāmarā iti | ete bhūtendriyavaśino dviguṇadviguṇottarāyuṣaḥ | dvitīye tapasi loke trividho devanikāyaḥ | ābhāsvarā mahābhāsvarāḥ satyamahābhāsvarā iti | te bhūtendriyaprakṛtivaśino dviguṇadviguṇottarāyuṣaḥ sarve dhyānāhārā ūrdhvaretasa ūrdhvamapratihatajñānā adharabhūmiṣvanāvṛtajñānaviṣayāḥ | tṛtīye brahmaṇaḥ satyaloke catvāro devanikāyaḥ | acyutāḥ śūddhanivāsāḥ satyābhāḥ saṃjñāsaṃjñinaśceti | te cākṛtabhavananyāsāḥ svapratiṣṭhā uparyuparisthitāḥ pradhānavaśino yāvatsargāyuṣaḥ | tatrācyutāḥ savitarkadhyānasukhāḥ śuddhanivāsāḥ savicāradhyānasukhāḥ satyābhā ānandamātradhyānasukhāḥ saṃjñāsaṃjñāninaścāsmitāmātradhyānasukhāḥ | te'pi trailokyamadhye pratitiṣṭhante |

ta ete sapta lokāḥ sarva eva brahmakāḥ | videhaprakṛtilayāstu mokṣapade vartante iti na

subsist on meditation, and live for 1,000 *kalpas* (4,294,080,000,000 years).

In *janaloka*, the first of the worlds of Brahmā, there are four classes of divine being: the *brahmapurohitas*, the *brahmakāyikas*, the *brahmamahākāyikas*, the *ajarāmaras*. They have mastery over the elements and the senses, and each group lives twice as long as the preceding group. In the second world, *tapaloka*, there are three groups of divine beings: the *ābhāsvaras*, the *mahābhāsvaras*, the *satyamahābhāsvaras*. They have mastery over the elements, the senses and Nature. Each group lives twice as long as the preceding group. They all subsist on meditation. They are chaste. Their knowledge is unobstructed in the higher spheres. There is no boundary to their knowledge in the lower spheres. In *satyaloka*, the third world of Brahmā, there are four groups of divine beings: the *acyutas*, the *śuddhanivāsas*, the *satyābhas*, the *saṃjñāsaṃjñins*. They have no abode, for they reside within themselves, and are located one above the other. They have mastery over almighty Nature and live as long as the created universe. The *acyutas* enjoy the softest thinking levels of transcending in meditation. The *śuddhanivāsas* experience the finest feeling levels of transcending in meditation. The *satyābhas* enjoy only bliss in meditation. The *saṃjñāsaṃjñins* enjoy the level of Amness. They are also established in the three worlds.

These are the seven worlds. All are worlds of Brahmā. However, disembodied beings and those abiding within unmanifest Nature exist in a state of liberation and are not

lokamadhye nyastā iti | etadyoginā sākṣātkaraṇīyam | sūryadvāre saṃyamaṃ kṛtvā tato'nyatrāpi evaṃ tāvadabhyased yāvadidaṃ sarvaṃ dṛṣṭamiti | 3.26 |

to be found within the field of the visible universe. The yogi can have direct perception of all this by practising *saṃyama* on the portal of the sun and other sites. One should continue the practice until one has seen it all.

candre tārāvyūhajñānam || 3.27 ||

candre saṃyamaṃ kṛtvā tārāṇāṃ vyūhaṃ vijānīyāt | 3.27 |

III.27. On the moon — knowledge of the arrangement of the stars.

Having performed *saṃyama* on the moon, one may know the arrangement of the stars.

dhruve tadgatijñānam || *3.28* ||

tato dhruve saṃyamaṃ kṛtvā tārāṇāṃ gatiṃ vijānīyāt | ūrdhvavimāneṣu kṛtasaṃyamastāni vijānīyāt | 3.28 |

III.28. On the polestar — knowledge of their movement.

Then, having performed *saṃyama* on the polestar, one may know their movements. Performing *saṃyama* on their heavenly courses will make them known.

nābhicakre kāyavyūhajñānam || 3.29 ||

nābhicakre saṃyamaṃ kṛtvā kāyavyūhaṃ vijānīyāt | vātapittaśleṣmāṣastrayo doṣāḥ | dhātavaḥ sapta tvaglohitamāṃsasnāyvasthimajjāśukrāṇi pūrvaṃ pūrvameṣāṃ bahyamityeṣa vinyāsaḥ | 3.29 |

III.29. On the navel plexus — knowledge of the bodily systems.

Having performed *saṃyama* on the navel plexus, one may know the bodily systems. The three humours are air, bile and phlegm. The seven tissues are: plasma, blood, muscle, fat, bones, marrow, and reproductive fluids. They are structured in layers from the outside towards the inside.

kaṇṭhakūpe kṣutpipāsānivṛttiḥ || 3.30 ||

jihvāyā adhastāttantuḥ | tato'dhastātkaṇṭhaḥ | tato'dhastātkūpaḥ | tatra saṃyamātkṣutpipāse na bhādhete | 3.30 |

III.30. On the hollow in the throat — cessation of hunger and thirst.

Under the tongue there is a thread. Beneath that, there is the throat. Below that, there is a hollow. From *saṃyama* on that, one is not affected by hunger and thirst.

kūrmanāḍyāṃ sthairyam || 3.31 ||

kūpādadha urasi kūrmākārā nāḍī | tasyāṃ kṛtasaṃyamaḥ sthirapadaṃ labhate | yathā sarpo goghā ceti | 3.31 |

III.31. On the bronchial tube — calmness.

Below the hollow in the throat is a tube in the shape of a tortoise. *Saṃyama* practised on this produces a state of stillness, like that of a snake or an iguana.

mūrdhajyotiṣi siddhadarśanam || 3.32 ||

śiraḥ kapāle'rantaścidraṃ prabhāsvaraṃ jyotiḥ | tatra saṃyamaṃ kṛtvā siddhānāṃ dyāvāpṛthivyorantarāla-cāriṇāṃ darśanam | 3.32 |

III.32. On the light in the head — the vision of siddhas.

Through an opening in the cranium there is a radiant light. Having performed *saṃyama* on that, one can see *siddhas* as they roam the space between heaven and earth.

prātibhādvā sarvam || *3.33* ||

prātibha nāma tārakam | tadvivekajasya jñānasya pūrvarūpam yathodaye prabhā bhāskarasya | tena vā sarvameva jānāti yogī prātibhasya jñānasyotpattāviti | 3.33 |

III.33. From intuition — everything.

The role of the intuition is to fill in the gaps in knowledge. It is a form of knowledge that precedes the Pure Knowledge of the enlightened, just as dawn appears before the sun rises. With a fully developed intuition a yogi can really know anything.

hṛdaye cittasaṃvit || *3.34* ||

yadidamasminbrahmapure daharaṃ puṇḍarīkaṃ veśma tatra vijñānam | tasminsaṃyamāccittasaṃvit | 3.34 |

III.34. On the heart — complete knowledge of the mind.

Within the city of Brahma lies a cavity in the form of a small lotus. This is the home of all knowledge. *Saṃyama* on that develops one's full mental potential.

sattvapuruṣayoratyantāsaṃkīrṇayoḥ pratyayāviśeṣo bhogaḥ parārthatvātsvārthasaṃyamāt puruṣajñānam || 3.35 ||

buddhisattvaṃ prakhyāśīlaṃ samānasattvopanibandhane rajastamasī vaśīkṛtya sattvapuruṣānyatāpratyayena pariṇatam | tasmācca sattvātpariṇāmino'tyantavidharmā śuddho'nyaścitimātrarūpaḥ puruṣaḥ | tayoratyantāsaṃkīrṇayoḥ pratyayāviśeṣo bhogaḥ puruṣasya darśitaviṣayatvāt | sa bhogapratyayaḥ sattvasya parārthatvād dṛśyaḥ | yastu tasmādviśiṣṭaścitimātra-rūpo'nyaḥ pauruṣeyaḥ pratyayastatra saṃyamāt-puruṣaviṣayā prajñā jāyate | na ca puruṣapratyayena buddhisattvātmanā puruṣo dṛśyate | puruṣa eva taṃ pratyayaṃ svātmāvalambanaṃ paśyati | tathā hyuktam | vijñātāramare kena vijānīyād iti | 3.35 |

III.35. Experience occurs when, through object-referral, there is no distinction in the thinking process between the mind and the Self, which are completely separate. Saṃyama on Self-referral develops knowledge of the Self.

When the *rajas* and *tamas* components of the mind have subsided, the *sattva* in the mind, with its enlivening capacity, is altered by the thought of the difference between itself and the Self. The Self is self-sufficient Pure Consciousness, and it remains completely beyond those aspects of change which are inherent in the mind. Experience occurs as a result of the failure to distinguish between what are notwithstanding two distinct entities, because the mind is simply the object which is reflected in the Self. Because the mind's status is object-referral, this thought becomes the object of experience which is presented to the Self. *Saṃyama* on the thought of the Self as Pure Consciousness, uninvolved with the mind, develops knowledge of the Self. It is not that the Self can be experienced by entertaining the thought of the Self, because the thought is an activity that takes place only in the mind. But the Self experiences the thought which has 'Self' as its content. Thus it is said: 'Who knows the Knower?' (*Bṛhadāraṇyaka Upaniṣad IV.5.15*).

tataḥ prātibhaśrāvaṇavedanā'darśā'svādavārtā jāyante || 3.36 ||

prātibhātsūkṣmavyavahitaviprakṛṣṭātītānāgatajñānam | śrāvaṇād divyaśabdaśravaṇam | vedanād divyasparśādhigamaḥ | ādarśād divyarūpasaṃvit | āsvādād divyarasasaṃvid | vārtāto divyagandhavijñānamiti | etāni nityaṃ jāyante | 3.36 |

III.36. Then develop the powers of intuition, refined hearing, touch, sight, taste and smell.

From intuition comes knowledge of what is subtle, hidden or remote, and the past and the future. From developing the faculty of hearing comes divine hearing. From developing the faculty of touch, comes the capacity for divine touch. From developing the faculty of sight, comes full experience of divine sight. From developing the faculty of taste, comes full experience of divine taste. From developing the faculty of smell, comes the experience of divine smell. They develop spontaneously.

***te samādhāvupasargā vyutthāne siddhayaḥ* || *3.37* ||**

te prātibhādayaḥ samāhitacittasyotpadyamānā upasargāḥ | taddarśanapratyanīkatvāt | vyutthitacittasyotpadyamānāḥ siddhayaḥ | 3.37 |

III.37. These are by-products of transcendental consciousness, enrichments for activity.

As they arise when the mind is transcending, the intuition and the other powers are distractions, because they eclipse the experience of the Self. As they occur when the mind is active, they are enrichments.

***bandhakāraṇaśaithilyāt pracārasaṃvedanācca cittasya paraśarīrāveśaḥ* || *3.38* ||**

lolībhūtasya manaso'pratiṣṭhasya śarīre karmāśayavaśādbandhaḥ pratiṣṭhetyarthaḥ | tasya karmaṇo bandhakāraṇasya śaithilyaṃ samādhibalād bhavati | pracārasaṃvedanaṃ ca cittasya samādhijameva | karmabandhakṣayātsvacittasya pracārasaṃvedanācca yogī cittaṃ svaśarīrānniṣkṛṣya śarīrāntareṣu nikṣipati | nikṣiptaṃ cittaṃ cendriyāṇyanu patanti | yathā madhukararājānaṃ makṣikā utpatantamanutpatanti niviśamānamanu niviśante tathendriyāṇi paraśarīrāveśe cittamanu vidhīyanta iti | 3.38 |

III.38. By loosening the boundaries, and knowing the behaviour, of the mind, one may enter another's body.

The meaning is that, although the mind is mobile and flexible, the power of karma binds the mind to the body. The power of transcendental consciousness brings about a loosening of the boundaries that karma holds in place. Knowledge of the behaviour of the mind can only be had from the experience of transcendental consciousness. By loosening the ties of karma and by knowing the movements of the mind, the yogi can extricate his mind from his own body and project it into other bodies. Moreover, the senses follow the mind. As honey bees fly off when the queen bee takes off and alight when she alights, so the senses follow the mind when it enters another body.

udānajayājjalapaṅkakaṇṭakādiṣvasaṅga utkrāntiśca || 3.39 ||

samastendriyavṛttiḥ prāṇādilakṣaṇā jīvanaḥ | tasya kriyā pañcatayī | prāṇo mukhanāsikāgatirāhṛdayavṛttiḥ | samaṃ nayanāt samānaścā'nābhivṛttiḥ | apanayanādapāna āpādatalavṛttiḥ | unnayanādudāna āśirovṛttiḥ | vyāpi vyāna iti | eṣāṃ pradhānaṃ prāṇaḥ | udānajayājjalapaṅka-kaṇṭakādiṣvasaṅga utkrāntiśca prāyaṇakāle bhavati | tāṃ vaśitvena pratipadyate | 3.39 |

III.39. Mastering the upward breath one is untouched by water, mud, or thorns, and ascends at death.

The combined activity of the senses, characterised by breathing and related activities, constitutes the lifeforce. The activity of the lifeforce has five currents. 'Outward' breath (*prāṇa*) is the flow of life-force through the mouth and the nostrils to the heart. The 'even' breath (*samāna*) brings balance and flows to the navel. The 'downward' breath (*apāna*) aids elimination and flows to the heels. The 'upward' breath (*udāna*) uplifts and flows to the head. The 'diffusive' breath (*vyāna*) stimulates circulation. The 'outward' breath (*prāṇa*) is the fundamental one. Mastering the 'upward' breath means there is no contact with water, mud, thorns and the like, and having mastered it, at the time of death, one ascends.

***samānajayājjvalanam* || *3.40* ||**

jitasamānastejasa upadhmānaṃ kṛtvā jvalayati | 3.40 |

III.40. From mastery of the balancing breath — effulgence.

When the 'balancing' breath is mastered, breathing over fire, it blazes.

śrotrākāśayossaṃbandhasaṃyamāddivyaṃ śrotram || *3.41* ||

sarvaśrotrāṇāmākāśaṃ pratiṣṭhā sarvaśabdānāṃca | yathoktam | tulyadeśaśravaṇānāmekadeśaśrutitvaṃ sarveṣāṃ bhavatīti | taccaitadākāśasya liṅgam | anāvaraṇaṃ coktam | tathā'mūrtasyāpyanyatrānāvaraṇa-darśanādvibhutvamapi prakhyātamākāśasya | śabdagrahaṇanimittaṃ śrotram | badhirābadhirayorekaḥ śabdaṃ gṛhṇātyaparo na gṛhṇātīti | tasmātśrotrameva śabdaviṣayam | śrotrākāsayoḥ saṃbandhe kṛta-saṃyamasya yogino divyaṃ śrotraṃ pravartate | 3.41 |

III.41. Saṃyama on the relationship of hearing and the ether develops divine hearing.

The ether is the ground for all hearing and all sounds. Thus it is said: 'In that everyone hears sounds through the same organ (the ear), there must be one common medium through which sounds are propagated' (*Pañcaśikha*). This fact demonstrates the existence of the ether. It is also said to be unbounded. The all-pervasiveness of the ether is deduced from the fact that non-material objects do not absorb sound. Sound is perceived through the organ of hearing. Thus, a hearing man can hear, but a deaf man cannot. Therefore, hearing is the faculty concerned with sound. Having performed *saṃyama* on the relationship of hearing and the ether, a yogi experiences divine hearing.

kāyākāśossaṃbandhasaṃyamāllaghutūlasamāpatteścākāśa-gamanam || *3.42* ||

yatra kāyastatrā'kāśaṃ | tasyāvakāśadānātkāyasya tena saṃbandhaḥ prāptis | tatra kṛtasaṃyamo jītvā tatsaṃbandhaṃ laghuṣu vā tūlādiṣvāparamāṇubhyaḥ samāpattiṃ labdhvā jitasaṃbandho laghurbhavati | laghutvācca jale pādābhyāṃ viharati | tatastūrṇanābhitantumātre vihṛtya raśmiṣu viharati | tato yatheṣṭamākāśagatirasya bhavatīti | 3.42 |

III.42. From saṃyama on the relationship of the body and the ether, and becoming light as cotton fibre — the ability to move through the air.

Wherever the body may be, the ether is there. When the body moves, the ether makes room for it, and so a relationship between the two is established. Having performed *saṃyama* on this, and having mastered the relationship — or as the body's finest atoms become light, like cotton fibre, for example — becoming light, one can walk on water; then on spiders' webs; and then on sunbeams. Then one may travel through space wherever one wishes.

bahirakalpitā vṛttirmahāvidehā tataḥ prakāśāvaraṇakṣayaḥ || *3.43* ||

śārīrādbahirmanaso vṛttilābho videhā nāma dhāraṇā | sa yadi śarīrapratiṣṭhasya manaso bahirvṛttimātreṇa bhavati sā kalpitetyucyate | yā tu śarīranirapekṣā bahirbhūtasyaiva manaso bahirvṛttiḥ sā khalvakalpitā | tatra kalpitayā sādhyayantyakalpitāṃ mahāvidehāmiti yayā paraśarīrāṇyāviśanti yoginaḥ | tataśca dhāraṇātaḥ prakāśātmano buddhisattvasya yadāvaraṇaṃ kleśakarmavipākatrayaṃ rajastamomūlaṃ tasya ca kṣayo bhavati | 3.43 |

III.43. The ability to project outside the body becomes real and objective. Then the veil masking enlightenment is destroyed.

There is a technique called 'disincarnation' which involves the mind experiencing being out of the body. If this feeling of being outside occurs while the mind is yet connected to the body, it is considered to be only a subjective experience. But if the experience of being outside occurs independently of the body, when the mind is outside the body, it is not just a mental projection. Yogis perfect this latter objective ability to leave the actual body by means of the former mental experience of projection, and can then enter other bodies. This technique destroys the veil which is woven from the causes of suffering, the three aspects of karma, and *rajas* and *tamas*, and which masks the purity of the mind.

***sthūlasvarūpasūkṣmānvayārthavattvasaṃyamād-bhūtajayaḥ* || *3.44* ||**

tatra pārthivādyāḥ śabdādayo viśeṣāḥ sahā'kārādibhirdharmaiḥ sthūlaśabdena paribhāṣitāḥ | etadbhūtānāṃ prathamaṃ rūpam | dvitīyaṃ rūpaṃ svasāmānyaṃ mūrtirbhūmiḥ sneho jalaṃ vahniruṣṇatā vāyuḥ praṇāmī sarvatogatirākāśa ityetatsvarūpaśabdenocyate | asya sāmānyasya śabdādayo viśeṣāḥ | tathā coktam | ekajātisamanvitānāmeṣāṃ dharmamātravyāvṛttiriti | sāmānyaviśeṣasamudāyo'tra dravyam | dviṣṭho hi samūhaḥ | pratyastamitabhedāvayavānugataḥ śarīraṃ vṛkṣo yūthaṃ vanamiti | śabdenopāttabhedāvayavānugataḥ samūha ubhaye devamanuṣyāḥ | samūhasya deva eko bhāgo manuṣyā dvitīyo bhāgaḥ tābhyāmevābhidhīyate samūhaḥ | sa ca bhedābhedavivakṣitaḥ | āmrāṇāṃ vanaṃ brāhmaṇānāṃ saṃghaḥ āmravanaṃ brāhmaṇasaṃgha iti | sa punardvividho yutasiddhāvayavo'yutasiddhāvayavaśca | yutasiddhāvayavaḥ samūho vanaṃ saṃgha iti |

III.44. Saṃyama on their gross form, essential nature, subtle form, articulation, and purpose develops mastery of the elements.

According to the Teaching, the special qualities (sound, for example) together with their various properties (form, for example) are expressed values of the elements (earth, for example): these are called 'gross'. This is the first aspect of the elements.

The second aspect is the generic characteristic of each element. Earth has consistence; water wetness; fire heat; air motion; ether all-pervasiveness. This is called their essential nature. These generic characteristics are expressed properties of sound and the other special qualities. Thus it is said: 'It is only their individual properties which serve to distinguish the members of a given species.' For current purposes, a substance is a composite of generic and specific characteristics. There are two kinds of composite: one when the parts have lost their identity in the whole — for example: a body, a herd, a tree, a forest — and the other when the parts can be identified by name. In the case of 'gods and men' the 'gods' form one component of the whole and 'men' form the other component but the whole is only known via the component parts. The distinction between the two parts may be emphasised or not, as in the phrases 'mango-trees in a forest' or 'a group of Brahmans' as opposed to 'a mango forest' or 'a Brahman group'. This type of composite can itself be divided into two kinds, depending on whether the component parts can be distinguished, or not. The forest and the group are examples where the

ayutasiddhāvayavaḥ saṃghātaḥ śarīraṃ vṛkṣaḥ paramāṇuriti | ayutasiddhāvayavabhedānugataḥ samūho dravyamiti patañjaliḥ | etatsvarūpamityuktam | atha kimeṣāṃ sūkṣmarūpam | tanmātraṃ bhūtakāraṇam | tasyaiko'vayavaḥ paramāṇuḥ sāmānyaviśeṣātmā'yutasiddhāvayavabhedānugataḥ samudāya ityevam sarvatanmātrāṇi | etattṛtīyam | atha bhūtānāṃ caturthaṃ rūpaṃ khyātikriyāsthitiśīlā guṇāḥ kāryasvabhāvānupātino'nvayaśabdenoktāḥ | athaiṣāṃ pañcamaṃ rūpamarthavattvaṃ bhogāpavargārthatā guṇeṣvanvayinī guṇāstanmātrabhūtabhautikeṣviti sarvamarthavat | teṣvidānīṃ bhūteṣu pañcasu pañcarūpeṣu saṃyamāttasya tasya rūpasya svarūpadarśanaṃ jayaśca prādurbhavati | tatra pañcabhūtasvarūpāṇi jitvā bhūtajayī bhavati | tajjayādvatsānusāriṇya iva gāvo'sya saṃkalpānuvidhāyinyo bhūtaprakṛtayo bhavanti | 3.44 |

parts can be identified, whereas in the case of the body, a tree, or an atomic particle, their components cannot be distinguished. For Patañjali, a substance is a composite whose parts have no independent identity. This is called the 'essential nature'.

— What is the subtle form? — The essences (*tanmātras*) are at the basis of the elements. Its simplest form is the ultimate particle, a composite having both generic features and specific characteristics, whose components cannot exist independently. This is true for all the *tanmātras*. This is the third aspect.

The fourth aspect of the elements concerns the *guṇas*, which promote purity, activity and stability. They pursue their own natural course and are said to be the 'articulators'.

The fifth aspect of the elements is purposiveness. The objective of the *guṇas* is to provide experience and liberation. To this end, they are at work within the *tanmātras*, all the levels of the elements, and within created things; so everything has this goal.

Now, *saṃyama* on the five elements and their five aspects results in the cognition of the essential nature of each aspect and develops control over them. Having mastered the essential nature of the five elements, one becomes master of the elements. With this mastery, the elements and the laws of Nature move to support one's intentions as cows follow their calves.

tato'ṇimādiprādurbhāvaḥ kāyasampat-taddharmānabhighātaśca || 3.45 ||

tatrāṇimā bhavatyaṇuḥ | laghimā laghurbhavati | mahimā mahānbhavati | prāptiraṅgulyagreṇāpi sparśati candramasam | prākāmyamicchānabhighātaḥ | bhūmāvunmajjati nimajjati yathodake | vaśitvaṃ bhūtabhautikeṣu vaśī bhavati | avaśyaścānyeṣām | īśitṛtvaṃ teṣāṃ prabhavāpyayavyūhānāmīṣṭe | yatrakāmāvasāyitvaṃ satyasaṃkalpatā yathā saṅkalpastathā bhūtaprakṛtīnāmavasthānam | na ca śakto'pi padārthaviparyāsaṃ karoti | kasmāt | anyasya yatra kāmāvasāyinaḥ pūrvasiddhasya tathā bhūteṣu saṃkalpāditi | etānyaṣṭāvaisvaryāṇi | kāyasaṃpadvakṣyamāṇā | taddharmānabhighātaśca pṛthivī mūrtyā na niruṇaddhi yoginah śarīrādikriyām śilāmapyanuviśatīti | nā'paḥ snigdhāḥ kledayanti | nāgniruṣṇo dahati | na vāyuḥ praṇāmī vahati anāvaraṇātmake'pyākāśe bhavatyāvṛtakāyaḥ siddhānāmapyadṛśyo bhavati | 3.45 |

III.45. Then other powers develop, such as becoming as small as an atom. Also, perfection of the body and no resistance from the elements.

'Minuteness' is the ability to become as small as an atom. 'Lightness' is the ability to levitate. 'Greatness' is the ability to become large. 'Extension' means one can touch the moon with one's fingertips. 'Invincibility' is the absence of resistance to one's desires; for example, diving into or rising up out of the earth as if it were water. 'Mastery' is command of the elements and their creations, without being subject to any superior authority. 'Supremacy' is exercise of dominion over the source, course and goal of the universe. 'Fulfilment of desires' is the realisation of one's intentions: as is the intention, so is the ordering of the elements. However, though one may be capable, one does not upset the established order of things. — Why? — Because in the past, an earlier *siddha*, who had the same power to fulfil his desires, has already intended that the elements be as they are today.

These are the eight super-powers. Perfection of the body is described later. Experiencing no resistance from the elements means that the density of the earth cannot stop the passage of the yogi's body. So, for example, he can walk through walls. Water cannot wet him. Fire cannot burn him. Wind cannot blow him away. His body is not permeated by the ether, so he is invisible, even to *siddhas*.

rūpalāvaṇyabalavajrasaṃhananatvāni kāyasaṃpat || *3.46* ||

darśanīyaḥ kāntimān atiśayabalo
vajrasaṃhananaśceti | 3.46 |

III.46. Perfection of the body means beauty, radiance, strength, and the hardness of diamond.

The body is pleasing to behold, radiant in appearance, extremely powerful, and as hard as diamond.

grahaṇasvarūpāsmitānvayārthavattvasaṃyamād-indriyajayaḥ || *3.47* ||

sāmānyaviśeṣātmā śabdādirgrāhyaḥ | teṣvindriyāṇāṃ vṛttigrahaṇam | na ca tatsāmānyamātragrahaṇākāraṃ kathamanālocitaḥ sa viṣayaviśeṣa indriyeṇa manasā vānuvyavasīyeteti | svarūpaṃ punaḥ prakāśātmano buddhisattvasya sāmānyaviśeṣayorayutasiddhāvayava-bhedānugataḥ samūho dravyamindriyam | teṣāṃ tṛtīyaṃ rūpamasmitālakṣaṇo'hamkāraḥ | tasya sāmānyasyendriyāṇi viśeṣāḥ | caturthaṃ rūpaṃ vyavasāyātmakāḥ prakāśakriyāsthitiśīlā guṇā yeṣāmindriyāṇi sāhaṃkārāṇi pariṇāmāḥ | pañcamaṃ rūpaṃ guṇeṣu yadanugataṃ puruṣārthattvamiti | pañcasveteṣvindriyarūpeṣu yathākramaṃ saṃyamaḥ tatra tatra jayaṃ kṛtvā pañcarūpajayādindriyajayaḥ prādurbhavati yoginaḥ | 3.47 |

III.47. Saṃyama on their acts of perception, essential nature, Amness, articlation, and purpose develops mastery of the faculties of cognition.

The object perceived — sound and other sensory stimuli — has both generic and specific characteristics. 'Acts of perception' take place when the faculties of cognition are directed upon it. The act of perception does not just seize on the generic characteristics; otherwise how could the senses or the mind recognise an object if its specific characteristics had not been noted? The 'essential nature' is a self-sufficient whole whose constituent parts do not exist independently; it is itself made up of both generic and specific characteristics recognisable by the mind; a faculty of cognition is, therefore, an object in its own right. The third aspect is the sense of 'I' in the form of Amness. The faculties of cognition are individual expressions of this underlying form. The fourth aspect of 'articulation' refers to the *guṇas*, which promote purity, activity and stability, and to their combinatorial function. The faculties and the sense of Amness are the product of their interactions. The fifth aspect is the 'purpose' of the Self as it informs the *guṇas*. Performing *saṃyama* on these five aspects of the faculties, and mastering each one in turn, the yogi acquires mastery over the faculties of cognition.

***tato manojavitvaṃ vikaraṇabhāvaḥ pradhānajayaśca* || *3.48* ||**

kāyasyānuttamo gatilābho manojavitvam | videhānāmindriyāṇāmabhipretadeśakālaviṣayāpekṣo vṛttilābho vikaraṇabhāvaḥ | sarvaprakṛtivikāravaśitvaṃ pradhānajaya ityetāstisraḥ siddhayo madhupratīkā ucyante | etāśca karaṇapañcakarūpajayādadhigamyante | 3.48 |

III.48. Then come movement at the speed of thought, action at a distance, and mastery of the laws of Nature.

Movement at the speed of thought means the body travels as fast as it is possible. Action at a distance means performing an action upon a desired object within the framework of time and space but without the instrumentality of the body. Mastery of the laws of Nature means having power over the whole of the created universe and its evolution. It is said that these three perfections are like nectar. They are acquired by mastering the essence of the five instruments of cognition.

sattvapuruśānyatākhyātimātrasya sarvabhāvādhiṣṭhātṛtvaṃ sarvajñātṛtvaṃ ca || 3.49 ||

nirdhūtarajastamomalasya buddhisattvasya pare vaiśāradye parasyāṃ vaśikārasaṃjñāyāṃ vartamānasya sattvapuruṣānyatākhyātimātrarūpapratiṣṭhasya sarvabhāvādhiṣṭhātṛtvam | sarvātmāno guṇā vyavasāyavyavaseyātmakāḥ svāminaṃ kṣetrajñaṃ pratyaśeṣadṛśyātmatvenopasthitā ityarthaḥ | sarvajñātṛtvaṃ sarvātmanāṃ guṇānāṃ śāntoditāvyapadeśyadharmatvena vyavasthitānāmakramopārūḍhaṃ vivekajaṃ jñānamityarthaḥ | ityeṣā viśokā nāma siddhiḥ yāṃ prāpya yogī sarvajñaḥ kṣīṇakleśabandhano vaśī viharati | 3.49 |

III.49. With the permanent realisation of the difference between the mind and the Self come omnipotence and omniscience.

When the mind has been cleansed of the impurities of *rajas* and *tamas*, in the state of absolute purity, and with the supreme power of Pure Consciousness, established in the simplest level of awareness of the difference between the mind and the Self, comes omnipotence. The meaning is that the *guṇas*, which underlie all things and are responsible for the maintenance and evolution of the universe, surrender to their master — the Knower of the field of the Relative, of the whole of creation. The meaning is also that omniscience is the Pure Knowledge of enlightened vision that is simultaneously aware of all the operations of the *guṇas*, past, present and future. This state of perfection is free from sorrow, and having achieved it, the yogi is omniscient. The bondage at the basis of suffering is undone. The master is free.

tadvairāgyādapi doṣabījakṣaye kaivalyam || 3.50 ||

yadā'syaivaṃ bhavati kleśakarmakṣaye sattvasyāyaṃ vivekapratyayo dharmaḥ | sattvaṃ ca heyapakṣe nyastaṃ puruṣaścāpariṇāmī śuddho'nyaḥ sattvāditi | evamasya tato virajyamānasya yāni kleśabījāni dagdhaśālibījakalpānyaprasavasamarthāni tāni saha manasā pratyastaṃ gacchanti | teṣu pralīneṣu puruṣaḥ punaridaṃ tāpatrayaṃ bhuṅkte | tadeteṣāṃ guṇānāṃ manasi karmakleśavipākasvarūpeṇābhivyaktānāṃ caritārthānāṃ pratiprasave puruṣasyā'tyantiko guṇaviyogaḥ kaivalyam | tadā svarūpapratiṣṭhā citiśaktireva puruṣa iti | 3.50 |

III.50. When even these are let go, all possibility of lack of fulfilment has been removed — this is enlightenment.

When this state has been achieved, when the basis for suffering and action has been destroyed, one realises that the experience of separation itself is also all within the mind, and that the mind is part of the realm of existence to be free of, and that the Self alone is 'unchanging, pure, uninvolved'. As this realisation dawns, one begins to free oneself of it, the very potential for suffering becomes as roasted grains of rice, sterile, no longer capable of germinating, and it vanishes along with the mind. When this trace has dissolved, the Self no longer experiences the three modes of suffering. When the *guṇas*, which formerly manifested in the mind as activity, suffering and its effects, since their role is completed, are decommissioned, there is the total separation of the *guṇas* and the Self: singularity. Then the Self is restored to Itself, to Its own true nature — Pure Consciousness.

sthānyupanimantraṇe saṅgasmayākaraṇaṃ punaraniṣṭaprasaṅgāt || 3.51 ||

catvāraḥ khalvamī yoginaḥ | prathamakalpikaḥ madhubhūmikaḥ prajñājyotiḥ atikrāntabhāvanīyaśceti | tatrābhyāsī pravṛttamātrajyotiḥ prathamaḥ | ṛtaṃbharaprajño dvitīyaḥ | bhūtendriyajayī tṛtīyaḥ sarveṣu bhāviteṣu bhāvanīyeṣu kṛtarakṣābandhaḥ kṛtakartavyasādhanādinām | caturtho tastvatikrāntabhāvanīyaḥ | tasya cittapratisarga eko'rthaḥ | saptavidhā'sya prāntabhūmiprajñā | tatra madhumatīṃ bhūmiṃ sākṣātkurvato brāhmaṇasya sthānino devāḥ sattvaviśuddhimanupaśyantaḥ sthānairupanimantrayante | bho ihā'syatām | iha ramyatāṃ kamanīyo'yaṃ bhogaḥ kamanīyeyaṃ kanyā rasāyanamidaṃ jarāmṛtyū bādhate | vaihāyasamidaṃ yānamamī kalpadrumāḥ puṇyā mandākinī siddhā maharṣaya uttamā anukūlā apsaraso divye śrotracakṣuṣī vajropamaḥ kāyaḥ svaguṇaiḥ sarvamidamupārjitamāyuṣmatā

III.51. Being solicited by the inhabitants of the celestial realms is no reason for getting involved or feeling conceited, as the consequences risk being undesirable.

Now, there are four types of yogi: the newly initiate; those enjoying the sweetness of success; those guided by the light of consciousness; and those graduated beyond what there is to achieve. The first level is that of the seeker who has just embarked upon the path to enlightenment. The second level is where the seeker has developed *ṛtaṃbharaprajñā*. The third is the level of those who have mastered the elements and the senses, by making use of the technologies of enlightenment and other means to secure all their achievements to date and those to come. The fourth type is the yogi who has passed beyond all that there is to achieve. For him the only remaining step is the reabsorption of the mind. He has risen to the highest of the seven levels of development.

The gods in their abode, seeing the purity of consciousness achieved by the Brahman who has gained direct experience of this level of sweet blissfulness, solicit him with the delights of their realm: 'Hail! Please come and stay with us here. Come and enjoy yourself. Here is a beautiful young virgin. Here is an elixir which abolishes old age and death. This chariot flies through the skies. These trees of plenty will grant your every wish. Here is the auspicious *Mandākinī* river. Here are *siddhas* and *maharṣis*. Here are compliant, gorgeous nymphs. Here is divine hearing and sight. Here, an indestructible body. All this is yours as reward for your efforts. Your life will be

pratipadyatāmidamakṣayamajaramamarasthānaṃ devānāṃ priyamiti | evamabhidhīyamānaḥ saṅgadoṣānbhāvayed | ghoreṣu saṃsārāṅgāreṣu pacyamānena mayā jananamaraṇāndhakāre viparivartamānena kathañcitāsāditaḥ kleśatimiravināśī yogapradīpaḥ | tasya caite tṛṣṇāyonayo viṣayavāyavaḥ pratipakṣāḥ | sa khalvahaṃ labdhālokaḥ | kathamanayā viṣayamṛgatṛṣṇayā vañcitastasyaiva punaḥ pradīptasya saṃsārāgnerātmānamindhanī kuryāmiti | svasti vaḥ svapnopamebhyaḥ kṛpanajanaprārthanīyebhyo viṣayebhya ityevaṃ niścitamatiḥ samādhiṃ bhāvayet |

saṅgamakṛtvā smayamapi na kuryāt | evamahaṃ devānāmapi prārthanīya iti | smayādayaṃ susthitaṃ manyatayā mṛtyunā keśeṣu gṛhītamivā'tmānaṃ na bhāvayiṣyati | tathā cāsya cchidrāntaraprekṣī nityaṃ yatnopacaryaḥ pramādo labdhavivaraḥ kleśānuttambhayiṣyati | tataḥ punaraniṣṭaprasaṅgaḥ | evamasya saṅgasmayāvakurvato bhāvito'rtho dṛḍhī bhaviṣyati | bhāvanīyaścārtho'bhimukhī bhaviṣyati | 3.51 |

long. So enjoy! This realm is the delight of the gods, free from decay, age and death.'

If addressed in this way, one should think of the disadvantages of getting involved: 'I have been burning in the terrifying coals of Becoming, tossed hither and thither in the blind chaos of living and dying. Somehow I have managed to stumble upon the lamp of yoga which dispels the darkness of suffering. The storms of the Relative whipped up by desire now threaten its flickering flame. I happened upon this illustrious world. How should I now be dragged down by the pull of the Relative, which is but a mirage? How could I make of myself the fuel to rekindle the fires of the cycle of birth and death?' He should reply: 'I am most grateful for the delights you offer. But they are mere dreams coveted only by fools.' With this resolve, let him transcend. And in his conceit, let him not flatter himself: 'The very gods seek my company!' Fooling himself that he is unmoved, though puffed up with pride, he is unaware that death has seized him firmly by the scruff of the neck. For one must always guard against a lapse in vigilance, lest it discover an Achilles' heel and through that chink incite fresh suffering.

Whence the risk of undesired consequences. Thus, eschewing involvement and self-deception, the progress made to date can be consolidated, while the goal ahead lies within easy reach.

kṣaṇatatkramayoḥ saṃyamādvivekajaṃ jñānam || *3.52* ||

yathā'pakarṣaparyantaṃ dravyaṃ paramaṇurevaṃ paramāpakarṣaparyantaḥ kālaḥ kṣaṇaḥ | yāvatā vā samayena calitaḥ paramāṇuḥ pūrvadeśaṃ jahyāduttaradeśamupasaṃpadyeta sa kālaḥ kṣaṇaḥ | tatpravāhāvicchedastu kramaḥ | kṣaṇatatkramayornāsti vastusamāhāra iti | buddhisamāhāro muhūrtāhorātrādayaḥ | sa khalvayaṃ kālo vastuśūnyo'pi buddhinirmāṇaḥ śabdajñānānupātī laukikānāṃ vyutthitadarśanānāṃ vastusvarūpa ivāvabhāsate | kṣaṇastu vastupatitaḥ kramāvalambī | kramaśca kṣaṇānantaryātmā | taṃ kālavidaḥ kāla ityācakṣate yoginaḥ | na ca dvau kṣaṇau saha bhavataḥ kramaśca na dvayoḥ sahabhuvorasaṃbhavāt pūrvasmāduttarasya bhāvino yadānantaryaṃ kṣaṇasya sa kramaḥ | tasmādvartamāna evaikaḥ kṣaṇo na pūrvottarakṣaṇāḥ santīti | tasmānnāsti tatsamāhāraḥ | ye tu bhūtabhāvinaḥ kṣaṇāste pariṇāmānvitā vyākhyeyāḥ | tenaikena kṣaṇena kṛtsno lokaḥ pariṇāmamanubhavati | tatkṣaṇopārūḍhāḥ khalvamī sarve dharmāḥ | tayoḥ kṣaṇatatkramayoḥ saṃyamāttayos sākṣātkaraṇam | tataśca vivekajaṃ jñānaṃ prādurbhavati | 3.52 |

III.52. Saṃyama on instants in time and their sequence develops the power of discrimination.

Just as a particle is the smallest unit of matter, so an instant is the shortest unit of time. An instant is measured as the time it takes for a particle to move from one point in space to another. An uninterrupted succession of instants forms a sequence. However, an accumulation of such instants into a sequence has no reality. Hours, days, nights and other periods of time are just calculations made up by the mind. The fact is that time is not real. It is just a mental construct. It corresponds to daily experience and to language usage, but it only appears real to those whose awareness is caught up in worldly affairs. Nonetheless, the instant has a reality in the sense that it serves as the support for a sequence of instants. A sequence is in essence a continuity of instants. This is how yogis who know Reality talk about time.

Two instants do not occur at the same time, nor is it possible to form a sequence from two events that occur simultaneously. There is a sequence when one moment follows immediately upon another moment. Moreover, only the present moment exists; the previous moment and the next moment do not exist. Therefore, moments do not accumulate. Nevertheless, past and future moments can be understood as inherent components of the process of change; and the whole universe undergoes change at every moment in time. In fact, the totality of all phenomena manifests in the instant. From *saṃyama* on instants in time and their sequence, they can be directly cognised. And then the power of discrimination is developed.

tasya viṣayaviśeṣa upakṣipyate |

jātilakṣaṇadeśairanyatānavacchedāttulyayostataḥ pratipattiḥ || *3.53* ||

tulyayoḥ deśalakṣaṇasārūpye jātibhedo'nyatatāyā hetuḥ gauriti iyaṃ vaḍaveyamiti | tulyadeśajātīyatve lakṣaṇamanyatvakaraṃ kālākṣi gauḥ svastimatī gauriti | dvayorāmalakayorjātilakṣaṇasārūpyāddeśabhedo'nyatvakara idaṃ pūrvamidamuttaramiti | yadā tu pūrvamāmalakamanyavyagrasya jñāturuttaradeśa upāvartyate tadā tulyadeśatve pūrvametaduttarametaditi pravibhāgānupapattiḥ | asaṃdigdhena ca tattvajñānena bhavitavyamityata idamuktam | tataḥ pratipattir-vivekajñānāditi | katham | pūrvāmalakasahakṣaṇo deśa uttarāmalakasahakṣaṇāddeśādbhinnaḥ | te cāmalake svadeśakṣaṇānubhavabhinne | anyadeśakṣaṇānubhavastu tayoranyatve heturiti | etena dṛṣṭāntena paramāṇostulyajātilakṣaṇadeśasya pūrvaparamāṇu-deśasahakṣaṇasākṣātkaraṇāduttarasya paramāṇos taddeśānupapattāvuttarasya taddeśānubhavo bhinnaḥ sahakṣaṇabhedāttayorīsvarasya

The special nature of this discrimination is described:

III.53. Then comes the ability to distinguish between two objects which are identical in type, characteristics and location.

Two objects which are alike in terms of location and appearance can nonetheless be identified by type. Thus, we can say: 'This is a cow, and this is a mare.' If the location and the type are the same, the appearance helps to distinguish them. So we can say: 'This cow has blue eyes, and that cow has auspicious markings.' Two cherry plums share the same type and the same appearance but they occupy different positions in space. So we say: 'This one is in front, and that one is behind'. But if the plum in front is swapped with the one behind while the observer is looking away, then because the relative positions remain unchanged, it is no longer possible to tell which is which. Now, if knowledge of Reality is to be complete, it must be free from doubt; and it is said that this is possible through the exercise of discrimination. — How? — At a given moment, the point in space occupied by the first plum is different to the point in space occupied by the other plum. The two plums are different therefore in terms of their respective coordinates in space and in time. Mapping their space-time coordinates reveals that they are different. From this example, given the impossibility of two particles occupying the same point in space at the same moment in time, the direct cognition of the coordinates in space and time of one particle establishes that the spatial coordinate of the other particle is different. By picking up on the impulse of the divergence in the temporal axis, the accomplished yogi can draw the

yogino'nyatvapratyayo bhavatīti | apare tu varṇayanti | ye'ntyā viśeṣāste'nyatāpratyayaṃ kurvantīti | tatrāpi deśalakṣaṇabhedo mūrtivyavadhijātibhedaścānyatve hetuḥ | kṣaṇabhedastu yogibuddhigamya evetyata uktaṃ mūrtivyavadhijātibhedābhāvānnāsti mūlapṛthaktvamiti vārṣagaṇyaḥ | 3.53 |

distinction. Others maintain that the finest 'special qualities' inform the cognition. On this view, it is because of the difference in position and characteristics, together with differences in material composition, spatial extension and structural morphology, that the distinction may be discerned. But it has been stated that it is the difference in the temporal axis which appears in the yogi's mind. As Vārṣagaṇya says, at the level where there is no (material, spatial, structural) 'difference', there is no (serial) 'differance'.

tārakaṃ sarvaviṣayaṃ sarvathāviṣayamakramaṃ ceti vivekajaṃ jñānam || 3.54 ||

tārakamiti svapratibhotthamanaupadeśikamityarthaḥ | sarvaviṣayam nāsya kiñcidaviṣayībhūtamityarthaḥ | sarvathāviṣayamatītānāgatapratyutpannaṃ sarvaṃ paryāyaiḥ sarvathā jānātītyarthaḥ | akramamiti ekakṣaṇopārūḍhaṃ sarvaṃ sarvathā gṛhṇātītyarthaḥ | etadvivekajaṃ jñānaṃ paripūrṇam asyaivāṃśo yogapradīpaḥ madhumatīṃ bhūmimupādāya yāvadasya parisamāptiriti | 3.54 |

III.54. Pure Knowledge is complete, holistic, universal and instantaneous.

'Complete' means that there are no gaps, that it is intuitive, spontaneous and unmediated. 'Holistic' means that it is all-encompassing so that nothing lies beyond its reach. 'Universal' means that it knows all the past, present and future in all their stages of evolution and in all their details. 'Instantaneous' means that it knows the totality of all things simultaneously. This Pure Knowledge is full and complete. The lamp of yoga is but a tiny portion of It, lighting the way from the first steps of progress to final fulfilment.

prāptavivekajajñānasyāprāptavivekajajñānasya vā |

sattvapuruṣayoḥ śuddhisāmye kaivalyamiti || *3.55* ||

yadā nirdhūtarajastamomalaṃ buddhisattvaṃ puruṣasyānyatāpratītimātrādhikāraṃ dagdhakleśabījaṃ bhavati tadā puruṣasya śuddhisārūpyamivā'pannaṃ bhavati tadā puruṣasyopacaritabhogābhāvaḥ śuddhiḥ | etasyāmavasthāyāṃ kaivalyaṃ bhavatīśvarasyānīsvarasya vā vivekajñānabhāgina itarasya vā | na hi dagdhakleśabījasya jñāne punarapekṣā kācidasti | sattvaśuddhidvāreṇaitatsamādhijamaiśvaryaṃ jñānaṃ copakrāntam | paramārthatastu jñānādadarśanaṃ nivartate | tasminnivṛtte na santyuttare kleśāḥ | kleśābhāvātkarmavipākābhāvaḥ | caritādhikārāścaitasyāmavasthāyāṃ guṇā na puruṣasya dṛśyatvena punarupatiṣṭhante | tat puruṣasya kaivalyam | tadā puruṣaḥ svarūpamātrajyotiramalaḥ kevalī bhavati | 3.55 |

iti śrīpātañjale sāṃkhyapravacane sāṃkhyaśāstre tṛtīyaḥ vibhūtipādaḥ || **3** ||

Whether Pure Knowledge has been attained or not:

III.55. When the mind and the Self are both pure, there is enlightenment.

When the *sattva* in the mind is cleansed of the impurities of *rajas* and *tamas*, and when it reflects only the self-sufficient non-involvement of the Self, and when the seeds of suffering are roasted, then the mind achieves a state of purity that is like the purity of the Self — so pure that the phenomenon of experience is no longer erroneously attributed to the Self. In this state, there is Unity, with or without God consciousness, with or without awareness of Pure Knowledge. The seeds of suffering are destroyed. Nothing is lacking within that awareness. This supreme knowledge is born of transcendental consciousness and enters through the portal of the purified mind. The final goal is achieved when ignorance has been replaced by knowledge. When ignorance is destroyed, there is no more suffering. When suffering ends, karma ends. In this state too, the role of the *guṇas* is over and they no longer appear in the form of objects observed for the Self. Then the Self resides in the light of Its own true nature, immaculate, in Unity.

End of the Third Chapter on
'All Possibilities' in Maharṣi Patañjali's
Treatise on the Teaching on Yoga

|| 4 ||

kaivalyapāda

Chapter 4

Cosmic Consciousness

janmauṣadhimantratapaḥsamādhijāḥ siddhayaḥ || *4.1* ||

dehāntaritā janmanā siddhiḥ | oṣadhibhiḥ asurabhavaneṣu rasāyanenetyevamādiḥ | mantraiḥ ākāśagamanāṇimādi-siddhilābhaḥ | tapasā saṃkalpasiddhiḥ | kāmarūpī yatra tatra kāmaga ityevamādi | samādhijāḥ siddhayo vyākhyātāḥ | 4.1 |

IV.1. The powers can come from birth, drugs, mantras, techniques of self-purification, or transcendental consciousness.

'Powers from birth' means upon incarnating in a new nervous system. 'From drugs' means with potions concocted in the strongholds of the Asuras, and other sources. Passage through space, or becoming as small as an atom, and other powers, can be developed through the use of mantras. Techniques of self-purification can develop the power to realise one's intentions, such as adopting whatever appearance one wishes, teleportation, and so on. Powers that develop from transcendental consciousness have already been described.

tatra kāyendriyāṇāmanyajātīyapariṇatānām |

jātyantarapariṇāmaḥ prakṛtyāpūrāt || *4.2* ||

pūrvapariṇāmāpāya uttarapariṇāmopajanasteṣām-apūrvāvayavānupraveśād bhavati | kāyendriyaprakṛtayaśca svaṃ svaṃ vikāramanugṛhnantyāpūreṇa dharmādinimittamapekṣamāṇā iti | 4.2 |

As to the different order of mind-body co-ordination which they display:

IV.2. Evolution to new levels is upheld by the fullness of Nature.

When one stage of evolution is discarded, the next one comes along, incorporating the previous structure. And the laws of Nature responsible for the physiology and the machinery of experience ensure their continuing development, as appropriate, given their evolutionary status and other factors, towards more and more fulfilment.

nimittamaprayojakaṃ prakṛtīnāṃ varaṇabhedastu tataḥ kṣetrikavat || *4.3* ||

na hi dharmādinimittaṃ tatprayojakam prakṛtīnāṃ bhavati | na kāryeṇa kāraṇaṃ pravartyate iti | kathaṃ tarhi | varaṇabhedastu tataḥ kṣetrikavat | yathā kṣetrikaḥ kedārādapāṃ pūraṇāt kedārāntaraṃ piplāvayiṣuḥ samaṃ nimnaṃ nimnataraṃ vā nāpaḥ pāṇinā’pakarṣati | āvaraṇaṃ tvāsāṃ bhinatti tasminbhinne svayamevā’paḥ kedārāntaramāplāvayanti | tathā dharmaḥ prakṛtīnāmāvaraṇamadharmaṃ bhinatti tasminbhinne svayameva prakṛtayaḥ svaṃ svaṃ vikāramāplāvayanti | yathā vā sa eva kṣetrikastasminneva kedāre na prabhavatyaudakānbhaumānvā rasāndhānyamūlānyanupraveṣayituṃ kiṃ tarhi mudgagavedhukaśyāmākādīṃstato’pakarṣati | aprakṛṣṭeṣu teṣu svayameva rasā dhānyamūlanyanupraviśanti | tathā dharmo nivṛttimātre kāraṇadharmasya śuddhyaśuddyoratyantavirodhāt | na tu prakṛtipravṛttau dharmo heturbhavatīti | atra nandīśvarādaya udāhāryāḥ | viparyayeṇāpyadharmo dharmaṃ bhādate | tataścāśuddipariṇāma iti | tatrāpi nahuṣājagarādaya udāhāryāḥ | 4.3 |

IV.3. For the support of the laws of Nature flows spontaneously, as when the farmer breaches a dyke.

The laws of Nature are not stirred into action by an individual's seeking to evolve or other factors. The effect does not provoke the cause. — Then how? — 'As when the farmer breaches a dyke': when a farmer wants to irrigate a paddy-field with the water that is filling another field on a higher terrace or on the same level, he does not carry the water in his hands; he makes a breach in the bank separating the fields. Once the breach is made, the water flows into the other field by itself. Like that, evolving breaches the dyke of stagnation that has been holding the laws of Nature back, and when the dyke is breached, the laws of Nature flow by themselves to lend their support. Or it is like the same farmer who cannot get the nutrients to fertilise the roots of his crops. So what he does is to pull up the shoots of mung beans, prickly sida, winter cherry and other weeds, and the nutrients penetrate the roots of his cereals by themselves. Like that, action in accord with Nature eliminates action which is not in accord with Nature, because purity and impurity are mutually exclusive. It is not that taking steps to evolve stirs the laws of Nature into action. The example of Nandīśvara and others like him illustrates this point. Conversely, failure to evolve prevents evolution; then the result is an increase in negativity. An example of this, among others, is Nahuṣa when he was turned into a boa constrictor.

yadā tu yogī bahūnkāyānnirmimīte tadā kimekamanaskāste bhavantyathānekamanaskā iti |

nirmāṇacittānyasmitāmātrāt || *4.4* ||

asmitāmātraṃ cittakāraṇamupādāya nirmāṇacittāni karoti | tataḥ sacittāni bhavantīti | 4.4 |

— But as the yogi evolves different physiologies, do they involve the same, or several different, minds? —

IV.4. Individual expressions of consciousness are structured from the level of Amness.

He generates individual expressions of consciousness from the source of consciousness, which is the level of Amness. So they involve the same mind.

pravṛttibhede prayojakaṃ cittamekamanekeṣām || *4.5* ||

bāhūnāṃ cittānāṃ kathamekacittābhiprāyapuraḥsarā pravṛttiriti sarvacittānāṃ prayojakaṃ cittamekaṃ nirmimīte tataḥ pravṛttibhedaḥ | 4.5 |

IV.5. The wholeness of awareness underlies the diversity of its expressions.

— How can different mental states be generated by the intentions of an earlier mental state? — A single unified awareness brings forth all mental states; hence the diversity of mental activity.

***tatra dhyānajamanāśayam* || *4.6* ||**

pañcavidhaṃ nirmāṇacittaṃ janmauśadhimantratapaḥ-samādhijāḥ siddhaya iti | tatra yadeva dhyānajaṃ cittaṃ tadevānāśayam | tasyaiva nāstyāśayo rāgādipravṛttirnātaḥ puṇyapāpābhisaṃbandhaḥ kṣīṇakleśatvādyogina iti | itareṣāṃ tu vidyate karmāśayaḥ | 4.6 |

IV.6. A mind cultured by meditation is free of the remains of impressions.

There are five styles of individual neurophysiology, since the powers are developed through the circumstances of birth, by drugs, by mantras, by self-purification, or by transcendental consciousness. Only the mind which has been cultured by meditation is free from the deposits of impressions. Only in such a mind do desire and other activities not leave impressions. Consequently, the yogi who has destroyed the roots of suffering has no tie to good or to evil. But other kinds of mind do contain the residue of previous actions.

yataḥ |

***karmāśuklākṛṣṇaṃ yoginastrividhamitareṣām* || *4.7* ||**

catuṣpātkhalviyaṃ karmajātayaḥ | kṛṣṇā śuklakṛṣṇā śuklā aśuklākṛṣṇā ceti | tatra kṛṣṇā durātmanām | śuklakṛṣṇā bahiḥ sādhanasādhyā tatra parapīḍānugrahadvāreṇaiva karmāśayapracayaḥ | śuklā tapaḥsvādhyāyadhyānavatām | sā hi kevale manasyāyattatvādbahiḥsādhanānadhīnā na parān pīḍayitvā bhavati | aśuklākṛṣṇā saṃnyāsināṃ kṣīṇakleśānāṃ caramadehānāmiti | tatrāśuklaṃ yogina eva phalasaṃnyāsād akṛṣṇaṃ cānupādānāt | itareṣāṃ tu bhūtānāṃ pūrvameva trividhamiti | 4.7 |

So:

IV.7. The actions of a yogi are neither black nor white. There are three types of action for others.

In fact, there are four types of action: black; white and black; white; neither black nor white. The actions of the wicked are 'black'. Actions performed on the surface of life are 'white and black', for they create deposits of impressions depending on whether they harm or benefit others. 'White' actions are performed by those who practise self-purification, Vedic recitation, and meditation. Such actions are purely mental in nature; they do not involve the outer levels of activity and so they do no harm to others. Actions which are 'neither black nor white' are those undertaken by renunciates — those who have destroyed the roots of suffering and are in their final physical incarnation. The actions of a yogi are not 'white' because he has renounced the fruits of action and they are not 'black' either because he does not indulge in them. The three other types of action belong to everyone else.

tatastadvipākānuguṇānāmevābhivyaktirvāsanānām || 4.8 ||

tata iti trividhāt karmaṇaḥ | tadvipākānuguṇānāmeveti yajjātīyasya karmaṇo yo vipākastasyānuguṇā yā vāsanāḥ karmavipākamanuśerate tāsāmevābhivyaktiḥ | na hi daivaṃ karma vipacyamānaṃ nārakatiryaṅmanuṣyavāsanābhivyaktinimittaṃ saṃbhavati | kiṃtu daivānuguṇā evāsya vāsanā vyajyante | nārakatiryaṅmanuṣyeṣu caivaṃ samānaścarcaḥ | 4.8 |

IV.8. As a result, when impressions resurface, they have the same structure as the actions which created them.

'As a result': add 'of these three types of action'. 'The same structure': the imprint created by the remains of an action produces an impression which duplicates its structure. When the impression resurfaces, it has the same structure as the deposit which formed it. An action whose reward is heaven does not ensue in the manifestation of impressions which lead to rebirth in hell, or as an animal, or as a human. This is because only impressions befitting heavenly existence get expressed. The same mechanics applies to rebirth in hell, or as an animal, or as a human.

jātideśakālavyavahitānāmapyānantaryaṃ smṛtisaṃskārayorekarūpatvāt || *4.9* ||

vṛṣadaṃśavipākodayaḥ svavyañjakāñjanābhivyaktaḥ | sa yadi jātiśatena vā dūradeśatayā vā kalpaśatena vā vyavahitaḥ punaśca svavyañjakāñjana evodiyād drāgityeva pūrvānubhūtavṛṣadaṃśavipākābhisaṃskṛtā vāsanā upādāya vyajyeta | kasmāt | yato vyavahitānāmapyāsāṃ sadṛśyaṃ karmābhivyañjakaṃ nimittībhūtam-ityānantaryameva | kutaśca | smṛtisaṃskārayorekarūpatvāt | yathā'nubhavāstathā saṃskārāḥ | te ca karmavāsanānurūpāḥ | yathā ca vāsanāstathā smṛtiriti jātideśakālavyavahitebhyaḥ saṃskārebhyaḥ smṛtiḥ | smṛteśca punaḥ saṃskārā ityevam-ete smṛtisaṃskārāḥ karmāśayavṛttilābhavaśādvyajyante | ataśca vyavahitānāmapi nimittanaimittikabhāvānucchedād-ānantaryameva siddhamiti | 4.9 |

IV.9. Because memory and impressions have the same structure, the connection between them remains unbroken in spite of being separated by time and place, and across lifetimes.

Rebirth as a cat occurs as the underlying factors become ready to take on material expression. Even if it is separated by a hundred lifetimes, or great distances, or a hundred *kalpas* (429,408,000,000 years), it nonetheless happens speedily once the underlying causes come to manifestation by activating the storehouse of impressions which were created by the experience of a previous life as a cat. — Why? — Because, although they are at a remove, the underlying factor remains the same and becomes the cause of the remanifestation. The relay mechanism is not broken. — How is that? — 'Because memory and impressions have the same structure.' As is the initial experience, so is the impression it leaves; it has the same structure as the deposit left by the experience. And then as is the impression, so is the memory that it calls forth. The memory is formed by the impression even though the latter was created a long way away, or a long time ago, or even in a former lifetime. And then new impressions are formed by the experience of the memory. In this way, memory and impression surface under the influence of the residue of action, and appear in the mind as a thought. Consequently, the mechanism which ensures the articulation between cause and effect never fails.

***tāsāmanāditvaṃ cāśiṣo nityatvāt* || *4.10* ||**

tāsāṃ vāsanānāmāśiṣo nityatvādanāditvam | yeyamātmāśiḥ na bhūvaṃ bhūyāsamiti sarvasya dṛśyate sā na svābhāvikī | kasmāt | jātamātrasya jantorananubhūtamaraṇadharmakasya dveṣaduḥkhānusmṛtinimitto maraṇatrāsaḥ kathaṃ bhavet | na ca svābhāvikaṃ vastu nimittamupādatte | tasmādanādivāsanānuviddhamidaṃ cittaṃ nimittavaśāt kāścideva vāsanāḥ pratilabhya puruṣasya bhogāyopāvartata iti | ghāṭaprāsādapradīpakalpaṃ saṃkocavikāsi cittaṃ śarīraparimāṇākāramātramityapare pratipannāḥ | tathā cāntarābhāvaḥ saṃsāraśca yukta iti | vṛttirevāsya vibhunaścittasya saṃkocavikāsinī ityācāryaḥ | tacca dharmādinimittāpekṣam | nimittaṃ ca dvividham | bāhyamādhyātmikaṃ ca | śarīrādisādhanāpekṣaṃ bāhyam stutidānābhivādanādi | cittamātrādhīnaṃ śraddhādyadhyātmikam | tathā coktam | ye caite maitryādayo dhyānināṃ vihāraste bāhyasādhananiranugrahātmanaḥ prakṛṣṭaṃ dharmamabhinirvartayanti | tayormānasaṃ balīyaḥ | katham | jñānavairagye kenātiṣayyete |

IV.10. And these have no beginning, because desire is eternal.

Because desire is eternal, there never was a time when impressions began. Everyone has the desire, 'May I not not live; please let me live'. This desire is not innate. — Why? — How could the terror at the thought of dying afflict a new-born creature who has not experienced dying before unless it were aroused by the recurring memory of its painfulness? Moreover, properly speaking, something innate has no cause. Consequently, the mind, being replete with beginningless impressions, and experiencing certain impressions under the influence of some cause, remanifests and the Self has experience of it. Some maintain that the mind is influenced by the constraints of the body, like the light of a lamp which flickers when confined within a jar but casts its radiance throughout an open palace hall. This simile explains the mind's withdrawal between lifetimes and its reappearance upon reincarnation. Master Patañjali's view is that it is only the impulses of the mind which persist and which contract and expand, according to the evolutionary need. There are two kinds of motivation for evolution: outward and inward. When the motivation comes from the outside, it involves the instrumentality of the body; for example, worship, charitable giving, acts of reverence. When the motivation is internal, it is anchored in the mind; faith is an example. Thus it is said: 'The cultivation of friendliness and other positive emotions are pure delights for those who meditate, because there is no need to go outside of oneself, and yet they greatly speed up one's evolution.' Of the two, the inward motivation is the more powerful. — How? — What can be greater than Pure Knowledge and

daṇḍakāraṇyaṃ ca cittabalavyatirekeṇa kaḥ śārīreṇa karmaṇā śūnyaṃ kartumutsaheta samudramagastyavadvā pibet | 4.10 |

non-involvement? Without the support of the power of the mind, using only physical means, who could clear the Forest of Daṇḍaka or, like Agastya, drink the ocean dry? (*Rāmāyaṇa VII.81.8-10 and Mahābhārata III.101-5*).

hetuphalāśrayālambanaiḥ saṃgṛhītatvādeṣāmabhāve tadabhāvaḥ || *4.11* ||

hetuḥ dharmātsukhamadharmādduḥkham | sukhādrāgo duḥkhād dveśaḥ tataśca prayatnaḥ tena manasā vācā kāyena vā parispandamānaḥ paramanugṛhṇātyupahanti vā | tataḥ punaḥ dharmādharmau sukhaduḥkhe rāgadveṣau iti pravṛttamidaṃ ṣaḍaraṃ saṃsāracakram | asya ca pratikṣaṇamāvartamānasyāvidyā netrī mūlaṃ sarvakleśānāmityeṣa hetuḥ | phalaṃ tu yamāśritya yasya pratyutpannatā dharmādeḥ na hyapūrvopajanaḥ | manastu sādhikāramāśrayo vāsanānām | na hyavasitādhikāre manasi nirāśrayā vāsanāḥ sthātumutsahante | yadabhimukhībhūtaṃ vastu yāṃ vāsanāṃ vyanakti tasyāstadālambanam | evaṃ hetuphalāśrayālambanairetaiḥ saṃgṛhītāḥ sarvā vāsanāḥ | eṣāmabhāve tatsaṃśrayāṇāmapi vāsanānāmabhāvaḥ | 4.11 |

IV.11. Without the nexus of cause, effect, medium and catalyst, they do not resurface.

'Cause': as life-supporting activity brings pleasure, so non-evolutionary action brings pain. From pleasure springs desire, and from pain comes aversion. Consequently, our attempts to secure the former and avoid the latter compel us, in thought, word and deed, to do good, or harm, to others. Thus is set in motion the wheel of fate with its six spokes: evolution and non-evolution, joy and sorrow, desire and loathing. At all times it is ignorance which drives the wheel, and is the root of suffering. So much for 'cause'. 'Effect' describes a phenomenon which appears in reaction to another phenomenon which provokes it, for nothing occurs that does not already exist. The function of the mind is to provide a 'medium' where impressions can be stored. When the role of the mind is over, impressions do not survive without a repository. A 'catalyst' is any object which triggers the reactivation of an impression. This is how all impressions are articulated via cause, effect, medium and catalyst. When these do not exist, associated impressions are not reactivated.

nāstyasataḥ saṃbhavaḥ na cāsti sato vināśa iti dravyatvena saṃbhavantyaḥ kathaṃ nivartiṣyante vāsanā iti |

atītānāgataṃ svarūpato'styadhvabhedād-dharmāṇām || 4.12 ||

bhaviṣyadvyaktikamanāgatam | anubhūtavyaktikamatītam | svavyāpāropārūḍhaṃ vartamānam | trayaṃ caitadvastu jñānasya jñeyam | yadi caitatsvarūpato nābhaviṣayannedaṃ nirviṣayaṃ jñānamudapatsyata | tasmādatītānāgataṃ svarūpataḥ astīti | kiṃca bhogabhāgīyasya vā'pavargabhāgīyasya vā karmaṇaḥ phalamutpitsu yadi nirupākhyamiti taduddeśena tena nimittena kuśalānuṣṭhānaṃ na yujyate | sataśca phalasya nimittaṃ vartamānīkaraṇe samarthaṃ nāpūrvopajanane | siddhaṃ nimittaṃ naimittikasya viśeṣānugrahaṇaṃ kurute nāpūrvamutpādayatīti | dharmī cānekadharmasvabhavaḥ tasya cādhvabhedena dharmāḥ pratyavasthitāḥ | na ca yathā vartamānaṃ vyaktiviśeṣāpannaṃ dravyato'styevamatītamanāgataṃ ca | kathaṃ tarhi | svenaiva vyaṅgyena svarūpeṇānāgatamasti | svena cānubhūtavyaktikena svarūpeṇātītamiti | vartamānasyaivādhvanaḥ svarūpavyaktiriti | na sā bhavatyatītānāgatayoradhvanoḥ | ekasya cādhvanaḥ samaye dvāvadhvānau dharmisamanvāgatau bhavata eveti | nā'bhūtvā bhāvastrayāṇāmadhvānāmiti | 4.12 |

— Nothing comes from nothing; and no thing can be destroyed. So how can impressions, once created, cease to exist? —

IV.12. The past and the future have their reality, and are based on the sequential expression of an object's properties.

The future is what will happen. The past is what has happened. The present is what is currently taking place. This trio of temporal aspects forms an object of knowledge. If these phases did not have a basic reality, then knowledge of them would be baseless and so would not be possible. So the past and the future are real. Moreover, if the outcome of an action were irreal, it would lead neither to experience nor to liberation, and the efforts of the experts to determine which of these two ends it might serve would be pointless. An action can actualise an outcome for something that already exists, but not if that something has no prior existence. Once activated, a cause elicits a specific effect, but it does not create something that did not exist before. Now, a substance has many properties, and these properties appear separately in sequential expression. The past and the future have no material reality as does the present, which takes on various specific forms. — So do they exist? — The future has potentiality, and the past, once experienced, has completeness. The present is manifested as it takes its course. But past and future time do not become manifest. As one temporal mode occupies the present, the other two modes remain latent within the object. So these three phases do not just spring into existence out of nothingness.

te vyaktasūkṣmā guṇātmānaḥ || *4.13* ||

te khalvamī tryadhvāno dharmā vartamānā vyaktātmano'tītānāgatāḥ sūkṣmātmānaḥ ṣaḍaviśeṣarūpāḥ | sarvamidaṃ guṇānāṃ sanniveśaviśeṣamātramiti | paramārthato guṇātmānaḥ | tathā ca śāstrānuśāsanam | guṇānāṃ paramaṃ rūpaḥ na dṛṣṭipathamṛcchati | yattu dṛṣṭipathaṃ prāptaṃ tanmāyeva sutucchakamiti | 4.13 |

IV.13. They are products of the guṇas, and are either manifest or subtle.

In point of fact, the three temporal aspects are manifest when present, and subtle when past and future, being then structured within the six non-individuated agencies (the five *tanmātras* and Amness). Everything is a particular combination of the *guṇas*. In the final analysis, the basis of the aspects of time is just the *guṇas*. Thus the tradition of the Teaching states: 'The finest level of the *guṇas* is not available to perception; and what can be seen is as insubstantial as a ghostly apparition' (*Varṣagaṇya*).

yadā tu sarve guṇāḥ kathamekaḥ śabda ekamindriyamiti |

***pariṇāmaikatvādvastutattvam** || 4.14 ||*

prakhyākriyāsthitiśīlānāṃ guṇānāṃ grahaṇātmakānāṃ karaṇabhāvenaikaḥ pariṇāmaḥ śrotramindriyam | grāhyātmakānāṃ śabdatanmātrabhāvenaikaḥ pariṇāmaḥ śabdo viṣaya iti | śabdādīnāṃ mūrtisamānajātiyānāmekaḥ pariṇāmaḥ pṛthivīparamāṇustanmātrāvayavaḥ | teṣāñcaikaḥ pariṇāmaḥ pṛthivī gaurvṛkṣaḥ parvata ityevamādiḥ | bhūtāntareṣvapi snehoṣṇyapraṇāmitvāvakāśadānānyupādāya sāmānyamekavikārārambhaḥ samādheyaḥ | nāstyartho vijñānavisahacaro'sti tu jñānamarthavisahacaraṃ svapnādau kalpitamityanayā diśā ye vastusvarūpamapahnuvate jñānaparikalpanāmātraṃ vastu svapnaviṣayopamaṃ na paramārthato'stīti yā āhuḥ te tatheti pratyupasthitamidaṃ svamāhātmyena vastu kathamapramāṇātmakena vikalpajñānabalena vastusvarūpamutsṛjya tadevāpalapantaḥ śraddheyavacanāḥ syuḥ | 4.14 |

— If everything is the *guṇas*, how is there only one element of sound, and one sense of hearing? —

IV.14. The unity of an object is grounded in the integrated nature of change.

The *guṇas* promote purity, activity and stability. When they are concerned with the subjective side of the process of perception, one of their particular transformations, in the form of a faculty of cognition, produces the sense of hearing. When they are concerned with the objective side of the process of perception, they produce a particular transformation in the *tanmātra* of sound, and a sound is produced. A finest particle of earth is a composite of the *tanmātras*; it is a particular transformation of the *tanmātra* of sound and the other subtle elements as they are expressed in the forms of solid matter. The earth, a cow, a tree, a mountain and other objects are all particular products of the combinations of the *guṇas*. Taking into account the qualities of fluidity, heat, motion, and extension inherent in the other elements, the finest beginnings of the manifestation of objects emerging from the relevant *tanmātra* take place. Some object by saying that objects do not exist independently of thought, whereas thoughts do not need to be based on objects, as happens in dreams. For them, objects have no real existence, being mere mental constructs like the objects seen in dreams. It is without proof as to the force of their theory on mental fabrication that they deny any basis to objects which are clearly perceived as existing in their own right; so how can their views be taken seriously?

kutaścaitadanyāyyam |

vastusāmye cittabhedāttayorvibhaktaḥ panthāḥ || 4.15 ||

bahucittālambanībhūtamekaṃ vastu sādhāraṇaṃ | tatkhalu naikacittaparikalpitaṃ nāpyanekacitta-parikalpitaṃ | kiṃtu svapratiṣṭham | katham | vastusāmye cittabhedāt | dharmāpekṣaṃ cittasya vastusāmye'pi sukhajñānaṃ bhavatyadharmāpekṣaṃ tata eva duḥkhajñānamavidyāpekṣaṃ tata eva mūḍhajñānaṃ samyagdarśanāpekṣaṃ tata eva mādhyasthyajñānamiti | kasya taccittena parikalpitam | na cānyacittaparikalpit-enānarthenānyasya cittoparāgo yuktaḥ | tasmādvastujñānayorgrāhyagrahaṇabheda-bhinnayorvibhaktaḥ panthāḥ | nānayoḥ saṃkaragandho'pyastīti | sāṃkhyapakṣe vastu punastriguṇaṃ calaṃ ca guṇavṛttamiti | dharmādinimittāpekṣaṃ cittairabhisaṃbadhyate | nimittānurūpasya ca pratyayasyotpadyamānasya tena tenā'tmanā heturbhavati | 4.15 |

— And why is this illogical? —

IV.15. The object remains the same, but states of mind change. They function differently.

One object can become the object of thought in many minds. It is not fabricated by one mind, nor by a number of minds, but it is grounded in itself. — How? — The object remains the same; minds change. Although the object remains the same, when the mind is evolved, the experience of the object is a source of joy; when the mind is stressed, the experience is dull; when the mind is sunk into ignorance, it is a source of delusion; when the mind sees clearly, the experience is balanced. So what exactly is supposed to have been constructed by the mind? To claim that one person's mind can fall under the spell of what another person's mind has fabricated is absurd. Therefore, the behaviour of the object and that of the mind are unconnected, in the same way that the object observed and the process of observation are different. There can be no chance of confusion between the two. The Sāṃkhya school of philosophy declares that the object is made up of the three *guṇas* and the combinations of the *guṇas* are always changing. The object enters into contact with different states of mind, and in one way or another it stimulates a thought whose tone is determined by the factors just mentioned.

kecidāhuḥ | jñānasahabhūrevārtho bhogyatvātsukhādivad iti | ta etayā dvārā sādhāraṇatvaṃ bādhamānāḥ pūrvottareṣu kṣaṇeṣu vastusvarūpamevāpahnuvate |

***na caikacittatantraṃ cedvastu tadapramāṇakaṃ tadā kiṃ syāt* || *4.16* ||**

ekacittatantraṃ cedvastu syāttadā citte vyagre niruddhe vā svarūpameva tenāparāmṛṣṭamanyasyā'viṣayībhūtam-apramāṇakamagṛhītasvabhāvakaṃ kenacit tadānīṃ kiṃtatsyāt | saṃbhadyamānaṃ ca punaścittena kuta utpadyeta | ye cāsyānupasthita bhāgāste cāsya syuḥ evaṃ nāsti pṛṣṭhamityudaramapi na gṛhyeta | tasmāt-svatantro'rthaḥ sarvapuruṣasādhāraṇaḥ svatantrāṇi ca cittāni pratipuruṣaṃ pravartante | tayoḥ sambandhād-upalabdhiḥ puruṣasya bhoga iti | 4.16 |

Some say that the object is coeval with the experience of it, like pleasure, for example. On this view, in denying that the object is common to all minds, the existence of the object before and after it is experienced is denied.

IV.16. And the object is not based in the mind. Otherwise, what happens to it when it is not the object of thought?

If the object were dependent upon featuring in someone's mind, when their attention turns away, or transcends, then no longer being in contact with that mind, and not appearing either as an object of thought in anyone else's mind, being unnoticed by everybody, what becomes of it? Moreover, when it came to re-establish contact with a mind, where would it come back from? Its features would all be missing: and if its back cannot be seen, neither can its front. Therefore, the object enjoys an autonomous existence of its own. It is common to the experience of all Selfs and autonomous minds operate in regard to their respective Self. The relationship between the object and the mind creates a perception which is experienced by the Self.

taduparāgāpekṣitvāccittasya vastu jñātājñātam || 4.17 ||

ayaskāntamaṇikalpā viṣayāḥ | ayaḥsadharmakaṃ cittamabhisaṃbadhyoparañjayanti | yena ca viṣayeṇoparaktaṃ cittaṃ sa viṣayo jñātastato'nyaḥ punarajñātaḥ | vastuno jñātājñātasvarūpatvātpariṇāmi cittam | 4.17 |

IV.17. An object is known or not known, depending on whether it attracts the attention.

Objects are like magnets, and the mind is like a strip of iron. When they connect, the object drags the mind around. The mind knows the object it has latched on to, but no other. The mind is subject to change because it is the nature of the object that it be known or not known.

yasya tu tadeva cittaṃ viṣayastasya |

sadā jñātāścittavṛttayastatprabhoḥ puruṣasyāpariṇāmitvāt || *4.18* ||

yadi cittavat prabhurapi puruṣaḥ pariṇameta tatastadviṣayāścittavṛttayaḥ śabdādiviṣayavajjñātājñātāḥ syuḥ | sadājñātatvaṃ tu manasastatprabhoḥ puruṣasyāpariṇāmitatvamanumāpayati | 4.18 |

— But for whom is the mind an object? —

IV.18. Since all thoughts are known to It, the Self, which is the basis of the mind, is unchanging.

If, like the mind, the Self, which is the source of the mind, also changed, then Its objects — thoughts in the mind, such as sounds and other sensory input — would be variously known or not known. But since the source of the mind is eternal wakefulness, the unchanging nature of the Self can be inferred.

syādāśaṅkā cittameva svābhāsaṃ viṣayābhāsaṃ ca bhaviṣyati agnivat |

na tatsvābhāsaṃ dṛśyatvāt || 4.19 ||

yathetarāṇīndriyāṇi śabdādayaśca dṛśyatvānna svābhāsāni tathā mano'pi pratyetavyam | na cāgniratra driṣṭāntaḥ | na hyagnirātmasvarūpamaprakāśaṃ prakāśayati | prakāśaścāyaṃ prakāśyaprakāśakasaṃyoge dṛṣṭaḥ | na ca svarūpamātre'sti saṃyogaḥ | kiṃca svābhāsaṃ cittamityagrāhyameva kasyaciditi śabdārthaḥ | tadyathā svātmapratiṣṭhamākāśaṃ na parapratiṣṭhamityarthaḥ | svabuddhipracārapratisaṃvedanātsattvānāṃ pravṛttirdṛśyate | kruddho'haṃ bhīto'ham amutra me rāgo'mutra me krodha iti | etatsvabuddheragrahaṇe na yuktamiti | 4.19 |

— This is questionable. The mind is like fire: it sheds light both on itself and on its surroundings. —

IV.19. Because it is an object of perception, the mind is not self-aware.

The mind should be thought of as similar to the other faculties and the elements, such as sound and other sensory stimuli, in that they can become objects of perception and are not self-aware. Moreover, fire is not a good analogy; for fire does not illuminate itself before it burns. Light is seen when there is contact between the illuminating agent and the illuminated object. Such contact is not located within fire itself. Furthermore, to claim that the mind is self-aware is to say that it can only be perceived by itself. Just as one may say that space is self-supporting, the meaning is that it is not based on anything else. The behaviour of conscious beings is seen to be based on the reflective awareness they have of the functionings of their own minds: 'I am angry', 'I'm afraid', 'I love Ms X', 'I'm furious with Y'. This would not be possible if one's own perceiving mental state was not itself an object of perception.

***ekasamaye cobhayānavadhāraṇam* || *4.20* ||**

na caikasminkṣaṇe svapararūpāvadhāraṇaṃ yuktam | kṣaṇikavādino yad bhavanaṃ saiva kriyā tadeva ca kārakamityabhyupagamaḥ | 4.20 |

IV.20. The mind cannot focus on itself and another object at the same time.

It is not possible to perceive oneself and another at the same time. It is mere fancy on the part of the proponents of the theory of momentaneity to claim that a created thing can be both action and agent.

syānmatiḥ svarasanirudhaṃ cittaṃ cittāntareṇa samanantareṇa gṛhyata |

cittāntaradṛśye buddhibuddheratiprasaṅgaḥ smṛtisaṅkaraśca || 4.21 ||

atha cittaṃ ceccittāntareṇa gṛhyate buddhibuddhiḥ kena gṛhyate | sā'pyanyayā sā'pyanyayetyatiprasaṅgaḥ | smṛtisaṅkaraśca | yāvanto buddhibuddhīnāmanubhavās-tāvatyaḥ smṛtayaḥ prāpnuvanti | tatsaṅkarāccaikasmṛty-anavadhāraṇaṃ ca syāditi | evaṃ buddhipratisaṃvedinaṃ puruṣamapalapadbhirvaināśikaiḥ sarvamevā'kulīkṛtam | te tu bhoktṛsvarūpaṃ yatra kvacana kalpayanto na nyāyena saṃgacchante | kecittu sattvamātramapi parikalpyāsti sa sattvo ya etānpañca skandhānnikṣipyānyāṃśca pratisaṃdadhātītyuktvā tata eva punastrasyanti | tathā skhandhānāṃ mahānirvedāya virāgāyānutpādāya praśāntaye gurorantike brahmacaryaṃ cariṣyāmītyuktvā sattvasya punaḥ sattvamevāpahnuvate | sāṃkhyayogādayastu pravādāḥ svaśabdena puruṣameva svāminaṃ cittasya bhoktāramupayantīti | 4.21 |

— One may argue that as one impulse in the mind dissolves by itself, it may be perceived by another impulse, and then by another. —

IV.21. If one impulse in the mind perceived another, there would be infinite regression, and memory would be a chaos.

Now if one impulse in the mind were perceived by another, then what would perceive the thought of that thought? Regression from one to another would continue *ad infinitum*, and this would entail the collapse of memory since there would be as many memories as there were thoughts of thoughts. In this chaos there would be no way of determining which memory was accurate. Everything is set adrift by the deconstructionists who deny the Self knows the mind by reflection. There is no logic to their claim that the knower is located wherever. Others declare that some entity does exist, and this entity casts off one set of the five constituent elements in order to don another set — only then to take fright at their own theory. For, while they trumpet their desire to take up the life of a *brahmacari* with a *guru* — in their absolute indifference and dispassion towards the five constituent elements, and in order to prevent their re-occurrence and to gain peace of mind — they nonetheless deny that the said entity exists! The proponents of Sāṃkhya, of Yoga, and other philosophies, on the other hand, use the word '*sva*' ('own'/ 'self') to refer to the Self — the source of the mind, the Knower.

katham |

citerapratisamkramāyāstadākārāpattau svabuddhisaṃvedanam || 4.22 ||

apariṇāminī hi bhoktṛśaktirapratisaṃkramā ca pariṇāminyarthe pratisaṃkrānteva tadvṛttimanupatati | tasyāśca prāptacaitanyopagrahasvarūpāyā buddhivṛtteranukāramātratayā buddhivṛttyaviśiṣṭā hi jñānavṛttirākhyāyate | tathā coktam | na pātālaṃ na ca vivaraṃ girīṇāṃ naivāndhakāraṃ kukṣayo nodadhīnām | guhā yasyāṃ nihitaṃ brahma śāśvataṃ buddhivṛttimaviśiṣṭāṃ kavayo vedayante iti | 4.22 |

— How? —

IV.22. Though uninvolved, Pure Consciousness becomes conscious of Its mind by assuming its forms.

'The function of the Seer, while unchanging and unmoving, appears to move with the changing object of thought and to take on the form of that impulse in the mind. The resultant wave of awareness is taken to be not different to the impulse in the mind because It takes on the form of the impulse in the mind' (*Pañcaśikha: cf. Yoga-Sūtras II.20*).

Thus it is said:

'Not in hell, not in the mountain's chasm,
Not in darkness, not in the belly of the seas,
Is the secret hiding place of the eternal Brahman.
The wise know it is the source of thought.'

ataścaitadabhyupagamyate |

draṣṭṛdṛśyoparaktaṃ cittaṃ sarvārtham || 4.23 ||

mano hi mantavyenārthenoparaktaṃ | tatsvayaṃ viṣayatvād viṣayiṇā puruṣeṇā'tmīyayā vṛttyā'bhisaṃbaddhaṃ tadetaccittameva draṣṭṛdṛśyoparaktaṃ viṣayaviṣayinirbhāsaṃ cetanācetanasvarūpāpannaṃ viṣayātmakamapyaviṣayātmakamivācetanaṃ cetanamiva sphaṭikamaṇikalpaṃ sarvārthamityucyate | tadanena cittasārūpyeṇa bhrāntāḥ kecittadeva cetanamityāhuḥ | apare cittamātramevedaṃ sarvaṃ nāsti khalvayaṃ gavādir ghaṭādiśca sakāraṇo loka iti | anukampanīyāste | kasmāt | asti hi teṣāṃ bhrāntibījaṃ sarvarūpākāranirbhāsaṃ cittamiti | samādhiprajñāyāṃ prajñeyo'rthaḥ pratibimbībhūtastasyālambanībhūtatvādanyaḥ | sa cedarthaścittamātraṃ syāt kathaṃ prajñayaiva prajñārūpamavadhāryeta | tasmātpratibimbībhūto'rthaḥ prajñāyāṃ yenāvadhāryate sa puruṣa iti | evaṃ grahītṛgrahaṇagrāhyasvarūpacittabhedāttrayamapyetat jātitaḥ pravibhajante te samyagdarśinaḥ tairadhigataḥ puruṣa iti | 4.23 |

Then it follows that:

IV.23. The mind is all-embracing, drawn by the Seer and the seen.

The mind is taken over by the object of thought. And since it is also itself an object of perception, it is also connected to the Self. This is how the mind, reacting to the Seer and the seen, acts as both subject and object. Although properly speaking not consciousness, it assumes qualities of both consciousness and non-consciousness, and although properly speaking an object, it assumes the quality of subject. Without being conscious, it appears conscious. It is like the rock crystal, reflecting everything. Lured by this similarity, the ignorant mistake the mind for consciousness. Others believe that the whole universe is just mind and this contingent world with its cows, jars and all the rest does not really exist. How pitiable they are! — Why? — The source of their error lies in the fact that the mind absorbs the forms of everything. To be perceived, the external object is reflected into the settled level of the awareness, becoming then an object of thought, distinct from the mind. If the objective world existed only in the mind, how could that structure in the awareness be comprehended by that same awareness? Therefore, the external object is reflected into the awareness, whereby it can be appreciated by the Self. Those who recognise that the mind is divided into the three aspects of knower, known and process of knowing are right and their clarity of vision leads them to the Self.

kutaścaitat |

tadasaṃkhyeyavāsanābhiścitramapi parārthaṃ saṃhatyakāritvāt || 4.24 ||

tadetaccittamasaṃkhyeyābhirvāsanābhireva citrīkṛtamapi parārthaṃ parasya bhogāpavargārthaṃ na svārthaṃ saṃhatyakāritvād gṛhavat | sāmhatyakāriṇā cittena na svārthena bhavitavyam | na sukhacittaṃ sukhārthaṃ na jñānam jñānārtham | ubhayamapyetatparārtham | yaśca bhogenāpavargeṇa cārthenārthavānpuruṣaḥ sa eva paraḥ | na paraḥ sāmānyamātram | yattu kiñcitparaṃ sāmānyamātraṃ svarūpeṇodaharedvaināśikastatsarvaṃ saṃhatyakāritvātparārthameva syāt | yastvasau paro viśeṣaḥ sa na saṃhatyakārī puruṣa iti | 4.24 |

— Why is that? —

IV.24. Being overshadowed by the excitations of innumerable impressions, it is object-referral. Its role is to relay to the Self.

'It' means the mind. Being pulled all over by innumerable impressions, it is object-referral; that is, its function is to provide experience and liberation to another entity, and not for its own purposes. Its role is to relay. It is like a house, which is not put up for its own benefit: the mind provides a coordinating function. The point of happiness is not a happy mind. The point of knowledge is not to have a knowledgeable mind. Both serve another's purpose. The 'Other' in question is not some generalised 'other', but the Self whose objectives are realised through experience and liberation. Whatever it is that a deconstructionist may refer to as 'other' in some general sense, it will act to relay for a quite specific Other, which Itself does not engage with anything — namely, the Self.

viśeṣadarśina ātmabhāvabhāvanānivṛttiḥ || *4.25* ||

yathā prāvṛṣi tṛṇāṅkurasyodbhedena tadbījasattā'numīyate tathā mokṣamārgaśraveṇa yasya romaharṣāśrupātau dṛśyete tatrāpyasti viśeṣadarśanabījamapavargabhāgīyaṃ karmābhinirvartitamityanumīyate | tasyā'tmabhāvabhāvanā svābhāvikī pravartate | yasyābhāvād idamuktam | svabhāvaṃ muktvā doṣād yeṣāṃ pūrvapakṣe rucirbhavatyaruciśca nirṇaye bhavati | tatrā'tmabhāvabhāvanā ko'hamāsaṃ kathamahamāsaṃ kiṃsvididaṃ kathaṃ svididaṃ ke bhaviṣyāmaḥ kathaṃ vā bhaviṣyāma iti | sā tu viśeṣadarśino nivartate | kutaḥ | cittasyaivaiṣa vicitraḥ pariṇāmaḥ puruṣastvasatyām-avidyāyāṃ śuddhaścittadharmairaparāmṛṣṭa iti | tato'syā'tmabhāvabhāvanā kuśalasya nivartata iti | 4.25 |

IV.25. When separation is realised, concerns about individual identity evaporate.

In the rainy season green shoots spring up. From this can be inferred the presence of seeds in the soil. Like that, when a man first hears about the path to enlightenment, he is seen to break down and cry, and his heart beats faster. From this reaction it can be inferred that he has taken the first step towards realising the distinction between the mind and the Self which leads to liberation. Concerns about personal identity are natural. Of someone not at this stage it is said: 'Alienated from himself, in his inner emptiness, such a man adheres to a superficial view of things and is impervious to true understanding.' Such existential questions as: 'Who was I? What was I like? What is this life? What is it for? What shall become of us? What will happen to us?' — they stop when separation is realised. — How? — They are just so many passing thoughts. The Self, of course, remains ever pure, untouched by ignorance or the vagaries of the mind. So an advanced seeker has no concerns about his identity.

tadā vivekanimnaṃ kaivalyaprāgbhāraṃ cittam || 4.26 ||

tadānīṃ yadasya cittaṃ viṣayaprāgbhāram ajñānanimnamāsīttadasyānyathā bhavati kaivalyaprāgbhāraṃ vivekajñānanimnamiti | 4.26 |

IV.26. Then the mind is immersed in Pure Knowledge and is drawn towards enlightenment.

The mind used to be attracted towards the Relative and be immersed in ignorance. Now it takes a different turn. It is deeply immersed in the knowledge of enlightenment and is drawn towards liberation.

tacchidreṣu pratyayāntarāṇi saṃskārebhyaḥ || *4.27* ||

pratyayavivekanimnasya sattvapuruṣānyatākhyātimātra-pravāhārohiṇaścittasya tacchidreṣu pratyayāntaraṇi asmīti vā mameti vā jānāmi vā na jānāmīti vā | kutaḥ | kṣīyamāṇabījebhyaḥ pūrvasaṃskārebhya iti | 4.27 |

IV.27. In the remaining gaps, impressions still give rise to other thoughts.

In the gaps, while the mind is immersing itself in Pure Knowledge and is progressing towards permanent awareness of the separation of the Self, other thoughts still arise: the thought of 'I', 'mine', 'I know', 'I don't know'. — How is that? — Because there are still some previous impressions left, although their influence is on the wane.

***hānameṣāṃ kleśavaduktam* || *4.28* ||**

yathā kleśā dagdhabījabhāvā na prarohasamarthā bhavanti tathā jñānāgninā dagdhabījabhāvaḥ purvasaṃskāro na pratyayaprasūrbhavati | jñānasaṃskārāstu cittādhikārasamāptimanuśerata iti na cintyante | 4.28 |

IV.28. They come to an end in the same way as the causes of suffering.

The causes of suffering are roasted into sterile seeds. Like that, when impressions become like seeds roasted in the fire of Pure Knowledge, they no longer give rise to thoughts. This does not include the impressions which are created by Pure Knowledge itself, which remain until the role of the mind is fulfilled.

prasaṃkhyāne'pyakusīdasya sarvathā vivekakhyāter dharmameghaḥ samādhiḥ || 4.29 ||

yadā'yaṃ brāhmaṇaḥ prasaṃkhyāne'pyakusīdaḥ tato'pi na kiñcitprārthayate | tatrāpi viraktasya sarvathā vivekakhyātireva bhavatīti saṃskārabījakṣayānnāsya pratyayāntarāṇyutpadyante | tadāsya dharmamegho nāma samādhirbhavati | 4.29 |

IV.29. The fully enlightened is free from any interest in the benefits of such abundance. He enjoys the support of the Unified Field of Natural Law.

When the Brahman, uninvolved, has no concern for the benefits such abundance may bring, he has achieved full enlightenment. The destruction of the seeds of impressions means that other thoughts do not arise. Then he receives showers of blessings from Natural Law.

tataḥ kleśakarmanivṛttiḥ || *4.30* ||

tallābhādavidyādayaḥ kleśāḥ samūlakāṣaṃ kaṣitā bhavanti | kuśalākuśalāśca karmāśayāḥ samūlaghātaṃ hatā bhavanti | kleśakarmanivṛttau jīvanneva vidvān vimukto bhavati | kasmād | yasmād viparyayo bhavasya kāraṇam | na hi kṣīṇaviparyayaḥ kaścit kenacit kvacijjāto dṛśyata iti | 4.30 |

IV.30. Then suffering and action come to an end.

When that has been achieved, the causes of suffering — ignorance and so on — are uprooted. All remains of action, both positive and negative, are also extirpated. When the causes of suffering are gone, the Knower is liberated in this life. — Why? — Because illusion is the cause of Becoming. No man is born who is not seen to need to correct his mistaken view of Reality.

tadā sarvāvaraṇamalāpetasya jñānasyānantyāj-jñeyamalpam || 4.31 ||

sarvaiḥ kleśakarmāvaraṇairvimuktasya jñānasyā'nantyaṃ bhavati | tamasābhibhūtamāvṛtamanantaṃ jñānasattvaṃ kvacideva rajasā pravartitamudghāṭitaṃ grahaṇasamarthaṃ bhavati | tatra yadā sarvairāvaraṇamalairapagatamalaṃ bhavati tadā bhavatyasyānantyaṃ | jñānasyānantyājjñeyamalpaṃ saṃpadyate | yathākāśe khadyotaḥ | yatredamuktam | andho maṇimavidhyat | tamanaṅgulirāvayat | agrīvastaṃ pratyamuñcat | tamajihvo'bhyapūjayad iti | 4.31 |

IV.31. Then the field of Relative knowledge is a trifle compared to the totality of infinite Pure Knowledge.

Freed of the veils of all suffering and action, knowledge is unbounded. Infinite Pure Knowledge is overshadowed by *tamas* and lies hidden for a while. Stimulated by *rajas*, it is unlocked and is able to enjoy experience. Once all the impurities which served to obscure it are removed, its infinite nature is revealed. The infinity of Pure Knowledge makes the realm of Relative knowledge seem insignificant — like a firefly in the open skies. Thus it is said:

'A blind man pierced a pearl.
A man with no hands threaded it.
A man with no head wore it around his neck.
A man with no tongue sang about it.'
(*Taittirīya Araṇyaka I.II.5*)

tataḥ kṛtārthānāṃ pariṇāmakramaparisamāptir-guṇānām || 4.32 ||

tasya dharmameghasyodayātkṛtārthānāṃ guṇānāṃ pariṇāmakramaḥ parisamāpyate | na hi kṛtabhogāpavargāḥ parisamāptakramāḥ kṣaṇamapyavasthātumutsahante | 4.32 |

IV.32. Then the guṇas have fulfilled their duty of conducting the process of evolution.

The process of evolution is led by the *guṇas* and it is completed when one is secure in the support of the Unified Field of Natural Law. For the *guṇas* do not continue for a moment longer once the process of experience and liberation is complete.

atha ko'yaṃ kramo nāma iti |

kṣaṇapratiyogī pariṇāmāparāntanirgrāhyaḥ kramaḥ || *4.33* ||

kṣaṇānantaryātmā pariṇamasyāparāntenāvasānena gṛhyate kramaḥ | na hyananubhūtakramakṣaṇā navasya purāṇatā vastrasyānte bhavati | nityeṣu ca kramo dṛṣṭaḥ | dvayī ceyaṃ nityatā | kūṭasthanityatā pariṇāminityatā ca | tatra kūṭasthanityatā puruṣasya | pariṇāminityatā guṇānām | yasminpariṇāmyamāne tattvaṃ na vihanyate tannityam | ubhayasya ca tattvānabhighātānnityatvam | tatra guṇadharmeṣu buddhyādiṣu pariṇāmāparāntanirgrāhyaḥ kramo labdhaparyavasāno nityeṣu dharmiṣu guṇeṣvalabdhaparyavasānaḥ | kūṭasthanityeṣu svarūpamātrapratiṣṭheṣu muktapuruṣeṣu svarūpāstitā krameṇaivānubhūyata iti tatrāpyalabdhaparyavasānaḥ śabdapṛṣṭhenāstikriyāmupādāya kalpita iti | athāsya sāṃsārasya sthityā gatyā ca guṇeṣu vartamānasyāsti kramasamāptirna veti | avacanīyametat | katham | asti praśna ekāntavacanīyaḥ | sarvo jāto mariṣyati iti | om bho iti | atha sarvo mṛtvā janiṣyata iti | vibhajya vacanīyametat | pratyuditakhyātiḥ kṣīṇatṛṣṇaḥ kuśalo na janiṣyata

— So what of the 'process' of evolution then? —

IV.33. No further evolution involving time-bound process is conceivable.

Change is structured in a seamless succession of moments in time, and it only becomes perceptible when it is complete, at the end of the process. A new garment does not suddenly wear out, without passing through a series of stages of deterioration. Even eternal things are subject to this process. There are two kinds of eternity: immutable eternity and the eternity of change. The Self is ever non-changing. The *guṇas* are perpetual change. Something that is never destroyed in spite of the changes it goes through is eternal. Both are eternal since their essence is never destroyed. In the case of the products of the *guṇas* — such as the mind, for example — their evolution is complete when for them the process of change comes to an end. In the case of such eternal things as the *guṇas* themselves the end is never reached. In the case of the immutable eternal things that are liberated Selves re-established in Self-referral, when their mode of being is construed in terms of process, there is no end; but to speak of their 'continuing existence' is merely a construct of language. — So does the coming and going which constitutes the cycle of living and dying, thrown up by the *guṇas*, come to an end or not? — The question is unanswerable. — What? — Some questions have a determinate answer, such as: 'Do all living beings die?' Answer: Yes. So the next question is: 'Do all creatures that have died get reborn?' To which the reply is ambiguous. A clever man who has used his life to gain

itarastu janiṣyate | tathā manuṣyajātiḥ śreyasī na vā śreyasītyevaṃ paripṛṣṭhe vibhajya vacanīyaḥ praśnaḥ | paśūnadhikṛtya śreyasī devānṛṣinścādhikṛtya neti | ayaṃ tvavacanīyaḥ praśnaḥ | saṃsāro'yamantavānathānanta iti | kuśalasyāsti samsārakramaparisamāptirnetarasyeti | anyatarāvadhāraṇe'doṣaḥ | tasmādvyākaraṇīya evāyaṃ praśna iti | 4.33 |

enlightenment and has gone beyond desire will not be reborn, but others will. Another question requiring split answers is: 'Is the human race superior?' Compared to animals: yes. Compared to the gods or to *ṛṣis*: no. Like that, the present question — 'Does creation have an end?' — allows no unequivocal reply. For the happy few — the enlightened — the course of creation does have a term, but for everybody else it does not. It is not wrong to answer one way or the other; but the question has to be dissected first.

guṇādhikārakramasamāptau kaivalyamuktam | tatsvarūpamavadhāryate |

puruṣārthaśūnyānāṃ guṇānāṃ pratiprasavaḥ kaivalyaṃ svarūpapratiṣṭhā vā citiśaktiriti || 4.34 ||

kṛtabhogāpavargāṇāṃ puruṣḥārthaśūnyānāṃ yaḥ pratiprasavaḥ kāryakaraṇātmakānāṃ guṇānāṃ tat kaivalyam | svarūpapratiṣṭhā punarbuddhisattvānabhisaṃbandhātpuruṣasya citiśaktireva kevalā tasyāḥ sadā tathaivāvasthānaṃ kaivalyamiti | 4.34 |

iti śrīpātañjale sāṃkhyapravacane sāṃkhyaśāstre caturthaḥ kaivalyapādaḥ || 4 ||

When the *guṇas* have fulfilled the role of evolution, it is called Cosmic Consciousness. The nature of this state is described as follows:

IV.34. When they have fulfilled the purposes of the Self, the role of the guṇas is complete. Pure Consciousness established in Self-referral — this is Cosmic Consciousness.

When the *guṇas*, which underlie all cause and effect, have fulfilled the objective of the Self, which is to gain experience and then liberation, their role is complete — that is enlightenment.

The uninvolved Pure Consciousness of the Self is realised as separate from the mind and re-established in Self-referral. When this state is a permanent living reality — that is Cosmic Consciousness.

End of the Fourth Chapter on 'Cosmic Consciousness' in Maharṣi Patañjali's Treatise on the Teaching on Yoga

The Yoga-Sūtras

samādhipāda || 1 ||

atha yogānuśāsanam | 1.1 |

yogaścittavṛttinirodhaḥ | 1. 2 |

tadā draṣṭuḥ svarūpe'vasthānam | 1.3 |

vṛttisārūpyamitaratra | 1.4 |

vṛttayaḥ pañcatayyaḥ kliṣṭākliṣṭāḥ | 1.5 |

pramāṇaviparyayavikalpanidrāsmṛtayaḥ | 1.6 |

pratyakṣānumānāgamāḥ pramāṇāni | 1.7 |

viparyayo mithyājñānamatadrūpapratiṣṭham | 1.8 |

śabdajñānānupātī vastuśūnyo vikalpaḥ | 1.9 |

abhāvapratyayālambanā vṛttirnidrā | 1.10 |

anubhūtaviṣayāsaṃpramoṣaḥ smṛtiḥ | 1.11 |

abhyāsavairāgbhyāṃ tannirodhaḥ | 1.12 |

tatra sthitau yatno'bhyāsaḥ | 1.13 |

sa tu dīrghakālanairantaryasatkārāsevito dṛḍhabhūmiḥ | 1.14 |

dṛṣṭānuśravikaviṣayavitṛṣṇasya vaśīkārasaṃjñā vairāgyam | 1.15 |

Chapter 1: THE TRANSCENDENT

1. So: this is the exposition of yoga.

2. Yoga is the settling of the impulses of the mind.

3. Then consciousness is established in Self-referral.

4. Otherwise, it takes on the form of mental activity.

5. Mental activity, negative and positive, is of five kinds.

6. These are: true knowledge, false knowledge, mental constructs, sleep, memory.

7. The types of true knowledge are: direct perception, inference, and authoritative testimony.

8. False knowledge is not based on reality, and is flawed.

9. Mental constructs are devoid of reality, being derived from language.

10. The mental activity based on the experience of non-presence is sleep.

11. Non-loss of the object experienced is memory.

12. To transcend these, repeat and take it as it comes.

13. To achieve integration in life, a commitment to regular practice is required.

14. But it can be steadily acquired over time when practised carefully and consistently.

15. Inner freedom, known as 'self-sufficiency', is acquired when the thirst for personal experience and for the goals enjoined by the Veda is quenched.

tatparaṃ puruṣakhyāterguṇavaitṛṣṇyam | 1.16 |

vitarkavicārānandāsmitārūpānugamāt saṃprajñātaḥ | 1.17 |

virāmapratyayābhyāsapūrvaḥ saṃskāraśeṣo'nyaḥ | 1.18 |

bhavapratyayo videhaprakṛtilayānām | 1.19 |

śraddhāvīryasmṛtisamādhiprajñāpūrvaka itareṣām | 1. 20 |

tīvrasaṃvegānāmāsannaḥ | 1.21 |

mṛdumadhyādhimātratvāttato'pi viśeṣaḥ | 1.22 |

īśvarapraṇidhānādvā | 1.23 |

kleśakarmavipākāśayairaparāmṛṣṭaḥ puruṣaviśeṣa īśvaraḥ | 1.24 |

tatra niratiśayaṃ sarvajñabījam | 1.25 |

sa eṣa pūrveṣāmapi guruḥ kālenānavacchedāt | 1.26 |

tasya vācakaḥ praṇavaḥ | 1.27 |

tajjapastadarthabhāvanam | 1.28 |

tataḥ pratyak cetanādhigamo'pi antarāyābhāvaśca | 1.29 |

16. Beyond that, the realisation of the Self brings complete freedom from the Relative.

17. Transcending the levels of thought ranges from gross, to subtle, to bliss, to Amness.

18. The repeated experience of the state of least excitation culminates in Pure Consciousness, where only impressions remain.

19. Disembodied beings and those immersed in the subtle levels of Nature experience this by virtue of their status.

20. For others, confidence, vigour, focus, practice of transcending, and clear experience lead to it.

21. For the serious-minded, it is easy to attain.

22. Although there is a difference between less, somewhat and highly committed.

23. Or the mind may be settled by surrendering to the Absolute.

24. The Absolute is a special Self that is untouched by suffering, action, its results and impressions.

25. Within It is located the supreme home of all knowledge.

26. It is the teacher of the sages of old, beyond time.

27. The cosmic hum is Its expression.

28. Repeating it realises Its meaning.

29. Then the attention can dive within and obstacles dissolve.

vyādhistyānasaṃśayapramādālasyāviratibhrānti-
darśanālabhabhūmikatvānavasthitatvāni
cittavikṣepāste'ntarāyāḥ | 1.30 |

duḥkhadaurmanasyāṅgamejayatvaśvāsāpraśvāsā
vikṣepasahabhuvaḥ | 1.31 |

tatpratiṣedhārthamekatattvābhyāsaḥ | 1.32 |

maitrīkaruṇāmuditopekṣāṇāṃ
sukhaduḥkhapuṇyāpuṇyaviṣayāṇāṃ
bhāvanātaścittaprasādanam | 1.33 |

pracchardanavidhāraṇābhyāṃ vā prāṇasya | 1.34 |

viṣayavatī vā pravṛttirutpannā manasaḥ
sthitinibandhanī | 1.35 |

viśokā vā jyotiṣmatī | 1.36 |

vītarāgaviṣayaṃ vā cittam | 1.37 |

svapnanidrājñānālambanaṃ vā | 1.38 |

yathābhimatadhyānādvā | 1.39 |

paramāṇuparamamahattvānto'sya vaśīkāraḥ | 1.40 |

30. Sickness, apathy, doubt, neglect, listlessness, intemperance, confused misunderstandings, failure to make progress, failure to integrate, are the obstacles which distract the mind.

31. Pain, frustration, restlessness in the body, coarseness of the inward and the outward breath, accompany such distractions.

32. Repeated exposure to the wholeness of Reality removes them.

33. Clarity of mind comes from cultivating friendliness, compassion, good will, and indifference towards the happy, the unhappy, the deserving and the undeserving.

34. Or the mind may be settled by exhaling and suspending the breath.

35. Or directing the attention to have the refined experience of certain objects also helps to settle the mind swiftly.

36. Or by attending to a pleasing, luminous object.

37. Or by attuning oneself to the level of consciousness of one who is free from desire.

38. Or by the experience of witnessing dreaming or sleep.

39. Or with a recognised technique of meditation.

40. The range of experience extends from the smallest to the greatest.

kṣīṇavṛtterabhijātasyeva maṇergrahītṛgrahaṇagrāhyeṣu tatsthatadañjanatā samāpattiḥ | 1.41 |

tatra śadbārthajñānavikalpaiḥ saṃkīrṇā savitarkā samāpattiḥ | 1.42 |

smṛtipariśuddhau svarūpaśūnyevārthamātranirbhāsā nirvitarkā | 1.43 |

etayaiva savicārā nirvicārā ca sūkṣmaviṣaya vyākhyātā | 1.44 |

sūkṣmaviṣayatvaṃ cāliṅgaparyavasānam | 1.45 |

tā eva sabījaḥ samādhiḥ | 1.46 |

nirvicāravaiśāradye'dhyātmaprasādaḥ | 1.47 |

ṛtaṃbharā tatra prajñā | 1.48 |

śrutānumānaprajñābhyamanyaviṣayā viśeṣārthatvāt | 1.49 |

tajjaḥ saṃskāro'nyasaṃskārapratibandhī | 1.50 |

tasyāpi nirodhe sarvanirodhānnirbījassamādhiḥ | 1.51 |

41. As mental activity is refined, the mind is like a precious stone, absorbing the image of whatever object is presented — be it observer, process of observation or object observed.

42. The attention may be absorbed in meanings, caught up in the associations of words, objects and ideas.

43. When the thinking refines into the vacuum state beyond the level of meaning, the awareness is lively just with the object of thought.

44. From this, the subtler experiences of expansion and unboundedness can be understood.

45. And the finest subtle level in turn dissolves into undifferentiated pure Being.

46. All these experiences occur at relative transcendental levels.

47. Familiarity with the calm of unboundedness brings sublime peacefulness.

48. Then the awareness is in accord with cosmic law.

49. This state is qualitatively different to knowledge gained from authoritative testimony and inference.

50. The effect of this experience is to prevent other impressions caused by stress.

51. When this awareness also dissolves, everything has dissolved, and there is Pure Consciousness.

sādhanapāda || 2 ||

tapaḥsvādhyāyeśvarapraṇidhānāni kriyāyogaḥ | 2.1 |

samādhibhāvanārthaḥ kleśatanūkaraṇārthaśca | 2.2 |

avidyā'smitārāgadveṣābhiniveśāḥ kleśāḥ | 2.3 |

avidyā kṣetramuttareṣāṃ prasuptatanuvicchinno-
dārāṇām | 2.4 |

anityāśuciduḥkhānātmasu
nityaśucisukhātmakhyātiravidyā | 2.5 |

dṛgdarśanaśaktyorekātmatevā'smitā | 2.6 |

sukhānuśayī rāgaḥ | 2.7 |

duḥkhānuśayī dveṣaḥ | 2.8 |

svarasavāhī viduṣo'pi tathārūḍho'bhiniveśaḥ | 2.9 |

te pratiprasavaheyāḥ sūkṣmāḥ | 2.10 |

dhyānaheyāstadvṛttayaḥ | 2.11 |

kleśamūlaḥ karmāśayo dṛṣṭādṛṣṭajanmavedanīyaḥ | 2.12 |

Chapter 2: TECHNOLOGIES OF ENLIGHTENMENT

1. Self-purification, study and surrender to the Absolute are the technologies for yoga.

2. Their purpose is to integrate the Transcendent and to relieve suffering.

3. Suffering is caused by ignorance, the sense of separate individuality, desire, aversion, and the will to live.

4. Ignorance is the breeding ground for the other causes, which may be dormant, attenuated, recurrent or active.

5. Ignorance mistakes impermanence, impurity, suffering, and the non-Self for eternity, purity, happiness, and the Self.

6. The sense of individual identity comes from thinking that the functions of Seer and seeing are the same.

7. Desire follows pleasure.

8. Aversion follows pain.

9. The will to live is spontaneous and inborn, even among the wise.

10. The subtle aspects of suffering can be released by returning to the source of thought.

11. Release these deposits through meditation.

12. At the basis of suffering is the storehouse of karma which has to be worked out either in the present or in future lives.

sati mūle tadvipāko jātyāyurbhogāḥ | 2.13 |

te hlādaparitāpaphalāḥ puṇyāpuṇyahetutvāt | 2.14 |

pariṇāmatāpasaṃskāraduḥkhairguṇavṛttivirodhācca duḥkhameva sarvaṃ vivekinaḥ | 2.15 |

heyaṃ duḥkhamanāgatam | 2.16 |

draṣṭṛdṛśyayoḥ saṃyogo heyahetuḥ | 2.17 |

prakāśakriyāsthitiśīlaṃ bhūtendriyātmakaṃ bhogāpavargārthaṃ dṛśyam | 2.18 |

viśeṣāviśeṣaliṅgamātrāliṅgāni guṇaparvāṇi | 2.19 |

draṣṭā dṛśimātraḥ śuddho'pi pratyayānupaśyaḥ | 2.20 |

tadartha eva dṛśyasyātmā | 2.21 |

kṛtārthaṃ prati naṣṭamapyanaṣṭaṃ tadanyasādharaṇatvāt | 2.22 |

13. While the roots of suffering subsist, the resolution of karma is expressed in the birth-chart, the lifespan, and the types of experience undergone.

14. As one's deeds are positive or negative, so the rewards are joy or sorrow.

15. One who has learnt Pure Knowledge knows that nothing in the Relative can be fulfilling, because of the banes of transience, pain, stress, and the implacable operations of the *guṇas*.

16. Avert the pain before it arises.

17. Avoid confusing the Seer and the seen.

18. The observable universe (the forms taken by the elements and the faculties of cognition) is produced by the interplay of the creative, upholding and destructive tendencies of the *guṇas*; its purpose is the enjoyment of life and to gain enlightenment.

19. The combinations of the *guṇas* operate at gross, subtle, subtlest and unmanifest levels.

20. Ever pure, the Seer is the observer who just witnesses thoughts.

21. The role of creation is to serve the Self.

22. It disappears from view when this role is fulfilled, but it is not destroyed since it continues to exist for other Selves.

svasvāmiśaktyoḥ svarūpopalabdhihetuḥ saṃyogaḥ | 2.23 |

tasya heturavidyā | 2.24 |

tadabhāvāt saṃyogābhāvo hānaṃ taddṛśeḥ kaivalyam | 2.25 |

vivekakhyātiraviplavā hānopāyaḥ | 2.26 |

tasya saptadhā prāntabhūmiḥ prajñā | 2.27 |

yogāṅgānuṣṭhānādaśuddhikṣaye jñānadīptirāvivekakhyāteḥ | 2.28 |

yamaniyamāsanaprāṇāyāmapratyāhāradhāraṇādhyāna-samādhayo'ṣṭāvaṅgāni | 2.29 |

tatrāhiṃsāsatyāsteyabrahmacaryāparigrahā yamāḥ | 2.30 |

jātideśakālasamayānavacchinnāḥ sārvabhaumā mahāvratam | 2.31 |

śaucasaṃtoṣatapaḥsvādhyāyeṣvarapraṇidhānāni niyamāḥ | 2.32 |

vitarkabādhane pratipakṣabhāvanam | 2.33 |

23. It is the link that makes possible the conscious experience of the real nature of the mechanics of the 'property' (the object of perception) and of the 'owner' (the Self).

24. Ignorance causes the link.

25. When ignorance is removed, there is no link. This means freedom — singularity of consciousness.

26. The way to end bondage is with the unbroken awareness of separation.

27. One's experience of this progresses through seven stages.

28. Exercising the limbs of yoga removes impurities and brings the light of consciousness to full realisation.

29. The eight limbs of yoga are: observances, rules of living, posture, breathing, withdrawal, turning within, meditation, transcendence.

30. The observances are: non-violence, truthfulness, non-covetousness, celibacy, non-acceptance of others' possessions.

31. They apply in all circumstances, irrespective of class, place, time, or duty: this great law of life is universal.

32. The rules of living are: purity, contentment, purification, study, surrender to the Absolute.

33. Neutralise negative thoughts if they arise.

vitarkā hiṃsādayaḥ kṛtakāritānumoditā lobhakrodhamohapūrvakā mṛdumadhyādhimātrā duḥkhājñānānantaphalā iti pratipakṣabhāvanam | 2.34 |

ahiṃsāpratiṣṭhāyāṃ tatsaṃnidhau vairatyāgaḥ | 2.35 |

satyapratiṣṭhāyāṃ kriyāphalāśrayatvam | 2.36 |

asteyapratiṣṭhāyāṃ sarvaratnopasthānam | 2.37 |

brahmacaryapratiṣṭhāyāṃ vīryalābhaḥ | 2.38 |

aparigrahasthairye janmakathaṃtā saṃbodhaḥ | 2.39 |

śaucātsvāṅgajugupsā parairasaṃsargaḥ | 2.40 |

sattvaśuddhisaumanasyaikāgryendriyajayātmadarśanayogyatvāni ca | 2.41 |

saṃtoṣādanuttamasukhalābhaḥ | 2.42 |

kāyendriyasiddhiraśuddhikṣayāttapasaḥ | 2.43 |

svādhyāyādiṣṭadevatāsaṃprayogaḥ | 2.44 |

34. Negative thoughts — about acts of violence and similar, which one has performed, caused, or condoned — come from lust, anger, and delusion. They can be mild, moderate or high in intensity, and they lead to unending suffering and ignorance. Neutralise them.

35. When non-violence is established, hostility melts away in its presence.

36. When truthfulness is established, action is guaranteed success.

37. When non-covetousness is established, affluence accrues.

38. Established in celibacy, potency develops.

39. With constancy in non-acceptance comes clear understanding of one's purpose in life.

40. Purity entails attentiveness to the physiology and self-reliance from others.

41. And one enjoys clarity of mind, positivity in outlook, the ability to concentrate, control of the senses, and witnessing.

42. From contentment comes unsurpassable joy.

43. With the elimination of impurities through the practice of purification comes perfection of the body and the senses.

44. In Vedic recitation one enjoys communion with the desired deity.

samādhisiddhirīśvarapraṇidhānāt | 2.45 |

sthirasukhamāsanam | 2.46 |

prayatnaśaitilyānantasamāpattibhyām | 2.47 |

tato dvandvānabhighātaḥ | 2.48 |

tasminsati śvāsapraśvāsayorgativicchedaḥ prāṇāyāmaḥ | 2.49 |

bāhyābhyantarastambhavṛttirdeśakālasaṃkhyābhiḥ paridṛṣṭo dīrghasūkṣmaḥ | 2.50 |

bāhyābhyantaraviṣayākṣepī caturthaḥ | 2.51 |

tataḥ kṣīyate prakāśāvaraṇam | 2.52 |

dhāraṇāsu ca yogyatā manasaḥ | 2.53 |

svaviṣayāsaṃprayoge cittasya svarūpānukāra ivendriyāṇāṃ pratyāhāraḥ | 2.54 |

tataḥ paramā vaśyatendriyāṇām | 2.55 |

45. From surrender to the Absolute comes perfect transcending.

46. Posture involves comfortably holding certain positions.

47. Perform this without straining and with the awareness on unboundedness.

48. Then one is not perturbed by the opposites.

49. Next come exercises to refine the breathing, inward and outward.

50. When the breathing — in, out and the pause between — is regulated by depth, rhythm, and count, it becomes relaxed and subtle.

51. The fourth aspect of the breath transcends the outward and the inward strokes.

52. Then the veil over the light is destroyed.

53. And the mind is ready to dive within.

54. The senses copy the mind and withdraw contact with their objects.

55. Then comes complete control of the senses.

vibhūtipāda || 3 ||

deśabandhaścittasya dhāraṇā | 3.1 |

tatra pratyayaikatānatā dhyānam |3.2 |

tadevārthamātranirbhāsaṃ svarūpaśūnyamiva samādhiḥ | 3.3 |

trayamekatra saṃyamaḥ | 3.4 |

tajjayātprajñālokaḥ | 3.5 |

tasya bhūmiṣu viniyogaḥ | 3.6 |

trayamantaraṅgaṃ pūrvebhyaḥ | 3.7 |

tadapi bahiraṅgaṃ nirbījasya | 3.8 |

vyutthānanirodhasaṃskārayorabhibhavaprādurbhāvau nirodhakṣaṇacittānvayo nirodhapariṇāmaḥ | 3.9 |

tasya praśāntavāhitā saṃskārāt | 3.10 |

sarvārthataikāgratayoḥ kṣayodayau cittasya samādhipariṇāmaḥ | 3.11 |

tataḥ punaḥ śāntoditau tulyapratyayau cittasyaikāgratāpariṇāmaḥ | 3.12 |

Chapter 3: ALL POSSIBILITIES

1. The mind dives within by entertaining a specific impulse of thought.

2. Meditation involves the uniform flow of awareness on that thought.

3. Transcending occurs when the vehicle of meditation is experienced as in a vacuum state of restful alertness.

4. These three together is *saṃyama* — non-extravagance.

5. Mastering this enlivens the finest transcendental level of the awareness.

6. It can be applied across a range of all possibilities.

7. These three aspects are more intimate that the earlier limbs.

8. Although they are grosser than Pure Consciousness.

9. At the junction point between the inward stroke of the mind settling and the outward stroke of mental activity, the experience of silence deepens the silence which infuses the mind.

10. The effect of transcending is to produce restful alertness.

11. Transcendental consciousness is stabilised as the mind moves between the diversified state of awareness and the state of one-pointedness.

12. And then the one-pointedness is transformed as the mind becomes able to maintain rest and activity both together.

etena bhūtendriyeṣu dharmalakṣanāvasthāpariṇāmā vyākhyātāḥ | 3.13 |

śāntoditāvyapadeśyadharmānupātī dharmī | 3.14 |

kramānyatvaṃ pariṇāmānyatve hetuḥ | 3.15 |

pariṇāmatrayasaṃyamādatītānāgatajñānam | 3.16 |

śabdārthapratyayānāmitaretarādhyāsātsaṅkaras-tatpravibhāgasaṃyamātsarvabhūtarutajñānam | 3.17 |

saṃskārasākṣātkaraṇātpūrvajātijñānam | 3.18 |

pratyayasya paracittajñānam | 3.19 |

na ca tatsālambanaṃ tasyāviṣayībhūtatvāt | 3.20 |

kāyarūpasaṃyamāttadgrāhyaśaktistambhe cakṣuḥprakāśā'saṃprayoge'ntardhānam | 3.21 |

sopakramaṃ nirupakramaṃ ca karma tatsaṃyamādaparāntajñānamariṣṭebhyo vā | 3.22 |

maitryādiṣu balāni | 3.23 |

13. From this, changes in the qualities, temporal phases and states among the elements and the faculties of cognition can be understood.

14. An object contains within itself its own potential: past, present and future.

15. Change is due to modulation in their sequence.

16. *Saṃyama* on the three aspects of change develops knowledge of the past and future.

17. The word, the meaning and the idea are confused because they are superimposed one upon the other; *saṃyama* on the distinction between them develops understanding of the sounds of all creatures.

18. The direct cognition of impressions provides knowledge of previous lives.

19. *Saṃyama* on an impulse of thought provides knowledge of another's mind.

20. But not its content, because that is not the object.

21. *Saṃyama* on the form of the body, blocking its ability to be seen, with no contact between its light and the eye, develops invisibility.

22. The effects of actions are slow or quick to return. From *saṃyama* on both — or from omens — comes knowledge of one's death.

23. On friendliness and other feelings — the corresponding qualities.

baleṣu hastibalādīni | 3.24 |

pravṛttyālokanyāsātsūkṣmavyavahitaviprakṛṣṭa-
jñānam | 3.25 |

bhuvanajñānaṃ sūrye saṃyamāt | 3.26 |

candre tārāvyūhajñānam | 3.27 |

dhruve tadgatijñānam | 3.28 |

nābhicakre kāyavyūhajñānam | 3.29 |

kaṇṭhakūpe kṣutpipāsānivṛttiḥ | 3.30 |

kūrmanāḍyāṃ sthairyam | 3.31 |

mūrdhajyotiṣi siddhadarśanam | 3.32 |

prātibhādvā sarvam | 3.33 |

hṛdaye cittasaṃvit | 3.34 |

sattvapuruṣayoratyantāsaṃkīrṇayoḥ pratyayāviśeṣo bhogaḥ parārthatvātsvārthasaṃyamāt puruṣajñānam | 3.35 |

tataḥ prātibhaṣrāvaṇavedanā'darśā'svādavārtā jāyante | 3.36 |

24. On the strength of an elephant, and other forms — the corresponding qualities.

25. Directing the faculty of attention develops knowledge of what is subtle, hidden, or distant.

26. *Saṃyama* on the sun develops knowledge of the universe.

27. On the moon — knowledge of the arrangement of the stars.

28. On the polestar — knowledge of their movement.

29. On the navel plexus — knowledge of the bodily systems.

30. On the hollow in the throat — cessation of hunger and thirst.

31. On the bronchial tube — calmness.

32. On the light in the head — the vision of *siddhas*.

33. From intuition — everything.

34. On the heart — complete knowledge of the mind.

35. Experience occurs when, through object-referral, there is no distinction in the thinking process between the mind and the Self, which are completely separate; *saṃyama* on Self-referral develops knowledge of the Self.

36. Then develop the powers of intuition, refined hearing, touch, sight, taste and smell.

te samādhāvupasargā vyutthāne siddhayaḥ | 3.37 |

bandhakāraṇaśaithilyāt pracārasaṃvedanācca cittasya paraśarīrāveśaḥ | 3.38 |

udānajayājjalapaṅkakaṇṭakādiṣvasaṅga utkrāntiśca | 3.39 |

samānajayājjvalanam | 3.40 |

śrotrākāśayossaṃbandhasaṃyamāddivyaṃ śrotram | 3.41 |

kāyākāśossaṃbandhasaṃyamāllaghutūla-samāpatteścākāśagamanam | 3.42 |

bahirakalpitā vṛttirmahāvidehā tataḥ prakāśāvaraṇakṣayaḥ | 3.43 |

sthūlasvarūpasūkṣmānvayārthavattvasaṃyamād-bhūtajayaḥ | 3.44 |

tato'ṇimādiprādurbhavaḥ kāyasaṃpattaddharmānabhighātaśca | 3.45 |

rūpalāvaṇyabalavajrasaṃhananatvāni kāyasaṃpat | 3.46 |

37. These are by-products of transcendental consciousness, enrichments for activity.

38. By loosening the boundaries, and knowing the behaviour, of the mind, one may enter into another's body.

39. Mastering the upward breath one is untouched by water, mud, or thorns, and ascends at death.

40. From mastery of the balancing breath comes effulgence.

41. *Saṃyama* on the relationship of hearing and the ether develops divine hearing.

42. From *saṃyama* on the relationship of the body and the ether, and becoming light as cotton fibre — the ability to move through the air.

43. The ability to project outside the body becomes real and objective. Then the veil masking enlightenment is destroyed.

44. *Saṃyama* on their gross form, essential nature, subtle form, articulation, and purpose develops mastery of the elements.

45. Then other powers develop, such as becoming as small as an atom. Also, perfection of the body and no resistance from the elements.

46. Perfection of the body means beauty, radiance, strength, and the hardness of diamond.

grahaṇasvarūpāsmitānvayārthavattvasaṃyamādindriya-
jayaḥ | 3.47 |

tato manojavitvaṃ vikaraṇabhāvaḥ pradhānajayaśca | 3.48 |

sattvapuruśānyatākhyātimātrasya sarvabhāvādhiṣṭhātṛtvaṃ sarvajñātṛtvaṃ ca | 3.49 |

tadvairāgyādapi doṣabījakṣaye kaivalyam | 3.50 |

sthānyupanimantraṇe saṅgasmayākaraṇaṃ punaraniṣṭaprasaṅgāt | 3.51 |

kṣaṇatatkramayoḥ saṃyamādvivekajaṃ jñānam | 3.52 |

jātilakṣaṇadeśairanyatānavacchedāttulyayostataḥ pratipattiḥ | 3.53 |

tārakaṃ sarvaviṣayaṃ sarvathāviṣayamakramaṃ ceti vivekajaṃ jñānam | 3.54 |

sattvapuruṣayoḥ śuddhisāmye kaivalyamiti | 3.55 |

47. *Saṃyama* on their acts of perception, essential nature, Amness, articulation, and purpose develops mastery of the faculties of cognition.

48. Then come movement at the speed of thought, action at a distance, and mastery of the laws of Nature.

49. With the permanent realisation of the difference between the mind and the Self come omnipotence and omniscience.

50. When even these are let go, all possibility of lack of fulfilment has been removed — this is enlightenment.

51. Being solicited by the inhabitants of the celestial realms is no reason for getting involved or feeling conceited, as the consequences risk being undesirable.

52. *Saṃyama* on instants in time and their sequence develops the power of discrimination.

53. Then comes the ability to distinguish between two objects which are identical in type, characteristics and location.

54. Pure Knowledge is complete, holistic, universal and instantaneous.

55. When the mind and the Self are both pure, there is enlightenment.

kaivalyapāda || 4 ||

janmauṣadhimantratapaḥsamādhijāḥ siddhayaḥ | 4.1 |

jātyantarapariṇāmaḥ prakṛtyāpūrāt | 4.2 |

nimittamaprayojakaṃ prakṛtīnāṃ varaṇabhedastu tataḥ kṣetrikavat | 4.3 |

nirmāṇacittānyasmitāmātrāt | 4.4 |

pravṛttibhede prayojakaṃ cittamekamanekeṣām | 4.5 |

tatra dhyānajamanāśayam | 4.6 |

karmāśuklākṛṣṇaṃ yoginastrividhamitareṣām | 4.7 |

tatastadvipākānuguṇānāmevābhivyaktirvāsanānām | 4.8 |

jātideśakālavyavahitānāmapyānantaryam smṛtisaṃskārayorekarūpatvāt | 4.9 |

tāsāmanāditvaṃ cāśiṣo nityatvāt | 4.10 |

hetuphalāśrayālambanaiḥ saṃgṛhītatvādeṣāmabhāve tadabhāvaḥ | 4.11 |

Chapter 4: COSMIC CONSCIOUSNESS

1. The powers can come from birth, drugs, mantras, techniques of self-purification, or transcendental consciousness.

2. Evolution to new levels of life is upheld by the fullness of Nature.

3. For the support of the laws of Nature flows spontaneously, as when the farmer breaches a dyke.

4. Individual expressions of consciousness are structured from the level of Amness.

5. The wholeness of awareness underlies the diversity of its expressions.

6. A mind cultured by meditation is free of the remains of impressions.

7. The actions of a yogi are neither black nor white. There are three types of action for others.

8. As a result, when impressions resurface, they have the same structure as the actions which created them.

9. Because memory and impressions have the same structure, the connection between them remains unbroken in spite of being separated by time and place, and across lifetimes.

10. And these have no beginning, because desire is eternal.

11. Without the nexus of cause, effect, medium and catalyst, they do not resurface.

atītānāgataṃ svarūpato'styadhvabhedāddharmāṇām | 4.12 |

te vyaktasūkṣmā guṇātmānaḥ | 4.13 |

pariṇāmaikatvādvastutattvam | 4.14 |

vastusāmye cittabhedāttayorvibhaktaḥ panthāḥ | 4.15 |

na caikacittatantraṃ cedvastu tadapramāṇakaṃ tadā kiṃ syāt | 4.16 |

taduparāgāpekṣitvāccittasya vastu jñātājñātam | 4.17 |

sadā jñātāścittavṛttayastatprabhoḥ puruṣasyāpariṇāmitvāt | 4.18 |

na tatsvābhāsaṃ dṛśyatvāt | 4.19 |

ekasamaye cobhayānavadhāraṇam | 4.20 |

cittāntaradṛśye buddhibuddheratiprasaṅgaḥ smṛtisaṅkaraśca | 4.21 |

citerapratisaṃkramāyāstadākārāpattau svabuddhisaṃvedanam | 4.22 |

draṣṭṛdṛśyoparaktaṃ cittaṃ sarvārtham | 4.23 |

12. The past and the future have their reality, and are based on the sequential expression of an object's properties.

13. They are the products of the *guṇas*, and are either manifest or subtle.

14. The unity of an object is grounded in the integrated nature of change.

15. The object remains the same; but states of mind change. They function differently.

16. And the object is not based in the mind. Otherwise, what happens to it when it is not the object of thought?

17. An object is known or not known, depending on whether it attracts the attention.

18. Since all thoughts are known to It, the Self, which is the basis of the mind, is unchanging.

19. Because it is an object of perception, the mind is not self-aware.

20. The mind cannot focus on itself and another object at the same time.

21. If one impulse in the mind perceived another, there would be infinite regression, and memory would be a chaos.

22. Though uninvolved, Pure Consciousness becomes conscious of Its mind by assuming its forms.

23. The mind is all-embracing, drawn by the Seer and the seen.

tadasaṃkhyeyavāsanābhiścitramapi parārthaṃ saṃhatyakāritvāt | 4.24 |

viśeṣadarśina ātmabhāvabhāvanānivṛttiḥ | 4.25 |

tadā vivekanimnaṃ kaivalyaprāgbhāraṃ cittam | 4.26 |

tacchidreṣu pratyayāntarāṇi saṃskārebhyaḥ | 4.27 |

hānameṣāṃ kleśavaduktam | 4.28 |

prasaṃkhyāne'pyakusīdasya sarvathā vivekakhyāter dharmameghaḥ samādhiḥ | 4.29 |

tataḥ kleśakarmanivṛttiḥ | 4.30 |

tadā sarvāvaraṇamalāpetasya jñānasyānantyājjñeyamalpam | 4.31 |

tataḥ kṛtārthānāṃ pariṇāmakramaparisamāptir-guṇānām | 4.32 |

kṣaṇapratiyogī pariṇāmāparāntanirgrāhyaḥ kramaḥ | 4.33 |

puruṣārthaśūnyānāṃ guṇānāṃ pratiprasavaḥ kaivalyaṃ svarūpapratiṣṭhā vā citiśaktiriti | 4.34 |

24. Being overshadowed by the excitations of innumerable impressions, the mind is object-referral. Its role is to relay to the Self.

25. When separation is realised, concerns about individual identity evaporate.

26. Then the mind is immersed in Pure Knowledge and is drawn towards enlightenment.

27. In the remaining gaps, impressions still give rise to other thoughts.

28. They come to an end in the same way as the causes of suffering.

29. The fully enlightened is free from any interest in the benefits of such abundance. He enjoys the support of the Unified Field of Natural Law.

30. Then suffering and action come to an end.

31. Then the field of Relative knowledge is a trifle compared to the totality of infinite Pure Knowledge.

32. Then the *guṇas* have fulfilled their duty of conducting the process of evolution.

33. No further evolution involving time-bound process is conceivable.

34. When they have fulfilled the purposes of the Self, the role of the *guṇas* is complete. Pure Consciousness established in Self-referral — this is Cosmic Consciousness.

Glossary

abhiniveśa	will to live.
abhyāsa	repetition; regular practice.
adarśana	distorted vision; ignorance.
ālambana	vehicle of thought; object of thought.
aliṅga	undifferentiated; pure Being.
anādi	beginningless; having no inaugural moment; 'from time immemorial'.
anubhava	coordinate.
anupātī	attuned; copying.
apavarga	enlightenment; fulfilment.
āpūra	'more and more'; fullness.
artha	object; meaning.
asaṃprajñāta	beyond thought.
āsana	posture.
āśaya	storehouse.
asmitā	Amness; sense of separateness.
avastha	state.
avidyā	ignorance.
bhūmi	ground; level; area; channel.
bhūta	element.

brahmacarya	celibacy.
buddhi	mind; intellect.
caitanya	consciousness.
citi	consciousness.
citiśakti	Pure Consciousness.
citta	mind; thinking.
darśana	enlightened awareness.
dhāraṇā	directed attention; focus; turning within.
dharma	property; quality; evolution; Natural Law.
dharmamegha	Unified Field of Natural Law; shower of blessings.
dharmī	object; substance.
dhyāna	meditation.
draṣṭṛ	Seer; consciousness.
dvandhva	opposites.
gomayapāyasa	fallacy; false syllogism.
grahaṇa	process of observation; act of perception.
grahitṛ	observer.
grahya	object observed.

guṇa	basic constituent.
indriya	organ of sense; faculty of cognition.
īśvara	the Absolute.
īśvaraprasāda	support of the laws of Nature.
jñāna	knowledge; understanding.
kaivalya	singularity of consciousness; enlightenment; Cosmic Consciousness.
kalpa	4,294,080,000 years. (Calculated as: 14 *manvantaras*; 1 *manvantara* = 71 *caturyugis*; 1 *caturyugi* = 1 *satyuga* + 1 *tretayuga* (= 0.75 *satyuga*) + 1 *dvapārayuga* (= 0.50 *satyuga*) + 1 *kaliyuga* (= 0.25 *satyuga* = 432,000 years).
karma	action; karma.
karmāśaya	remains, deposit, residue of action; return of karma.
khyāti	understanding; experience; awareness; realisation.
kleśa	cause of suffering; stress.
krama	sequence; process; evolution.
kṣaṇa	moment; time.
lakṣaṇa	stage; phase; aspect.

liṅga	differentiated; finest relative.
mahāvideha	disincarnation.
mahāvratam	the great law of life.
manas	mind.
mūlapṛthaktvam	differance; foundational seriality.
nirodha	settled state; silence; simplest state of awareness; restful alertness.
nirvicāra	unbounded awareness.
nirvitarka	beyond surface meaning.
niyama	rule of living.
parārthattva	object-referral.
pariṇāma	change; evolution; progress.
pradhāna	almighty Nature.
prajñā	(finest) awareness; experience.
prajñāloka	enlightenment; enlivened awareness.
pramāna	mode of true knowledge.
prāṇayama	breathing exercise.
praṇidhāna	surrender; focus.
pratisaṃvedī	by reflection.
pratyak(cetana)	own; immediate; intimate (awareness).

pratyaya	thought; mental activity; impulse.
puruṣa	the Self.
ṛtam	cosmic order.
ṛtambhāraprajñā	awareness in accord with Cosmic Law.
rūpa	form; appearance.
sādhana	technology; technique.
samādhi	the Transcendent; transcendence; transcending; transcendental consciousness.
samāpatti	experience; absorption; entrainment; attunement.
saṃhita	integration; coherence.
saṃprajñāta	accompanied by thought.
saṃskāra	impression; stress.
saṃyama	(*technical*) non-extravagance; synthesis.
sattva	*sattva*; purity; mind.
sthitipada	simplest state of awareness; restful alertness.
śūnya	vacuum state; empty.
svārtha	Self-referral.
svarūpa	essential nature; Self-referral.

tanmātra	basic element.
tapas	self-purification; refinement.
tattvam	ultimate Reality.
vairāgya	innocence; with no expectation; 'taking it as it comes'.
vāsanā	(deep) impression; tendency.
vaśikāra	mastery; self-possession; self-sufficiency.
vastu	object.
vibhūti	all-pervading; 'all possibilities'.
vicāra	expanded awareness.
vikalpa	mental construct.
vikalpita	imagined; constructed.
vipāka	fruition; return of karma.
viparyaya	false knowledge; misunderstanding.
virakta	overshadowed; coloured.
viṣaya	object; object of thought.
vitarka	surface level of meaning.
viveka	separation; discrimination.
vivekajñāna	Pure Knowledge.
vivekakhyāti	enlightenment; Self-realisation.

vṛtti	thought; impulse; excitation; fluctuation.
vyutthāna	mental activity.
yama	observance.
yoga	transcendence.

Further Reading

The following publications are recommended:

Pātañjalayogasūtrāṇi, edited by Kāśīnāthaśāstrī Āgāśe (Ānandāśrama, Pune, 1904).

Le Yoga-Sūtra de Patañjali, le Yoga-Bhāṣya de Vyāsa, édition, traduction et présentation de Michel Angot (Les Belles Lettres, Paris, 2008).

The Yoga Sūtras of Patañjali: a New Edition, Translation and Commentary, by Edwin F. Bryant (North Point Press, New York, 2009).

The Yoga Sutras of Patanjali, translated and introduced by Alistair Shearer (Rider, London, 2002).

www.ingramcontent.com/pod-product-compliance
Lightning Source LLC
Chambersburg PA
CBHW022055150426
43195CB00008B/141
* 9 7 8 1 4 2 1 8 8 6 5 8 9 *